Designing Better Buildings

Designing is widely recognised as the key to improving the quality of the built environment. This well-illustrated book comprises 18 chapters written by leading practitioners, clients and academics, and presents the latest thinking on design quality and value. For designers and their clients alike, it provides evidence to justify greater emphasis on, and investment in, design. It summarises the benefits that arise from good design – such as civic pride and urban regeneration, corporate identity, occupant productivity and health in offices, improved learning outcomes in schools, better patient recovery rates in hospitals, as well as reduced environmental impact. And it illustrates these benefits through case study examples.

Part One describes the perspective of clients and what they expect from design. Part Two presents case studies in various sectors – offices, schools, healthcare buildings – to explain how and why the designs came about. Part Three addresses the processes necessary to achieve design quality. Part Four discusses the issue of whether and how design quality can be measured.

The book is intended for construction industry practitioners, particularly in architectural, engineering, planning, surveying and project management practices, as well as clients responsible for commissioning buildings and civil engineering projects. It will be an essential text book for many university courses in the built environment, including architecture, engineering, construction, planning and urban design.

Designing Better Buildings

Quality and Value in the Built Environment

Edited by Sebastian Macmillan

Spon Press
Taylor & Francis Group

LONDON AND NEW YORK

First published 2004 by Spon Press
11 New Fetter Lane, London EC4P 4EE

Simultaneously published in the USA and Canada
by Spon Press
29 West 35th Street, New York, NY 10001

Spon Press is an imprint of the Taylor & Francis Group

© 2004 Editorial and selection, Taylor & Francis, individual chapters – the authors

Typeset in Univers by Florence Production Ltd, Stoodleigh, Devon
Printed and bound in Great Britain by the Alden Group, Oxford

British Library Cataloguing in Publication Data
A catalogue record for this book is available from the British Library

Library of Congress Cataloging in Publication Data
Designing better buildings/edited by Sebastian Macmillan
     p. cm.
    Includes bibliographical references and index.
   1. Architectural design. I. Macmillan, Sebastian.
   NA2750.D4168 2003
   721–dc21   2003006275

ISBN   0–415–31525–5 (hb)
        0–415–31526–3 (pb)

Contents

Illustration acknowledgements

The authors and publisher wish to thank those listed below for their permission to reproduce material:

Figures

4.2 Raf Makda/VIEW; 4.3a and b Timothy Soar; 4.4 Raf Makda/VIEW; 6.1 Dennis Gilbert/VIEW; 6.2 Diana Edmunds; 6.3 Peter Cook/VIEW; 6.4 Richard Bryant/Arcaid; 6.5 Dennis Gilbert/VIEW; 6.6 Martine Hamilton Knight; 6.7 and 6.8 Peter Cook/VIEW; 7.1 Peter Cook/VIEW; 7.8 Adam Wilson; 7.9 Chris Gascoigne/VIEW; 8.4–8.7 Hampshire County Council Architects; 8.11 Brian Edwards; 8.12 Simon Doling; 14.1–14.3 Louis Hellman.

Plates

1 and 2 Raf Makda/VIEW; 3, 4 and 5 Dennis Gilbert/VIEW; 6 and 7 Peter Cook/VIEW; 8 and 9 Dennis Gilbert/VIEW; 10, 11 and 12 Peter Cook/VIEW; 13 Paul Rattigan/VIEW; 14 Tom Scott/VIEW.

Notes on contributors

Bill Bordass

Bill Bordass moved from science research to the multi-skilled design practice RMJM London. He worked on briefing, planning, and environmental impact, and became associate in charge of building services, energy and environmental design. Working on new, existing and historic buildings, he became particularly interested in monitoring environmental and energy performance, investigating technical problems, and using the results to inform briefing, design and management. In 1984 he set up William Bordass Associates, which does post-occupancy and energy surveys, monitoring, troubleshooting, briefing, research management and publication. His main interest is in how buildings and their engineering and control systems actually work, and the implications for clients, specification, design, benchmarking, procurement and management. He is a member of the Probe Team, which undertakes post-occupancy studies of technical and energy performance and occupant and management satisfaction in recent buildings, and publishes them in *Building Services Journal*. He is currently leading a project on feedback with the UK Confederation of Construction Clients.

Matthew Carmona

Matthew Carmona is a Reader in planning and urban design at the Bartlett School of Planning,

UCL. Previously he worked as a lecturer at the University of Nottingham and before that as a researcher and as an architect in private practice. He is particularly interested in the policy context for delivering better design quality in the built environment, having worked on a range of research projects examining design policies in local plans, residential design policy and guidance, best value in planning and urban design, the working relationships between housing providers and planners, and the management of public space. Currently, he holds a position on the CABE Urban Design Skills Working Group, and is a member of the RTPI Council. He is also on the editorial board of *Urban Design Quarterly*, and is Book Reviews Editor for the *Journal of Urban Design*.

Michael Dickson

Michael Dickson is an engineer who studied mechanical sciences at Cambridge University followed by structural engineering and town planning at Cornell University, USA. He has worked on a wide range of major building engineering and urban regeneration projects such as headquarters buildings for IBM and British Airways in England, headquarters for RWE Essen in Germany, a new main line station for Stuttgart 21, a large urban development in the centre of Shanghai, and the Japanese Pavilion in Hannover. Michael is

Founding Partner and Chairman of Buro Happold Consulting Engineers. He was recently Chairman of the IStructE Working Group Building for a Sustainable Future – Construction without Depletion and a member of Lord Justice Taylor's Working Group on the Safety of Sports Grounds. He is a Director of the Theatre Royal, Bath, and is Chairman of the Construction Industry Council, and of its Steering Group for the Design Quality Indicator.

Raymond Evans

Raymond Evans joined the building services industry in 1962 as a trainee mechanical engineer with a major contractor. He joined the consulting practice of Donald Smith Seymour and Rooley in 1974, was the resident overseas partner in the UK practice in 1985 and the managing partner of the London office in 1997. Major services projects undertaken include Canary Wharf Tower, North Terminal Gatwick, and Chelsea and Westminster Hospital.

Richard Feilden

Richard Feilden was a founding partner of Feilden Clegg Bradley in 1978. The practice has now grown to 75 staff, with offices in Bath and London. He developed particular interests in user involvement, environmental design and the creative re-use of buildings while studying at Cambridge and the Architectural Association. He has been involved with many of the practice's award-winning projects, including John Cabot CTC and student housing for Aston University and King Alfred's College. He has been extensively involved in the practice's work for education, and is a former convenor of the Higher Education Design Quality Forum. He was a special Advisor to the Urban Task Force chaired by Richard Rogers and this led to a particular interest in urban design. He was awarded an OBE in 1999 and is Visiting Professor of Architecture at the University of Central England. In 2000 he was appointed a Commissioner at the Commission for Architecture and the Built Environment (CABE)

where he has had particular responsibility for educational buildings and PFI schools projects.

Susan Francis

Susan Francis is a senior architectural advisor to the Future Healthcare Network at the NHS Confederation, and to the Centre for Health Architecture and Design at NHS Estates. She is also a research architect at the Medical Architecture Research Unit (MARU) at South Bank University, specialising in research and postgraduate training for the planning and design of health buildings. Studies include post-occupancy evaluations, design guidance and project reviews. She has contributed to national and international conferences and published articles in the medical and design press. Recent publications have focused on developing an understanding of hospital heritage in Europe and the relationship of art and architecture in making therapeutic environments. Susan was co-author of a recent study, *Building a 2020 Vision: Future healthcare environments*, that scanned current developments in the modernisation of care and design, setting out a blueprint for patient-centred care and quality of design. She is leading the team for the evaluation of the ongoing King's Fund Enhancing the Healing Environment programme.

David Gann

David Gann is director of the Innovation Studies Centre, Imperial College London, where he holds the Chair in Technology and Innovation Management. His main areas of research are on innovation in the built environment, and the management of technical change in project-based firms. He has been involved in the Design Quality Indicator project from its inception. He is a Board member of Rethinking Construction and the Housing Forum in the UK. He has worked extensively with government departments in the UK and in other countries and has provided advice to industry, and to agencies such as the OECD on policies for innovation and technical development.

Richard Haryott

Richard Haryott joined Arup in 1962 after graduating from Leeds University with a degree in Civil Engineering. He joined the Main Board in 1984, with responsibilities that included overseeing the firm's project management capabilities, education and training and quality systems. Major projects under his direction included the Sainsbury Wing of the National Gallery, the Glaxo Wellcome Medicines Research Centre at Stevenage, and the UK Pavilion at Expo 92 in Seville. In 1969 he helped create the multidisciplinary engineering design capability that is now a core business for the firm. He is currently Chairman of the firm's Corporate Services Division. He was Chairman of the Steel Construction Institute from 1994–1998. He is a Fellow of the Royal Academy of Engineering. He is also currently Chairman of the Joint Board of Moderators, which accredits engineering courses at over 100 universities in the UK and overseas on behalf of the Institutions of Civil, Structural and Building Services Engineers.

Norman Haste OBE

Norman Haste has spent most of his career working on major civil engineering projects and was Project Director for the Second Severn Crossing linking England and Wales. He was appointed Project Director for the proposed Terminal 5 Development at Heathrow and handled the infrastructure issues integrating the project with both the Heathrow Express and the Piccadilly line. He joined Crossrail as Chief Executive in 2002. His interest in the long-term cost of owning and operating buildings is mainly in the area of balancing capital costs with achieving flexibility for maintenance and adaptability for long-term use. Modular construction with standardisation in the use of components is of particular interest. He is a Fellow of the Royal Academy of Engineering, of the Institution of Civil Engineers and of the Institution of Highways and Transportation. He was awarded the OBE in 1996 for services to civil engineering.

Alan Jones

Alan Jones joined BICC plc as Chief Executive in April 1995. After taking an engineering degree at King's College Cambridge, he joined GEC in 1961. In 1973 he moved to Plessey where, in 1975, he was appointed MD of Plessey Marine and in 1980, additionally, MD of Plessey Radar. He joined the main Board as International Director in 1985 and from 1987 to 1989 was MD of Plessey Electronic Systems Group. In 1989 he was appointed Chief Executive of Westland. In 1994 Westland was taken over by GKN and Alan Jones joined the GKN Board. He is a Fellow of the Royal Academy of Engineering, a Fellow of the Institution of Electrical Engineers, a Fellow of the Royal Aeronautical Society, and a Member of the President's Committee at the CBI.

Bryan Lawson

Bryan Lawson is Professor of Architecture at the University of Sheffield. Formerly Head of the School of Architecture, he is now Dean of the Faculty of Architectural Studies. He is also Distinguished Visiting Professor to the Faculty of Design and Environment at the National University of Singapore. Bryan Lawson studied at the Oxford School of Architecture, followed by a period in the Applied Psychology Department at the University of Aston in Birmingham where he obtained his Masters and Doctorate. He is a qualified architect and has practised in both the public and private sectors. He has particular experience of design for healthcare. His research has been mainly concerned with the design process, computer-aided design, and architectural psychology. His books include *How Designers Think* and *Design in Mind*, which deal with the nature and practice of design, and *The Language of Space* which explores the psychology of spatial behaviour. His contemporary work concentrates on the briefing and feedback processes in design and how clients and users can contribute to those processes. His work has been funded by EPSRC, DETR, DTI, EEC, RIBA, ARCUK and NHS.

Adrian Leaman

Adrian Leaman is a social scientist who specialises in occupant feedback, briefing of building designers and managers, and strategic planning. His main interests are the behaviour and attitudes of building users, and design and management problems related to briefing, usability and human performance in buildings, the workplace and cities. He carried out pioneering and influential research work on occupant health in buildings in the 1980s. His current work now covers human, environmental and investment issues relating to buildings users' needs. He carried out the occupancy surveys for the internationally acknowledged Probe studies of building performance. He has presented his work at conferences around the world, and has written over 100 publications. He has been managing director of Building Use Studies (BUS) since 1987 and, between 1993 and 1997 he was a member of the Institute of Advanced Architectural Studies, University of York. In 1998 he was Visiting Professor at the Department of Real Estate and Project Management at the University of Delft, Netherlands. He has also worked at the Science Policy Research Unit (University of Sussex), the Royal Institute of British Architects and the Bartlett School of Architecture.

Sebastian Macmillan

Sebastian Macmillan trained as an architect at Liverpool University, before writing his Ph.D. at the Royal College of Art. He is a member of the Royal Institute of British Architects, and ran an architectural practice for ten years. In 1984 he set up Eclipse, a consultancy specialising in

research on the design and management of the built environment. He has written many publications for the government's Energy Efficiency Best Practice programme and, more recently, for the Construction Best Practice Programme. He has a part-time appointment at Cambridge University's Martin Centre where he is responsible for coordinating the Centre's research programme, and has studied the business process of interdisciplinary design. He wrote the technical manual *Environmental Management for Hotels: The industry guide to best practice*, and jointly edited a book on *Interdisciplinary Design in Practice*. He was seconded to the Engineering and Physical Sciences Research Council as Sector Programme Manager for Construction, 1999–2001. He is active in various construction sector improvement initiatives including Technology Foresight and the Construction Research and Innovation Strategy Panel.

Giles Oliver

Giles Oliver is an architect in practice with Penoyre and Prasad Architects. He is also an affiliated lecturer at the University of Cambridge School of Architecture where he is visiting tutor to the Interdisciplinary Design for the Built Environment Master's programme, for which he was founding coordinator in 1993. In July 1999 he was invited to chair the Construction Research and Innovation Strategy Panel's Design Task Group, and its report and recommendations form the basis of his contribution to this book (Chapter 12). His built work has included social housing, special needs housing, community and healthcare buildings and, more recently, master planning for urban regeneration in Gravesend and East London. His special interest is in deepening the terms within which health and the environment are understood, championed and realised in practice. He regularly contributes reviews of completed projects to *Architecture Today* and other architectural periodicals.

Tony Pollington

Tony Pollington was previously a Civil Servant, serving in the Ministry of Public Building and Works, the Department of Transport, the Department of the Environment, and the Property Services Agency. He gained experience in town and country planning as Regional Controller (Planning) for DoE Eastern Region, and in procurement for the PSA. He is a member of the Chartered Institute of Purchasing and Supply. In 1995, having retired from the Civil Service, he was asked to assist in establishing the Construction Clients Forum (CCF), now the Confederation of Construction Clients (CCC). The CCC brings together public and private sector clients of the construction industry to promote improvements in the industry through collaboration between suppliers and clients.

Sunand Prasad

Sunand Prasad is a founding partner of Penoyre and Prasad Architects, a London-based practice known for designing a diverse range of award-winning buidings. He is a Commissioner of CABE (the Commission for Architecture and the Built Environment) and founder of the Constructive Change group of the Royal Institute of British Architects which organised the conference that led to this book. He has been a member of the RIBA Awards Group and Health Clients Forum and a vice-president of the Architectural Association. Sunand's theoretical work includes architecture and cultural diversity, the exploration of the value of design, North Indian urbanism and domestic architecture and writings on Le Corbusier. He played a key part in the development of the Construction Industry Council's Design Quality Indicators and led the compilation of the standard guide: *Accommodating Diversity: Housing design in a multicultural society*. Sunand has taught and lectured in many schools of architecture in the UK and India, acted as external examiner and continues to be involved in teaching.

Dickon Robinson

Dickon Robinson started his career with a management consultancy engaged in environmental and behavioural research. He then worked as an architect in private practice, designing hospitals and housing schemes. During this period, he was a founder member and first Chair of the Soho Housing Association and was involved in community action groups in the West End, including the Save Piccadilly Campaign and the Soho Society. In 1975, he joined the London Borough of Camden Housing Department. As Assistant Director of Housing for Property Services he was responsible for the Council's Housing Investment Programme, building new homes and modernising older estates. He joined the Peabody Trust in 1988 as Director of Development and Technical Services and has been responsible for leading the greatly expanded new build and modernisation programmes which have repositioned Peabody as a key London regeneration agency. He was the Chair of the Foyer Federation between 1992/2001 and is a Board member of St Mungo's. He is a CABE Commissioner, a member of the English Heritage Urban Panel and patron of the Urban Design Group. As a West End resident for the past 25 years, he has a particular interest in mixed use developments, harnessing the arts to regeneration projects and promoting innovative construction and architectural excellence.

Jon Rouse

Jon Rouse is Chief Executive of the Commission for Architecture and the Built Environment. CABE is the Government's architecture champion for England, charged with facilitating improvements in the quality of the whole of the built environment – buildings and the spaces in between. Jon was previously Secretary to the Urban Task Force, and Policy and Communications Manager at the Government's urban regeneration agency, English Partnerships. Before that, he spent five years at the Department of the Environment, including a spell as Private Secretary to the Minister for Housing and Local Government, as well as secondments to the London Borough of Ealing and the Energy Savings Trust. He has a first degree in Law, and Masters in Urban Policy and Business Administration, specialising in corporate finance. He is an Honorary Fellow of RIBA and an Honorary Member of the RTPI.

Ammon Salter

Ammon Salter is a Research Fellow in the Innovation Studies Centre, the Business School, Imperial College London. He has a D.Phil in Science and Technology Policy Studies from the Science Policy Research Unit, University of Sussex. He has worked as a consultant and advisor on a number of innovation projects, including the Program on Globalisation and Regional Innovation Systems (Toronto University) and research on Ontario's Innovation Systems. He was involved in a study of the Economic Benefits of Basic Research for the UK Treasury. He is currently engaged in an EPSRC funded project on management of knowledge in dispersed and co-located teams

Peter Trebilcock

Peter Trebilcock is Head of Architecture with the AMEC Group, where he leads the architectural practice of over 60 architects and designers based in four UK offices. The Group's building projects extend across the UK and internationally, and serve the needs of the pharmaceutical, education, healthcare, defence, manufacturing and transport sectors. Peter is a consultant architect to the Steel Construction Institute and the author of several publications concerned with steelwork and modular construction. He has lectured widely in the UK and abroad, and been a competition judge in several national and regional architectural competitions. He is a regular contributor to the architectural press. Peter is actively involved in the Royal Institute of British Architects as Vice President (Membership 2001–2003); he served

on the RIBA Board, was a member of the National Council 1997–2003, and is chairman of the Membership and Regional Chairman's committees.

Paul Wheeler

Paul Wheeler is a senior consultant at DEGW and the Director of the Workplace Forum, a learning and research network exploring best practice in the workplace. He was one of the DEGW team responsible for running the first large-scale piloting of the Housing Quality Indicators system that DEGW developed for the Housing Corporation and the DETR. Since joining DEGW in 1999 he has worked in the Research and Methods team applying his interest in methodology, which dates back to his academic studies on internal and external research projects. He is the project coordinator for the SANE Project (Sustainable Accommodation for the New Economy), a multidisciplinary European Commission-funded research project into the future of the workplace. He is also closely involved with DEGW's client project teams reviewing international best practice and developing novel and innovative working environments. Prior to joining DEGW Paul worked in strategic research for Andersen Consulting and in business journalism. His interest in research, research approaches and methodologies developed as an undergraduate studying philosophy, particularly philosophy of science, at UCL, and as a postgraduate at the LSE studying politics and economics.

Jennifer Whyte

Jennifer Whyte is a Research Fellow in the Innovation Studies Centre at the Business School, Imperial College London. She is interested in the design and visualisation of the built environment. She has worked on a series of projects for sponsors such as the Construction Industry Council, Design Council and the Department of Trade and Industry (DTI), including the Design Quality Indicators (DQI), champion as a client; the building conceived as a driver for organisational change; an incremental process for exploring the costs and benefits of alternative environmental control systems; or formal value engineering and value management programmes.

The book is intended for those who are engaged in design, particularly within architectural, engineering, planning, surveying and project management practices, as well as clients responsible for commissioning buildings and civil engineering projects. It illustrates what 'good design' is and how to achieve it, and provides a vocabulary and evidence by which designers can argue the case for the importance of what they do and what they contribute. It should be a useful text book for many university courses in the built environment, including architecture, engineering, construction, planning and urban design.

The book's origins

The book's origins lie in two separate but intimately linked initiatives, as well as in a climate of opinion in which design is perceived as fundamental not only to the *Rethinking Construction* initiative (Construction Task Force, 1998), but also in relation to the urban renaissance (Urban Task Force, 1999; DETR, 2000).

In response to the publication of *Rethinking Construction*, the RIBA's Practice Committee formed the Constructive Change group in 1999, chaired by Sunand Prasad. The group put together a booklet, *Architects and the Changing Construction Industry* (RIBA, 2000), which was widely circulated, and decided to organise a one-day conference at the RIBA about the value of design.

In another part of the forest and in the same year, the Construction Research and Innovation Strategy Panel (CRISP) identified that *design* was an under-researched topic, and

formed a Task Group chaired by Giles Oliver. The Group commissioned a paper to identify and categorise academic research and industry initiatives relating to design as a value generator. The group's debates – updated to reflect subsequent events – are vividly captured in Chapter 12.

Other related initiatives were under way at the same time. The RIBA's Future Studies group had commissioned Ken Worpole and Eric Loe each to write a booklet on the value of architecture (Worpole, 2000; Loe, 2000). At the Movement for Innovation (M4I) conference in 1999 a group of architects became concerned that the M4I Key Performance Indicators (KPIs) – which focus on construction process issues such as timely completion, financial control and safety on site would become the de facto measure of design quality for new buildings. Robin Nicholson, then chair of the Construction Industry Council (CIC) was among them, and in consequence the CIC initiated a project to devise design quality indicators, appointing the Science Policy Research Unit as research contractor.

The Constructive Change group's conference, *Design Quality – the evidence*, was held at the RIBA in September 2000. Here, many of these initiatives came together for the first time. There were presentations about the CRISP Task Group's work, about recent and current research into design, about the emerging Design Quality Indicators; and also about the Clients' Charter and the work of the Commission for Architecture and the Built Environment (CABE).

Subsequently, the Constructive Change group determined that the emerging understanding about the relationship between *design*, *quality* and *value* in the built environment should be captured in the form of a publication, and the members of the group asked me to edit this book on their behalf. The chapters it contains go far beyond the presentations from the original conference and, of course, those from the conference have been updated. But it is important to record that the book owes its existence to the initiative taken by the group and particularly to the enthusiasm of Sunand Prasad.

Sebastian Macmillan
University of Cambridge
March 2003

References

Audit Commission (2003) *PFI in Schools: the quality and cost of buildings provided by early Private Finance Initiative schemes*, London: Audit Commission.

Construction Task Force (1998) *Rethinking Construction*, London: DETR.

DETR (2000) *Our Towns and Cities: the future – delivering an urban renaissance*, London: DETR.

Loe, E. (2000) *The Value of Architecture: context and current thinking*, London: RIBA.

RIBA (2000) *Architects and the Changing Construction Industry*, London: RIBA.

Urban Task Force (1999) *Towards an Urban Renaissance*, London: Thomas Telford.

Worpole, K. (2000) *The Value of Architecture: design, economy and the architectural imagination*, London: RIBA Future Studies.

Chapter 1

Design as a value generator

Sebastian Macmillan

There has never been a better time to address the issue of design quality and the value of design. Both are high on the political agenda. Government has endorsed the view that that everyone benefits from the buildings, towns and cities where we live and work providing efficiently constructed environments that promote health, productivity, and civic pride. And it is supporting initiatives to promote sustainable development, to improve the design of the built environment, and to raise the efficiency of the construction industry.

   Although there are antecedents, these three initiatives largely began with the election of New Labour in 1997, when sustainability, the built environment and the construction industry were all the subject of political attention. The Deputy Prime Minister commissioned both a Construction Task Force led by Sir John Egan, and an Urban Design Task Force led by Lord Rogers. The Urban Task Force report (1999) called for a design-led urban renaissance: 'Our analysis of successful urban design case studies emphasises how deeply quality of urban life is affected by good design,'

and

> Design is a core problem-solving activity that not only determines the quality of the built environment – the buildings, public spaces, landscape and infrastructure – but also delivers many of the instruments for the implementation of an urban renaissance.

The Construction Task Force report (1998) made a number of recommendations for improving the quality and efficiency of UK construction, though it had little to say about design, indeed little to say about the product of construction other than that it should be completed on time and within budget. It was left to the Deputy Prime Minister retrospectively to introduce design as a vital component:

> Good design is an integral and essential part of *Rethinking Construction*. It is a key to many of the performance targets; it is a key to reducing construction time and

defects; it is a key to sustainability and to respect for the environment. In the broadest sense it is the key to respect for people, whether they be users of a building or passers by . . .

(Rt Hon John Prescott, 1999)

These sentiments about design were subsequently picked up, endorsed and expanded by the government's Better Public Buildings Group. In the Foreword to the group's publication *Better Public Buildings*, the Prime Minister commits the government to making a step change in the quality of building design in the public sector (DCMS, 2000):

> We know that good design provides a host of benefits. The best designed schools encourage children to learn. The best designed hospitals help patients to recover their spirits and their health. Well-designed parks and town centres help to bring communities together. . . . That is why I have asked ministers and departments across government to work towards achieving a step change in the quality of building design in the public sector. . . . I am determined that good design should not be confined to high profile buildings in the big cities; all users of public services . . . should be able to benefit from better design.

However, the Foreword also makes it clear that it is the Egan view of 'good design' that is being endorsed:

> It is widely believed that good design is a costly luxury. But this is simply not true. As Sir John Egan's report *Rethinking Construction* demonstrated, best practice in integrating design and construction delivers better value for money as well as better buildings, particularly when attention is paid to the full costs of a building over its whole lifetime.

By effectively defining good design as 'integrated design and construction' the publication neatly implied that Private Finance Initiative (PFI) schemes, where design is integrated with construction, or often subsumed by it, are as able as conventionally-procured buildings to achieve design quality.

PFI is typically finance-led rather than design-led. In recognition of the risk that good design is sacrificed to financial concerns, the Treasury Task Force produced a guidance note in which the contribution of design was ringingly endorsed:

> At its broadest, design is the process in which intelligence and creativity are applied to a project in order to achieve an efficient and elegant solution. . . . good design is not an 'optional extra', rather it is inherent in the way the brief is responded to from the very beginning. Design encompasses functional efficiency, structural integrity, sustainability, lifetime costing, and flexibility as well as responsiveness to the site and to its setting. . . . Good design involves creativity, and it should lead to simplification and to savings in cost. . . . it can increase outputs and add to the quality of service. It can also give the facility a competitive advantage in attracting both customers and staff. Good design can also contribute to wider policy objectives, such as those relating to the protection of the environment. Good design . . . adds value in the following ways: functionality; reducing whole-life costs; service enhancement; architectural quality and wider social and environmental benefits.
>
> (Treasury Task Force, 2000)

CABE, the Movement for Innovation, and Sustainable Construction

To help industry meet the Construction Task Force objectives, the Movement for Innovation

(M4I) was established in 1998. Its mission was 'to lead radical improvement in the construction industry in: value for money, profitability, reliability, and respect for people; through the demonstration and dissemination of best practice and innovation' (from the M4I web site www.m4i.org.uk.).

To deliver the step change in the quality of public buildings and champion good quality architecture and urban design, the Commission for Architecture and the Built Environment was established in September 1999, replacing the Royal Fine Art Commission. Initially funded by the Department for Culture, Media and Sport (DCMS), it was subsequently recognised in the White Paper *Our Towns and Cities: the future* (DETR, 2000) as being relevant to the responsibilities of the DETR which became its joint sponsor (following government reorganisation, the Office of the Deputy Prime Minister became its joint sponsor with DCMS).

The White Paper itself largely endorsed the call by the Urban Task Force for good design:

> We want good planning and design in new development and renovation to be second nature for everyone, in both the public and private sectors. To achieve this we need to demonstrate the benefits of good practice through real life examples and encourage people to take the importance of good design and planning more seriously.
>
> (DETR, 2000)

CABE has stated that 'Good design is fundamental to achieving high-quality public buildings' and has identified a number of steps that are needed to encourage it, including: raising client commitment to achieving design quality, setting project budgets based on whole-life costs and benefits, setting benchmarks for design quality, communicating design needs, ensuring full stakeholder involvement in the design process, and signalling the importance of design to the procurement process (CABE, 2002a).

The original *Rethinking Construction* report made no reference to sustainability, but the government initiative on sustainable development identified construction as a sector where improvement was needed. In the daughter paper *Opportunities for Change: Sustainable Construction* (DETR, 1998), a call was made for progress in two areas that relate to quality, even though the term design was not used. These are:

- appropriate quality, durable, built environments that are flexible and adaptable; . . .
- the provision of buildings which are resource and energy efficient in their operation, and which provide pleasing and efficient environments for living, working and leisure.

Both were endorsed in the subsequent publication *A Better Quality of Life: A strategy for sustainable development for the UK* (DETR, 1999). As Bordass (2000) explains, there is an urgent need to make buildings more resource efficient while also contributing to human satisfaction and to business performance; and these ambitions need not conflict.

Establishing the principles of good design

CABE has the remit to promote good design in towns and cities and has begun to establish the principles of good design. This is by no means the first attempt to do so. 2000 years ago, the architect Vitruvius' *Ten Books on Architecture* (Morgan, 1960), were respectfully addressed to the Emperor, and sought to influence the design of public buildings. He argued for six fundamental principles to be followed – order, arrangement, eurythmy, symmetry, propriety, and economy.

In our own times, roles have been reversed as Prince Charles sought to influence architects. In his *Vision of Britain* (1989) he proposed 'Ten principles we can build upon'. These were: *sense of place*, *hierarchy*, *scale*, *harmony*, *enclosure*, *materials*, *decoration*, *art*, *signs and lights*, and *community*. Five years later, the Royal Fine Art Commission published its enquiry into *What Makes a Good Building?* (RFAC, 1994) and identified *order and unity*, *expression*, *integrity*, *plan and section*, *detail*, and *integration with neighbouring buildings* as the criteria for a good building.

Other authors have also prescribed the attributes that buildings should demonstrate at the urban scale. Punter and Carmona (1997) review them, comparing and contrasting principles proposed by the Prince of Wales with similar lists from authors like Kevin Lynch, Jane Jacobs, Francis Tibbalds, the Urban Design Group, and others. Perfect and Power (1997) cover some of the same ground.

The Urban Task Force (1999) offered its own set of 'key principles' for urban design:

1   Site and setting
2   Context, scale and character
3   Public realm
4   Access and permeability
5   Optimising land use and density
6   Mixing activities
7   Mixing tenures
8   Building to last
9   Sustainable buildings
10 Environmental responsibility.

CABE's emerging guides to good practice (CABE and DETR, 2000; CABE and DTLR, 2001) begin to identify and prescribe the principles of good design at both the individual building and urban levels (Table 1.1).

Many of the Urban Task Force prescriptions were based on advocacy rather

Table 1.1 Principles of good design as identified by CABE

CABE (2002b) **What makes a good project?**	CABE (2002c) **Principles of good design**	CABE (2002d) **What is a well-designed building?**	CABE (2002d) **What is a well-designed place?**
• order	• functionality in use	• appearance	• character
• clarity of organisation	• build quality	• context	• continuity and enclosure
• expression and representation	• efficiency and sustainability	• buildability	• quality of the public realm
• appropriateness of architectural ambition	• designing in context	• maintenance	• ease of movement legibility
• integrity and honesty	• aesthetic quality	• operation	• adaptability
• architectural language			• diversity
• conformity and contrast			
• orientation			
• detailing and materials			
• structure, environmental services and energy use			
• flexibility and adaptability			
• sustainability			
• beauty			

than evidence (Cooper, 2000) and similar criticisms may be levied at CABE; that the evidence base on which these prescriptions are being made is, as yet, slight. Nevertheless, there is a growing body of research about the value of design at the urban scale, and also at the individual building level.

The evidence base for valuing design in the public realm

In 1995, the Department of Environment launched its *Quality in Town and Country* initiative (DoE, 1995). Research was commissioned into the quality of urban design, as reported by Rowley (1998). This examined the role and importance of urban design considerations, the benefits of giving explicit attention to urban design considerations, the factors which constrain the promotion of good urban design, and the incentives and other measures that might encourage increased attention and contribution to urban design quality. Noting the difficulty of defining and discussing urban design quality, the researchers set out a list of fifty urban design considerations, grouped into four bundles:

- Functional and social use considerations
- Natural environment and sustainability considerations
- Visual considerations
- The urban experience.

Each of five developments was rated against all fifty criteria on a scale of 0 to 4, using a form of multicriteria analysis. The researchers admit a number of methodological limitations to the study (ranging from ambiguity, overlap and contradictions between the fifty considerations, to lack of input from local people, lack of quantitative assessment where considerations might allow, and so on) but nevertheless are able to claim that of the five case studies, Brindleyplace came closest to achieving a high

standard of urban design when assessed by this process. Rowley concludes:

> While it is easy to cost a development, it is much more difficult to place a value on what are often intangible qualities, all the more so if a particular solution is innovative. So developers are frequently driven back onto a 'gut feeling' although a few claim to be able to measure the returns on investment in design quality. For this reason, persuasive architects and masterplanners can have a significant influence on property developers, helping to convince them of the added value better design may realize even if this involves an increased cost initially.

In 1999 the RIBA Future Studies group commissioned Worpole and Loe to report on the value of architecture. Worpole's review (2000) put forward four principal arguments about the contribution that architecture and design can make at the urban level (Table 1.2)

Loe (2000) was more concerned with the economic value and impact of individual buildings. His wide-ranging review covers building rating methods and building industry award schemes, He cites four types of buildings that respond to differing requirements identified in the 1991/92 study by DEGW and Technibank on *Intelligent Buildings in Europe*:

- Use value building – custom-designed for the owner-occupier, maximises the use value for the end user organisation.
- Exchange value building – developed speculatively, and designed to maximise the building exchange value as a commodity to be traded.
- Image value building – designed to maximise the image value of the building, often at the expense of efficiency or other qualities.
- Business value building – use, exchange and image are synthesised into a building

Table 1.2 The contribution of architecture

Impact	Example
The wider economic impact of attractive buildings and settings	Flagship architectural projects that have clear economic impact on the towns and cities in which they are located.
Achieving greater value for money through technical and intellectual expertise	How the skills and expertise of the architect can provide cost-effective solutions to complex problems, not only saving money but providing extra benefits in terms of increased space, easier access, more efficient living and working conditions.
Enhanced individual and social well-being, and therefore quality of life	The ability of buildings and places to provide heat and coolness, light and shade, companionship and sanctuary, excitement and rest . . . safety and security, greater legibility and assurance, and a greater sense of locality, identity, civic pride and belonging . . . architecture can be a vital part of a wider notion of quality of life.
Greater adaptability, energy efficiency and environmental sustainability	Greater regard for the orientation of the site, local topographical and environmental factors . . . and designing and fine-tuning buildings that take advantage of these factors to minimise energy use – and therefore revenue costs – and provide comfortable and pleasant environments in which to work.

After Worpole (2000)

where technology is fully exploited to maximise the range of options for the end user.

In 2001, CABE followed up the research reported by Rowley by supporting and publishing *The Value of Urban Design* (CABE, 2001). In the introduction, Sir Stuart Lipton describes it as 'an excellent starting point from which to build up the evidential core of our work'. It includes a review of the literature on the value of urban design, drawing attention to the range of stakeholders who benefit from higher design standards. Many of its key findings are reported in Chapter 11.

Evidence on individual sectors and buildings

CABE has also begun to identify and publish studies into how buildings and spaces create economic and social value (CABE, 2002e) Collectively, these begin to provide evidence of the value of design in various sectors including healthcare, education, housing, and business. A more comprehensive literature survey is available on the CABE web site (www.cabe.org.uk). Separate publications cover key sectors – healthcare (Building Futures, 2002), education (CABE, 2002c), and housing (CABE, 2002f). CABE argues that

Good design is not just about the aesthetic improvement of our environment, it is as much about improved quality of life, equality of opportunity and economic growth. . . . Good design does not cost more when measured across the lifetime of the building or place; good design follows from the employment of skilled and multidisciplinary teams; the starting point of good design is client commitment.

(CABE, 2002e)

CABE's growing evidence base excludes building science research, although there is growing evidence about how the occupants of buildings interact and control their environment. The most prominent research of this type is provided by the Probe (post-occupancy review of buildings and their engineering) studies. These were concerned not with the public realm but with meeting clients' needs, with occupants' self-assessments of their own productivity, and with energy efficiency. An overview is provided in Chapter 3, while Chapter 13 also draws on some of the lessons from Probe. Probe identified some persistent problems and inefficiencies in new buildings including high levels of air infiltration, inadequate management of energy, and over-complicated controls – all leading to unnecessarily high energy consumption and reduced comfort for occupants.

What Probe and similar studies demonstrate is that the most successful buildings from the perspective of occupant comfort are those that offer *adaptive opportunities* (Baker, 1996) – openable windows, adjustable blinds, locally controlled mechanical services, task lighting and flexibility in furniture layout and seating positions. Shallow buildings that allow natural ventilation, views to the outside and good daylight levels inside are typically preferred to deep plan alternatives.

Indicators of design quality

Buildings have diverse impacts – ranging from civic pride to occupant comfort. These are all design issues, but only rarely are they discussed at one and the same time. We seem to decompose the built environment by discipline. More than thirty years ago, Hillier, Musgrove and O'Sullivan criticised this trend and proposed a four-function model for buildings which attempted to capture and classify all their effects (Table 1.3). It is a reminder of the breadth of the impact of buildings individually and in combination – not only on the health, welfare and behaviour of occupants, but on the use of natural resources, on microclimate, on land values, on transport needs, and on people and society.

The much more recently devised Design Quality Indicator (DQI) tool attempts something equally broad. The tool asks assessors to evaluate the performance of a building against a wide spectrum of attributes collected under three main headings of functionality, build quality and impact. The DQI system is reported fully in Chapters 15, 16 and 17.

Of course, there are major questions about the indicators and their use in practice. These questions relate to two broad areas – first, whether the system has been devised in accordance with accepted practice for *multicriteria analysis* (which is the basis of the hierarchical decomposition and weighting system employed by the tool) and second about the information that is needed by, and is available to, the assessors when making their value judgements. Multicriteria analysis is a well established technique with a substantial literature about procedural issues such as the need for independence of criteria from one another, and the bias that follows if they are instead interdependent. As for the information needed, in order to evaluate proposals adequately at the design stage with respect to attributes like lighting quality and energy use,

Table 1.3 The four-function model

Function	Effect
Climate modifier	A complex environment filter between inside and outside, it has a displacement effect on external climate and ecology, and it modifies by increasing, decreasing and specifying the sensory inputs into the human organism
Behaviour modifier	It both inhibits and facilitates activities, on occasion prompting or determining them. It locates behaviour and modifies the total behaviour of society
Cultural modifier	A symbolic and cultural object, not simply in terms of the intentions of the designer, but also in terms of the cognitive sets of those who encounter it
Resource modifier	A building is an addition of value to raw materials and a capital investment, a maximisation of scarce resources of material and manpower, and a use of resources over time.

After Hillier, Musgrove and O'Sullivan (1972)

these are fairly complex judgements requiring not only some expertise but also representations or models (together with proposals for building services controls and their operation and management) that allow judgements to be informed and reliable. How quickly reliable assessments can be made in practice remains to be seen.

Despite shortcomings the DQI system is being piloted by sixty trail-blazing organisations. While the originators of the DQIs wish to disassociate themselves from producing mere checklists, one of the strengths of the DQI is to act as prompts about the impacts of buildings – for the design team during the design process, but also for clients. If the DQI tool helps to stimulate constructive discussion and debate within design teams and between them and their clients – about issues like inspiration and delight and how these are to be balanced against functionality and performance – it will prove a valuable adjunct to the techniques that support design, almost regardless of any theoretical weakness. It is to be hoped that, if the DQI system becomes widespread, it will be

for this constructive use about design priorities, rather than as a mere point-scoring tool.

Good design as part of the construction industry vision

In 2001 the Strategic Forum was established, with Sir John Egan as its chairman, to bring together a number of rethinking construction initiatives. Although design had been conspicuous by its absence in the original Construction Task Force report, it reappeared in the report of the Forum's first year's work, *Accelerating Change* (2002). The Forum's vision for the industry now refers to the economic and social value of good design:

Our vision is for the UK construction industry to realise maximum value for all clients, end users and stakeholders and exceed their expectations through the consistent delivery of world class products and services. In order to achieve this the UK construction industry must:

- add value for its customers, whether occasional or experienced, large or small;
- exploit the economic and social value of good design to improve both the functionality and enjoyment for its end users of the environments it creates (for example, hospitals where patients recover more quickly, schools and work places which are more productive and more enjoyable to work in, and housing which raises the spirits and enhances the sense of self-worth).

This enlarged ambition and inclusive vision seem more likely than before to awaken the interest of design practitioners, who had demonstrated a lack of engagement in rethinking construction. It introduces into the initiative an interest in buildings as social assets rather than products to be delivered at a point in time, and in value in use as well as capital cost.

Design as a means to add social, economic and environmental value

Chapter 5 cites what has become a much quoted ratio – 1:5:200 – for the relationship between the capital cost of a building, the running costs and the staff costs of building occupants. Within the total capital cost, fees represent around 10 per cent, so the ratio could be rewritten in broad terms:

- Design   0.1
- Construction   1
- Running costs   5
- Occupancy costs   200

Viewed in this way, it can be seen there is a ratio of some 2000:1 between occupant costs and design costs. Often, much of the effort during the design and construction phases of a building is directed towards reducing the 1 and

reducing the 0.1. So-called value management is often treated as a means to reduce costs rather than, as the term implies, add value. Often this becomes a process of identifying the least capital cost option for each building element. At worst, this militates against buildings where, for example, the fabric is designed to be selective in how it deals with climate – using natural means as far as possible for ventilation, daylighting and heating – so as to minimise the need for mechanical services and applied energy. It is important to seek best value for money overall (EEBPp, 2000).

But there are further arguments designers need to make about their contribution. These relate to the economic and social value of design. Designers need to argue the case for buildings to be seen as means rather than as ends, and for greater investment in design so as to impact on the 5 and the 200.

One approach for assessing these benefits is the organisational performance matrix, described by Spencer and Winch (2002). This is derived from work by DEGW into how building performance contributes to organisational success, and by Heerwagen who used a balanced scorecard approach to evaluate building facilities (Figure 1.1).

What is also needed is to feed forward the results of these kinds of measurement exercises into valuation procedures. Current valuation systems focus on replacement cost and market value but, in consequence, often undervalue substantially the contribution of the asset to the organisation. Replacement cost and market value fail to account for the impact of buildings on corporate identity, on the health, well-being and productivity of staff, on staff retention and recruitment potential. Collectively these intangibles represent a variety of benefits to clients and other stakeholders which a building raises in terms of its design value. They are not taken into account by current valuation methods. Crucial investment in improving the quality of the built environment is held back through lack of knowledge of how to

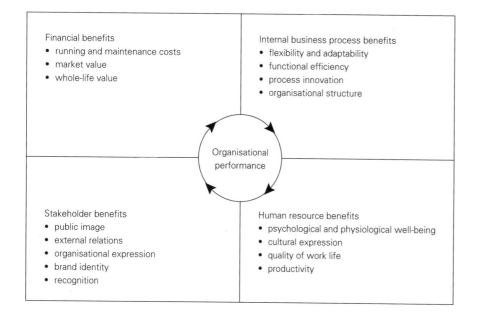

Financial benefits
- running and maintenance costs
- market value
- whole-life value

Internal business process benefits
- flexibility and adaptability
- functional efficiency
- process innovation
- organisational structure

Organisational performance

Stakeholder benefits
- public image
- external relations
- organisational expression
- brand identity
- recognition

Human resource benefits
- psychological and physiological well-being
- cultural expression
- quality of work life
- productivity

1.1
Organisational performance matrix
(after Spencer and Winch, 2002)

value these intangibles. This argument is explored further in Chapter 6.

However, measuring and valuing economic costs and benefits are only a part of a wider and longer-term issue of how to credit in some robust and measurable way the social and environmental advantages that arise from good design. CABE's collation of evidence, sector by sector, needs to be the start of an industry-supported knowledge base of research results demonstrating – defensibly and without special pleading – the full spectrum of benefits to all stakeholders arising from good design. To improve design practices and procedures and raise the profile and reputation of design within the built environment, there are at least four urgent needs:

- For continuing efforts by the research community to expand our knowledge of the added value of design
- For designers to embrace the emerging findings about how people use, react to, and value buildings, and to champion the ability of design to deliver environments within which people can pursue inspiring, meaningful, productive and happy lives

- For the industry itself to adopt and to promote to clients and to society a 'whole-life value' approach to the built environment that takes into account not just costs in use but also less tangible benefits
- For the development of valuation methods that reflect the full range of values in the built environment – including those of owners, users, developers, neighbours, and the general public – and relate to social, cultural, aesthetic, functional, environmental and economic criteria.

These actions will reinforce the emerging view that design should not be viewed as a cost, nor as costly. It is a vital activity that uses vision imagination to devise possible worlds that do not yet exist. Design exploits the skills of inventiveness and innovation not only to meet needs, to exceed the expectations of both clients and the public. Design provides ingenuity to solve problems in effective, efficient and previously unforeseen ways. Through design, alternative possibilities are devised that satisfy requirements to greater or lesser degrees and so clarify and illuminate the relationships between needs and wants, and make it possible to identify priorities among competing options. Design judgment determines the optimum balance between a wide range of attributes concerned with performance, functionality, appearance, longevity, robustness and ergonomics. Design is a generator of value and the key to ensuring the built environment provides wide-ranging benefits in which the whole of society shares.

References

Baker, N. (1996) 'The irritable occupant: recent developments in thermal comfort theory', *Architectural Research Quarterly*, vol. 2, no. 2, pp. 84–90.

Bordass, B. (2000) 'Cost and value: fact and fiction', *Building Research and Information*, vol. 28, no. 5/6, pp. 338–52.

Building Futures (2002) *2020 Vision: our future healthcare environments*, London: CABE.

CABE and DETR (2000) *By Design – urban design in the planning system: towards better practice*, London: Thomas Telford.

CABE and DTLR (2001) *By Design – better places to live*, London: Thomas Telford.

CABE (2001) *The Value of Urban Design*, London: Thomas Telford.

CABE (2002a) *Improving Standards of Design in the Procurement of Public Buildings*, London: CABE.

CABE (2002b) *Design Review: guidance on how CABE evaluates quality in architecture and urban design*, London: CABE.

CABE (2002c) *Client Guide: achieving well designed schools through PFI*, London: CABE.

CABE (2002d) *Better Civic Buildings and Spaces*, London: CABE.

CABE (2002e) *The Value of Good Design: how buildings and spaces create economic and social value*, London: CABE.

CABE (2002f) *The Value of Housing Design and Layout*, London: Thomas Telford.

Construction Task Force (1998) *Rethinking Construction: the report of the Construction Task Force*, London: DETR.

Cooper, I (2000) 'Inadequate grounds for a "design-led" approach to urban renaissance?' *Building Research and Information*, vol. 28, no. 3, pp. 212–19.

DCMS (2000) *Better Public Buildings: a proud legacy for the future*, London: Department of Culture, Media and Sport.

DETR (1998) *Sustainable Development: opportunities for change – sustainable construction*, London: DETR.

DETR (1999) *A Better Quality of Life: a strategy for sustainable development for the UK*, London: HMSO.

DETR (2000) *Our Towns and Cities: the future – delivering an urban renaissance*, London: HMSO.

DoE (1995) *Quality in Town and Country – urban design campaign*, London: Department of Environment.

EEBPp (2000) *The Design Team's Guide to Environmentally Smart Buildings*, Good Practice Guide 287, Energy Efficiency Best Practice programme, Watford: BRECSU.

Hillier, B., Musgrove, J. and O'Sullivan, P. (1972) 'Knowledge and design', reprinted in N. Cross, (ed.) *Developments in Design Methodology*, Chichester: Wiley, 1984.

Loe, E. (2000) *The Value of Architecture – context and current thinking*, London: RIBA Future Studies.

Morgan, M. (trans.) (1960) *Vitruvius – The Ten Books on Architecture*, New York: Dover Publications.

Parfect, M. and Power, G. (1997) *Planning for Urban Quality: urban design in towns and cities*, London: Routledge

Prince of Wales (1989) *A Vision of Britain*, London: Doubleday.

Punter, J. and Carmona, M. (1997) *The Design Dimension of Planning: theory, content and best practice for design policies*, London: E and FN Spon.

RFAC (1994) *What Makes a Good Building?* London: Royal Fine Art Commission.

Rowley, A. (1998) 'Private property decision makers and the quality of urban design', *Journal of Urban Design*, vol. 3, no. 2, pp. 151–73.

Rt Hon John Prescott (1999) DETR Press release, 19 July 1999.

Spencer, N. and Winch, G. (2002) *How Buildings Add Value for Clients*, London: Construction Industry Council, Thomas Telford.

Strategic Forum for Construction (2002) *Accelerating Change*, London: Strategic Forum.

Treasury Task Force (2000) *How to Achieve Design Quality in PFI Projects*, Technical Note 7, London: HM Treasury.

Urban Task Force (1999) *Towards an Urban Renaissance*, London: E and FN Spon.

Worpole, K. (2000) *The Value of Architecture: design economy and the architectural imagination*, London: RIBA Future Studies.

Part 1

The perspective of clients

Without clients, the construction industry cannot build. What do clients want from their buildings, and what steps can they take to ensure they receive it? This first section of the book discusses design quality as seen by clients. The opening chapter in this section is by Tony Pollington who assisted with establishing the Construction Clients Forum (CCF) – an umbrella body for a number of client organisations, and which later became the Confederation of Construction Clients (CCC). His chapter addresses the subject of clients and construction. His key point is that clients require buildings to support their own business processes – not as ends in themselves, but as means to an end. Designers therefore need to work with clients to understand the nature of those processes. His chapter also emphasises that feedback about the results is necessary to ensure the industry learns from experience.

In July 2000 the Deputy Prime Minister challenged the client community to draw up a charter that would set out the minimum standards they expected in construction procurement, as well as their aspirations for the future and a programme of steadily more demanding targets to drive up standards. The Charter was launched in December of that year, and Tony Pollington's chapter sets out its main features. The Charter commits clients, who agree to be bound to it, to adopt a number of good practices, such as providing leadership, treating the supply team fairly, promoting trust, identifying and managing risk, minimising waste, and respecting the health, safety and welfare of all those involved in the construction activity. The Charter expects clients to define measurable targets, many of which are design-related, and is widely recognised as a compendium of good client procurement practices, or good clientship. Together with other benchmarking initiatives – of the construction process through the M4I Key Performance Indicators, and of designs through Design Quality Indicators, the Clients' Charter emphasises the responsibilities as well as the rights of clients, and provides a way to benchmark them.

Once clients have decided to build, they need to understand the options open to them and the associated costs and benefits. To do this, they need knowledge of the effectiveness of their present facilities, and how their buildings help or hinder their business performance. The CCC initiated research to help clients and the industry review the performance of their buildings. The intentions behind this are to make the business case for undertaking feedback, to define what sort of feedback should be sought (for example, on the processes of procurement and delivery, and on the performance of the product) and to give practical advice to organisations on how to get started.

The Confederation of Construction Clients recognised the importance of learning from buildings both to improve their operation and to feed forward to new projects. In Chapter 3, *Learning more from what we build*, Bill Bordass presents a brief history of past research into building performance evaluation, summarises the benefits of such evaluations, and identifies different levels of approach. For organisations, the benefits of evaluating their facilities include: demonstrating their interest in occupants' welfare; helping managers to understand the potential of their facilities and how to fine-tune and operate buildings better; and improved space planning and asset management. In the longer-term, improved feedback has the potential to raise standards and provide design guidance, enhance performance over the whole-life cycle, and contribute to better designed and managed buildings. Yet where major evaluations have been undertaken these have most often been in response to some business driver, for example buildings having a negative impact on an organisation's customers; reactive rather than proactive.

Four levels of evaluation are set out: systematic walk-through observations; facilitated discussions in post-project review workshops; questionnaires and interviews; and physical monitoring, testing and analysis of performance facts and figures. Each has its own strengths, but it is in combination that they are at their most powerful, combining both *hard* and *soft* issues, and qualitative and quantitative evidence. The chapter ends with a call for closer links between the supply side and users and managers, particularly during the first year after handover of a building. While right first time is a commendable ambition, many buildings can benefit from a period of sea trials and fine tuning. These can help the client to understand better how the building operates and responds to controls, and the design team to learn from feedback and improve delivery on subsequent projects.

Chapter 4 is by Dickon Robinson of the Peabody Trust and discusses the client's perspective on the value of good design. The Peabody Trust is, of course, no ordinary client – this is the perspective of what is sometimes thought of as 'the enlightened client' – and Robinson champions innovation, design, long-term vision, people-based solutions, and partnering arrangements. He describes how the Trust has begun to explore mixed-use housing and to use leading edge architects, and has even promoted an architectural competition. Peabody has diversified into key worker housing and low cost home ownership, and has embraced innovative funding arrangements, procurement routes and construction techniques. At the same time, their ambition is also towards long-term fitness for purpose, and to construct buildings that contribute to urban regeneration. The author shares with Lord Rogers a view that urban design can be achieved through design-led construction projects – bespoke solutions with an ambitious vision. While commending the Egan report for its emphasis on innovation and involving people, he expresses concern that there is too much stress on building faster and more cheaply – on the product rather than on the process. He notes that, at worst, architects and engineers are losing influence under the new arrangements, and he questions whether the Egan agenda can deliver the Rogers' design-led vision.

Dickon Robinson then turns his attention to the importance of long-term working partnerships, where continuity of personnel creates mutual confidence and trust. That this is a gradual process should not be overlooked, it needs a period of joint working. He is also realistic about risk-sharing and accepts that at the end of the day it is the client who shoulders the risk – although he believes that increasingly all the parties will come to share in the risk, and that the allocation of rewards may also change. The right of designers to exert the dominant influence over the form and aesthetics of the building may have to be earned, and a share of the risk accepted. He concludes that design is about creating value, and high value leads to a lasting legacy – at its best the design process extracts the full potential of the site and adds both real and intangible values. The way forward for affordable housing and the creation of attractive neighbourhoods, he argues, is by a bespoke development-led approach, that exploits factory-based standardised construction technologies to achieve high quality.

Chapter 5, *The long-term costs of owning and using buildings*, was originally published by the Royal Academy of Engineering and is reproduced with their permission. Its authors are Raymond Evans, Richard Haryott, Norman Haste and Alan Jones. The authors reinforce the views expressed in Chapter 2 that clients primarily want buildings to support their own business process, whether these are concerned with generating wealth or providing a service. To do so effectively, facilities must create an environment where people feel motivated to give their best; and well-designed and well-managed buildings can lead to significant productivity gains. The authors provide a now much-quoted ratio – 1:5:200 – between the capital cost of a building, the cost of operating and owning it, and the overall cost

of the people working in it. They use this ratio to emphasise the importance of considering medium- and long-term issues in the design of buildings, and using a whole-life cost approach and life cycle analysis, rather than a short-term approach. The authors go on to review some of the evidence about the health and productivity of building occupants, particularly in relation to the issue of indoor air quality, and suggest that substantial productivity gains are possible through good design.

The authors also address the design and construction process and suggest ways of reducing building costs. They recommend a 'loose fit' approach between building fabric and building services for ease of installation, speed of construction, simplified maintenance and greater flexibility for future adaptations. They commend modularisation and standardisation, the early involvement of constructors, suppliers and installers, and computer-based modelling to help evaluate alternative options and reduce uncertainty about building performance. They recommend greater use of information and communication technologies for rapid data sharing and improved coordination.

The authors go on to discuss the operational phase of the building. They note the need for departmental adjacencies and functional space planning, for minimising energy consumption and environmental impact and for providing integrated IT systems. They recommend the involvement of the facilities manager in regular assessments of productivity, and propose reviews of the productivity benefits accruing from improved conditions – both complex tasks, as they freely admit. Nevertheless, the authors' wide-ranging prescriptions for improving the design, construction and operation phases of buildings serve to emphasise the substantial potential there is for better design processes, more efficient approaches to construction, and improved facilities management. Perhaps most valuable of all is their demonstration that all three phases are inextricably linked.

Chapter 2

Clients and quality

Tony Pollington

Today there is a much wider recognition that the construction industry's objective must be to provide the client with the best possible solution for the clients' own business. This seems a truism now, but it is only recently that the industry has truly accepted that its whole *raison d'être* is to provide a service to clients. Much has happened since 1994 but it was Sir Michael Latham (1994) who, as a result of a structured examination of the industry's approach to providing a service, first articulated that it would only change radically if the customers who pay the bills demand it. He spoke as a knowledgeable and experienced policy-maker in the industry, and his conclusions were both endorsed and given added impetus by Sir John Egan's Rethinking Construction Task Force (Construction Task Force, 1998). This identified the action programme necessary to achieve the improvements in the industry's performance defined by his experience as a major construction client, with continuing programmes of specialised works.

Few clients require buildings and/or constructions for their own sake. There are some examples of national memorials or decorative structures, but these are a small minority of projects. In the main, clients require buildings or constructions as an aid to successfully operating their own businesses, whether these are commercial operations or private assets. It is crucial, therefore, that clients know why they want a construction and what they want it to do to support the client's own operations. Unfortunately, not all clients recognise that they need expertise to identify these objectives successfully. It is not always the case that a construction solution is necessarily the optimum from a business point of view; perhaps the business objective might be better achieved by re-engineering the business, or by other management improvements. This is, after all, the stuff of everyday investment appraisal.

Where, however, a need for construction is properly established, it is essential that clients are aware of the options that are available to them and the costs and benefits associated with them. It is here that the development of appropriate systems of measurement is vital. Traditionally, perhaps, there has been some suspicion about the credibility of systems purporting to measure, for example, quality of design, or the costs in use of operating a construction. Clients in the main do not subscribe to this view. They expect to measure the effectiveness of their own operating processes, and express these in quantified terms, and they expect to be able to do this in relation to one of their most valuable assets – the facilities that they use. This is nothing new. Many years ago, at a time when the UK motorway programme was at its height, the Roads Divisions of the Ministry of Transport devised and used an assessment system which sought to give quantified monetary values to design options for road schemes, including not only relative savings in costs of accidents and reduced travel times, but more intangible benefits relating to preservation of landscape, settlements and heritage.

What clients want in relation to the product supplied to them by the industry, including the suppliers of specialised services such as design, is certainty about what it costs them to own an asset. This means that they need to know the full costs they will have to assume over the required life of the project. Unfortunately, the basis for knowledge of these whole-life costs is at present rudimentary in the extreme. Some attempts have been made, for example by BRE, to collect data relating to the performance over time of materials and components. But this is only partial, and needs to be recorded on a continuing basis.

Some technical information is of course also provided by manufacturers, but this is not always regarded, for obvious reasons, as truly objective. Clients acknowledge that they themselves need to develop expertise and methodologies for identifying and recording costs in use. These costs and benefits are not only the identified tangible ones – such as increased productivity in offices arising from a good quality internal working environment – but also less tangible and less easily measured external benefits reflecting the social impacts of the clients' construction project.

Feedback research

The Confederation of Construction Clients (CCC), with support from the Construction Industry Council, initiated a major research project, building upon and complementing existing and ongoing work, which was aimed at developing, testing and delivering a system of robust practical feedback techniques for use by a wide range of clients, and not just the large repeat clients. Chapter 3 presents an overview of the research and a summary of its interim findings.

Fortunately, despite the demise of the CCC in 2002, the research is to continue through to completion. Its aim is to record and interpret feedback information about the effectiveness of facilities in use. Those who stand to benefit most from such work are clients – because they will appreciate how feedback can improve their knowledge of how their facilities help or hinder their business performance. In turn this will lead to continuous improvement in their continuing building and construction programmes, and will help to direct how this improvement can be implemented, with the involvement of their suppliers.

The supply side will benefit because they will be able to improve their goods and services to meet better-defined client needs more effectively, and to supply information in ways which help clients and end users to carry out post-project evaluations more rapidly and consistently. The environment should also benefit, because the basic concepts of sustainability, environmental enhancement and pollution reduction will be better understood, implemented and reviewed. Finally, the national economy will benefit, because continuous improvement will give better value for money, reduce costs in use and increase the usefulness of facilities and the productivity of their occupants. Feedback will enhance the cumulative experience of clients, and in turn this experience can be evaluated and interpreted by the design and construction professional for the benefit of other users.

Client involvement will ensure that the benefits feed into the briefing and procurement system much faster than if feedback were undertaken solely by the supply side of the industry, or by intermediaries. Organisations will find the modest costs of beginning to implement feedback are soon repaid in added value and cost savings as better information becomes available, and is more easily acted upon. Once feedback becomes a habit, it will help turn construction into a learning process for everybody involved, rather than a succession of one-off achievements from which everyone escapes with a sigh of relief, often to make similar mistakes again.

The Clients' Charter

How confident can we be, however, that the clients are truly committed to advancing this measurement-based approach? The Construction Clients' Charter, launched by the Secretary of State for the Environment and the Construction Minister in December 2000 (CCC, 2000), expects real commitment from those clients seeking Charter registration. They commit to benchmarking their own performance in implementing programmes of improvement in their procurement processes, using an approach equivalent to those used to benchmark design achievement.

What is the Charter, and what relevance does it have? It is a commitment to action by clients – to adopt a culture of continuous improvement and to measure progress towards achieving this in relation to quantified performance indicators. It has the aim of

delivering for clients self-improvement in performance, higher productivity and profits for their businesses, recognition of their commitment to improved performance, and a better environment in which construction can take place.

It is important to identify the key cultural criteria which those clients seeking Charter status will be expected to adopt. There are four major generic areas of client emphasis:

1   Leadership and focus on the client
2   Product team integration
3   Quality
4   People.

Within these generic areas, clients are expected to identify programmes of improvement in their own processes which will achieve a culture aimed at working together towards high quality solutions. The cultural criteria which registered Charter clients have to adopt are:

Leadership and focus on the client:

- Providing client leadership, both for improvement in procurement processes and for the supply side to develop and innovate to meet clients' needs;
- Providing and setting clearly defined and, where possible, quantified objectives, scope and brief and realistic targets for achieving these;
- Fostering trust throughout the supply chain by treating suppliers fairly and ensuring a fair payment regime;
- Adopting a partnering approach wherever possible;
- Identifying risk and how best to manage it;
- Collecting and interpreting data on the performance in use of their construction solutions, for purposes of feedback.

Product team integration:

- Working in partnership with long-term relationships for all key suppliers;

- Involving all parties in the supply chain in the design process as far as possible;
- Promoting sustainability, use of renewable resources and the minimisation of waste in the construction process;
- Collecting and interpreting data on the performance of all the participants in the project;
- Maximising benefits from standardisation and off-site fabrication.

Quality:

- Aiming for quality-based solutions that yield maximum functionality for optimum whole-life cost, whilst preserving respect for the surroundings and the community;
- Promoting process and product improvements to minimise defects over the whole-life of the construction solution.

People:

- Adopting a policy of respect for all people involved in construction activity (health, safety, welfare, site conditions, diversity, training and certification);
- Training their own staff.

The measurement systems to be adopted reflect both the nationally adopted Key Performance Indicators (KPIs) promulgated by the Movement for Innovation (M4I), and the aspirations set out by the Commission for Architecture and the Built Environment (CABE).

Throughout the process, the importance to the client of recognising and incorporating the principles of good design is emphasised. For example, clients are asked to consider objectives that cannot readily be quantified, but which are intrinsic to creating corporate value from the project, such as design aspirations. They are asked to adopt a policy of involving the designer within the integrated project team throughout the project, and to involve suppliers in providing advice on

aspects of the design including functionality, whole-life costs and sustainability. Besides being encouraged to apply performance specifications wherever possible, clients are asked to set these, particularly for energy and materials use, in order to minimise waste. Altogether there are some ninety aspects of the clients' management of their construction interests which require clients to define measured targets over a period of time, and design considerations feature in most of them.

Initial responses to the Charter

How has the Charter been received? Evidence to date is that it is now widely recognised as a compendium of good client practice, possession of which assures the supply side that they are dealing with serious-minded clients genuinely committed to achieving quality solutions for their construction requirements, in full partnership with all elements of the supply chain.

Clients are of course sensitive to cynical reactions, that all this is merely aspiration, and that when the chips are down the determinative approach will be lowest cost, and acceptance of risk by the supplier only. Without appearing complacent, however, we believe that the Charter's operating framework will provide a method of assessing the reality of clients' commitment and will satisfy both suppliers and end-users. The aim is for Charter clients to be publicly recognised as adopters of good procurement practices, to establish genuine trust with their suppliers. Crucial to this is the commitment by clients to measuring their own progress in relation to a defined programme. We believe that the acceptance of the need to measure performance, including performance related to the effectiveness of design, is becoming widespread throughout the industry. Clients hope that as professionals begin to identify and apply methods of measurement in relation, for example, to the effectiveness of design, these will be developed in collaboration with clients, so that both professionals and their clients are committed from the earliest stage, both to the concepts and to their implementation.

References

CCC (2000) *Construction Clients' Charter*, Abingdon: Achilles Information Ltd.

Construction Task Force (1998) *Rethinking Construction*, London: DETR.

Latham, M. (1994) *Constructing the Team*, London: HMSO.

Chapter 3

Learning more from what we build

Bill Bordass

This chapter is based on an initial review undertaken in preparation for a project to improve feedback by construction clients and the industry in the UK. The review included a literature survey, a client questionnaire, and a series of workshops. The main output from the project is a Feedback Portfolio, providing access to a range of feedback techniques and results, and made available via the World Wide Web. A prototype can be seen at www.usable.buildings.co.uk. The project was initiated by the Confederation of Construction Clients and sponsored by the UK Department of Trade and Industry under its Partners in Innovation programme. However, the views expressed are those of the author.

There is clearly a perceived need for more feedback and not just in the UK. A review by the Federal Facilities Council in the USA (2001) presents a very similar picture and we have also had support from Canada, Australasia, and the Netherlands. Partly this seems to be because international trends have caused senior management to focus on core business, to outsource facilities expertise, and then to discover that facilities were more important to the business mission than they had thought. Organisations are now seeking to replace their lost expertise through post-project evaluation and making the supply side more accountable for performance delivery.

In spite of this, resources for feedback are still thin on the ground. Many clients don't see why they should pay. Nor, for the most part, do designers and builders, who also fear uncovering problems for which they may then be held responsible, at best giving them more (probably unpaid) work to do and at worst landing them in court and uninsurable. In addition, the hope that PFI[1] procurement would magically close the feedback loop has so far proved forlorn – PFI teams need feedback tools too.

In order to make feedback routine, there is a strong case for making a commitment to feedback (during briefing, design, construction and for at least a year afterwards) a contractual requirement; and for the processes and services to be defined and paid for accordingly. Proposals for project insurance may make this easier, as may a widespread demand for feedback services.

In our workshops and in some papers reviewed, there have also been pleas to regard feedback as much broader than the design and construction project – i.e. across a portfolio and from cradle to grave. Many clients are also particularly interested in looking at the full range of business benefits, and less concerned with the building-related ingredients such as occupant satisfaction and technical and environmental performance. While we appreciate these arguments, they do not fit well with the actuality of the scarce funds for feedback and the widespread ignorance of even the simplest issues. We fear that the best may be the enemy of the good; and that a more effective way to entrench feedback may be to find enthusiastic partners with whom one can demonstrate modest but robust successes, which then trigger virtuous circles in performance-driven organisations.

Regarding feedback techniques, there was a call for more clarity on the techniques available, how to get hold of them, how much they cost and the benefits they were likely to deliver. Here the proposed Feedback Portfolio will help, and this will also include examples of successful and cost-effective outcomes. We have identified four principal kinds of technique. These can be used separately or together – many people got the best results from combining hard and soft issues.

1 Observations
2 Questionnaires and interviews
3 Facilitated discussions
4 Physical monitoring, testing, and analysis of performance statistics.

Some history

The Building Performance Research Unit

Following a major review of architectural practice, in 1963 the RIBA (the Royal Institute of British Architects) published its Plan of Work for design team operation, which included Stage M – feedback. Later in the decade, twenty architectural and engineering practices, the RIBA, the *Architects' Journal* and the Ministry of Public Building and Works sponsored the Building Performance Research Unit (BPRU) to undertake feedback, bring together research, teaching and design on building performance, and publish the results.

BPRU only lasted four years in this form. Its work was largely on comprehensive schools. The results were published in 1972 in the book *Building Performance* (Markus *et al.*, 1972). While today the book strikes us as rather theoretical, its practical findings still ring true, for example an obsession with first cost, repeated mistakes (e.g. untreated timber windows failing and being replaced by the identical product), poor strategic fits between buildings and what goes on inside them (e.g. classroom sizes), and single issues (e.g. daylight factors) dominating the design, preventing effective integration (and the required daylight factors were not achieved anyway!).

The book included a plea for architects to be more involved in feedback. Ironically, in the year it was published (1972), the RIBA omitted Stage M from its publication on architects' appointment, reportedly because clients were not prepared to pay for feedback as an additional service; and the RIBA did not wish to create the impression that feedback would be undertaken as a matter of course. Today the wheel seems to have turned full circle, with the RIBA (1999) saying that

the biggest improvement to be made [in customer focus] is in systemising

- Identification of the likely users and how they will need the results communicated.
- A mixture of qualitative and quantitative, direct and indirect techniques.

If questionnaires were used, they must be designed by a skilled person, with items evaluated for usefulness, validity, discrimination and balance. Occupants must be told why it was happening, how the results would be used, if they would get them; and if so, what for and in how much detail.

Probe – Post-occupancy review of buildings and their engineering

This unique series of twenty published post-occupancy surveys ran in the CIBSE journal *Building Services* from 1995 to 2002. A special issue of *Building Research and Information* (Lorch, 2001) includes five papers on the method and conclusions. These in turn led to commentaries from experts around the world, and a response by the authors (Bordass, Leaman and Cohen, 2002).

Probe shows that it is possible to put feedback information on named buildings into the public domain. Its principal tools of an occupant questionnaire and an energy survey provided benchmark comparisons and rapidly unwrapped into other issues, e.g. briefing, procurement, build quality and business and facilities management.

Probe itself was oriented at extracting general messages for designers and their clients, rather than specifically feeding back to the building itself and the teams concerned.[9] Occupiers already operating monitoring and feedback systems used the Probe results to make further improvements, but those that weren't didn't necessarily react. Cultural change and incorporating feedback within routine design, construction, procurement and management practices are therefore important.

A major conclusion was that feedback would help to add value without increasing cost, by linking more closely the means (the constructed facility) to the client's ends, and thus stopping the project itself becoming the end and thereby losing touch with fundamental requirements. In addition:

- Clients should define their ends more clearly and undertake monitoring and reality-checks.
- Designers should seek to understand more about how buildings really work and make them better, more robust, more usable and more manageable.
- The supply side should establish 'no surprises' standards and provide support after handover, for example with provision for 'sea trials' periods in standard contracts, with much better proving of system performance and provision of aftercare to clients and occupants.
- FMs should monitor, be more responsive, and represent client requirements more strongly.
- Professional institutions should encourage feedback as part of normal practice.
- Government should encourage feedback and measures which lead to all-round improvement.

Types of feedback technique

From feedback to knowledge management

There are perhaps five levels to implementing feedback systems:

1   The will to do it, particularly at senior level.
2A Tools to help gather information on individual projects.
2B Tools to help people (clients, designers, users) get together to discuss how a

project went in a constructive way, to consider any data generated by 2A, and to learn from it.[10]

3 Means of turning the results of 2A and 2B into useful, actionable knowledge, starting with the parties concerned (e.g. client, design and construction team, users, managers).[11]

4 Consolidating this knowledge into organisational learning, or so-called Knowledge Management (KM) in 'learning organisations'. In our discussions, clients (even leading ones) said that they were not yet good at this – a problem shared with most construction industry companies, and also confirmed in the North American review (Federal Facilities Council, 2001).

5 Bringing all this together into industry learning.

Relevance to the current project

The project we are doing focuses on the nuts and bolts of data collection, i.e. Level 2, particularly 2A. However, many clients thought that the main problem was not a lack of techniques but of the will to use them (Level 1). Levels 3, 4 and 5 are largely beyond the scope of the current project, but are covered in others and will where appropriate be added to the Feedback Portfolio.

Four principal types of technique for collecting Level 2 information

We see four principal ways of collecting data, as outlined below. These can be used separately or together. There is widespread agreement that the most successful feedback exercises tend to combine both hard and soft issues, and both qualitative and quantitative methods.

Type 1 – Observation
Typically walk-through surveys, for example:

- Experts from Hereford and Worcester County Council used to walk through their recently completed projects and assess their impressions against a standard checklist.
- The Probe surveys make good use of walk-throughs of all parts of a building including service areas and plant rooms. These permit not only visual observations but spot tests, and spot measurements with hand-held instruments. At the same time they create opportunities for informal discussions with staff – from which much of value can emerge.

Systematic observations can also be undertaken, for example of how customers use a facility, or how staff undertake their work or, say, operate a control device.

Type 2 – Facilitated discussions for teams, clients and others
General guidelines have been developed and tested in the 'Learning from Experience' project (D. Bartholomew Associates, 2003) – not just to discuss the outcomes of a completed project (*hindsight reviews* in LFE's parlance), but during it (*insight reviews*), or before starting (*foresight reviews*). A format for post-project review workshops (fora) has also been developed by de Montfort University for the Higher Education Design Quality Forum (2000) and is now being applied in other sectors.

Type 3 – Questionnaires and interviews
Many techniques are already in use and will be reviewed in the course of the project (see Chappell and Willis, 1992). Workshop discussion suggested that there was scope for coordinating some key survey questions[12] in order to improve consistency, provide useful benchmarks and contribute to Key Performance Indicators (KPIs).

Type 4 – Physical monitoring, testing, and analysis of performance statistics
This can provide objective information, most easily on the internal environment and utility consumption – for which detailed information is increasingly available routinely from electronic building management systems (BMSs), at least in principle.

How can we get more feedback to happen?

Not enough feedback is happening

The construction industry is often slow to learn from its completed projects – particularly how they perform in the hands of their users. Problems can therefore persist, successes be overlooked, and innovations miss their targets. Feedback is not routine in the industry: there are many barriers and not enough drivers; and in this the US experience reviewed above sounds very similar to the UK's. Perhaps the greatest barrier is that the benefits are spread around, so no one party sees themselves as reaping enough of the benefit to bear the cost. The supply side also fears that they may expose problems which they will then get blamed for.

But shouldn't the supply side get things right first time?

Ideally perhaps they should, but this is unrealistic in the present situation where they do not routinely examine how their products really perform in practice. In addition, by their very nature, innovations cannot always be 'right first time'. However careful you are in planning and testing, there will always be surprises, as is well known in R&D with its all-pervasive 'Murphy's Laws'.[13] That is why scientific method is based on hypothesis, followed by experimental testing.

Most construction projects have experimental aspects

Except for the most standardised and repetitive projects (and even these need monitoring and feedback for quality control purposes), every new piece of construction is to some extent a hypothesis and its performance in practice is the experiment. But where are the designer/experimenters? In the distant past, when technology and user requirements changed slowly, one could perhaps rely on evolutionary feedback and the occasional catastrophe. More recently, one could look to academic study and the test of time. But today, when things are changing so fast, there is really no alternative to learning on the job.

The problem for clients

Clients are becoming aware that insufficient feedback within the industry is a problem for them too; particularly now they are coming to understand that facilities cannot be taken for granted – but can add value to (or subtract it from) their core businesses. At the same time, many have outsourced their feedback loops and find themselves more at the mercy of the supply side of an industry which frequently does not ask the right questions and does not know enough about what happens to its products after they have been handed over. While abject failures will come back to haunt them, disappointments often do not, and can even be regarded as successes and repeated virtually indefinitely.

Will clients have the time?

How can we make feedback happen in a world where clients seem to be increasingly short of time? Many clients do not even have time to make their requirements clear to design teams and to get involved in the necessary dialogue as the project progresses. How will they fit in feedback too? And how will the results be managed, not just for the clients and teams concerned, but for buildings which will also be in the public interest and to meet the challenges of sustainability, which stretch far into the future and well beyond the business concerns of today's customers?

Does post-occupancy evaluation get in the way of feedback?

We started the project seeing close parallels between feedback from completed projects and post-occupancy evaluation (POE). While undoubtedly there are, our research suggests that we should distance feedback from POE, as revealed in our workshops and in the FFC review in the USA (Federal Facilities Council, 2001). Rightly or wrongly, for many people POE has an aura of being somewhat academic and remote from clients, practice and project delivery. Instead, feedback – together with follow-through beyond project delivery into aftercare support – needs to be seen much more as a routine part of any project.

Feedback in the real world

For the current project, we are therefore promoting feedback as something practical, relevant and immediate. We suggest it is regarded as what Robson (1993) calls real-world research. Some principles (developed from Box 1.2 of Robson's book) are summarised in Figure 3.1. This is not to say that feedback cannot be used to test and develop theories – far from it – but that its focus should be on results and improvement.

Where should we start?

In our discussions and in some of the papers reviewed, people have mentioned the need for a cradle to grave approach, with a construction or refurbishment project being merely a small incident in a facility's life cycle; and an even tinier one in that of the organisations involved. People also mention a comprehensive approach, covering not just construction-related issues but overall business benefits.

Is the best the enemy of the good?

We agree with these sentiments, but also see that – in spite of the undoubted benefits –

Solving problems	rather than	just gaining knowledge
Predicting effects	rather than	finding causes
Getting large effects	rather than	relationships between variables
Looking for robust results and actionable factors	rather than	assessing statistical significance
Developing and testing programmes, interventions, services etc.	rather than	developing and testing theories
Field	rather than	laboratory
Outside organisation	rather than	research institution
Strict time constraints	rather than	as long as the problem needs
Strict cost constraints	rather than	as much finance as the problem needs
Little consistency of topic	rather than	high consistency of topic
Topic initiated by sponsor	rather than	topic initiated by researcher
Often generalist researchers	rather than	typically highly specialist researchers
Little use of 'true' experiments	rather than	much use of 'true' experiments
Multiple methods	rather than	single methods
Oriented to the client (particularly in reporting)	rather than	oriented to academic peers
Viewed as dubious by many academics	rather than	high academic prestige
Need for well developed social skills	rather than	some need of social skills

3.1
Real-world research
(after Robson, 1993)

many organisations are not prepared to invest in feedback systems. These may be two sides of the same coin: they fear elaborate feedback exercises because of their likely complexity, expense and risk. To stop the best becoming the enemy of the good, we suggest starting small and simple: even a little useful feedback can begin to turn what are so often vicious circles into virtuous ones, so starting small and simple may be the best way of developing effective systems which become comprehensive over time. As Probe has shown, looking at just a few things begins to unwrap into many other issues. The agenda soon becomes longer than most organisations can cope with – so the problem rapidly becomes one of prioritisation, and of identifying specific issues which need to be explored in more depth if the parties involved are sufficiently interested in them.

Business benefits, or just better buildings?

Just getting sounder buildings would be a good start. As said in a CRISP review (Blyth, 2000), most designers only notice that something is wrong when they are asked to investigate a failure. For example, in 1998, on the basis of Probe results, we warned a developer to look to the airtightness of their new buildings. Initially their designers said all was well when clearly it wasn't. Then they said it would cost more, but the developer did not want to pay as their customers wouldn't. But then the developer had a problem building. Further analysis then showed that over one-quarter of all complaints from their tenants were related to draughts, arising either from unwanted air infiltration, from HVAC system and control problems, or a combination of the two. In turn, questionnaire surveys reveal that complaints of this kind are statistically correlated with reductions in occupants' perceived productivity. The developer is now in the vanguard of those

seriously preparing their consultants and contractors to meet the pressure test requirements newly incorporated in Approved Document Part L2 of the Building Regulations for England and Wales (DETR, 2000).

Feedback and project delivery

The US experience (Federal Facilities Council, 2001) is that where POEs are done routinely, they nearly always happen in the first year after practical completion. To get closer links between the supply side, users and managers during this vital year is also a conclusion of the Probe team (sea trials) and other authors (e.g. the 'soft landings' idea of RMJM and the University of Cambridge, the 'continuous commissioning' process developed by ABS, and the RIBA's plea for more involvement in POE). It is time for clients and the industry to consider making a commitment to feedback (right through the project as well as in first year of operation) a standard part of project delivery.

Notes

1 The UK Government's Private Finance Initiative, in which public works are financed, designed, built and operated by the private sector.
2 For example, in a hospital where designers had provided demountable ceilings for 'flexibility', the ceilings could not be demounted owing to concerns about infection control.
3 For example, research by the Medical Architecture Research Unit, quoted in (Blyth, 2002), indicated that Nightingale hospital wards had proved more efficient in healthcare than many new alternative layouts introduced in the past 30 years.
4 An exception is Probe – a series of twenty POEs published between 1995 and 2002. This also gives priority to building services and environmental performance.
5 Some of these are already on www.usablebuildings.co.uk
6 However, time moves on, so techniques based on yesterday's priorities must also be alert to emerging new issues.
7 Interestingly, even Disney did not have an integrated knowledge management database, but three separate specialist systems. Much dissemination was by personal involvement, with the engineers who were

particularly involved in feedback acting as information carriers and being invited by teams to attend their meetings to inject their experience.

8   Iterative techniques can also be useful here. For example, for overseas building operations, the US Department of State first sends out a postal questionnaire to identify the occupants' views and concerns before deciding who will be on the team which goes to survey the building. The CIBSE TM 22 energy survey used in the UK Probe studies is also iterative, so a small amount of effort already gets a useful result, which can then be improved if everybody agrees it is worth doing so.

9   Clients do commission Probe-type surveys too, but as a rule the results of these are used internally and not published.

10 We are liaising closely with the parallel PII project on this aspect – Learning from Experience (LFE) (D. Bartholomew Associates, 2003).

11 Reviews of demonstration projects by the UK Movement for Innovation (M4I) and similar activities suggest that participation and word of mouth are much more effective in practice than databases and the printed word, at least in the early stages.

12 For example of staff, users, business managers, facilities managers, customers, and community interests.

13 Murphy's First Law: If it can go wrong, it will. Murphy's Second Law: Murphy was an optimist.

References

D. Bartholomew Associates (2003) *Learning from Experience: the Manual*, Cheltenham: David Bartholomew Associates.

Blyth, A. (2000) CRISP Consultancy Commission 00/02, *How can Long Term Building Performance be Built in?* Blyth Consulting (August 2000). Available on the CRISP website at www.crisp_uk.org.uk

Bordass, W. (2003) 'Learning more from our buildings, or just forgetting less?' *Building Research and Information*, in press.

Bordass, W., Leaman, A. and Cohen, R. (2002) 'Walking the tightrope: the Probe team's response to BRI commentaries', *Building Research and Information*, vol. 30, no. 1, 62–72.

Chappell, C. D. and Willis, C. (1992) *The Architect in Practice*, Oxford: Blackwell Science.

Cooper, I. (2001) 'Post-occupancy evaluation – where are you?' *Building Research and Information*, vol. 29, no. 2, 158–63.

DETR (2000) *The Building Regulations 2000, Approved Document Part L2: Conservation of fuel and power*, London: The Stationery Office.

Federal Facilities Council (2001) Technical Report 145, *Learning from our Buildings: a state-of-the-practice summary of post-occupancy evaluation*, Washington, DC: National Academy Press.

Higher Education Design Quality Forum (2000) *Post-occupancy review of buildings* (July 2000), downloadable from the HEFCE website, www.heestates.ac.uk.

Jaunzens, D., Hadi, M. and Graves, H. (2001) CRISP Commission 00/12, *Encouraging Post Occupancy Evaluation*, Environment Division, BRE, February 2001. Available on the CRISP website at www.crisp_uk.org.uk.

Lorch, R. (2001) Special issue on post-occupancy evaluation, *Building Research and Information* vol. 29, no. 2, March–April.

Markus, T., Whyman, P., Morgan, J., Whitton, D., Maver, T., Canter, D. and Fleming, J. (1972) *Building Performance*, London: Applied Science Publishers.

RIBA (1963) *Plan of Work for Design Team Operation*, London: Royal Institute of British Architects.

RIBA (1999) *Architects and the Changing Construction Industry*, London: RIBA.

RIBA (2000) *The Architect's Plan of Work*, London: RIBA Publications.

Robson, C. (1993) *Real World Research*, Oxford: Blackwell.

Warner, P. (2001) CRISP Consultancy Commission 00/04, *Matching Design Assumptions and Conditions in Use*, Geoffrey Reid Associates. Available on the CRISP website at www.crisp_uk.org.uk.

Chapter 4

A client's perspective on the value of good design

Dickon Robinson

Future generations will look back on the years immediately before and after the millennium and marvel at the number of major cultural and engineering projects completed in such a short time. These are exciting times architecturally, and London in particular is enjoying magnificent new structures and buildings which show what the design professions can achieve. Am I alone in feeling that by and large this upsurge of creativity and ambition has passed the world of housing by?

In the twenty-five years since the Housing Corporation was established, Housing Associations have spent billions of pounds of public subsidy and private finance. In many ways it has been a period of great achievement. There are several hundred thousand households who have a decent home and a roof over their head as a result. However, unlike the new towns programme, or the early estates of the LCC, or even the high-rise towers and slabs of post-war reconstruction, there is little sense that this investment has created a significant built legacy. No doubt

some will consider that, in the context of the popular view of post-war local housing estates, the self-effacement of much recent social housing built by Housing Associations is a good thing. I must admit, however, that I am uneasy about this. While there are some extremely good Housing Association refurbishment and infill new developments, there is also a great deal of unexciting and frankly rather indifferent development. I think too often an opportunity has been missed to make a major impact on improving the environment of our towns and cities through this massive investment in the urban fabric.

A legacy of housing design

Charles Handy has memorably remarked that organisations can look as far forward as they can look back – which puts my organisation, the Peabody Trust, at a distinct advantage. A quick look at our history is instructive. It was created by a bequest of half a million pounds in the 1860s, and became for the next twenty years the leading housing organisation in the country in terms of public health, development volume, influence of its Trustees and sheer energy. By the end of that first twenty years the Trust was housing over 20,000 people, albeit in conditions which would be regarded as unacceptably crowded today.

However, the story of the Peabody Trust in this century has been one of eclipse, first by local authority building programmes, then in the post-war period by an internal preoccupation with repairing wartime destruction, and later with modernising its stock in an external climate where socialism emphasised individual rights and charitable philanthropy was regarded with suspicion. At the beginning of the 1990s the Trust was often referred to as London's sleeping giant, and regarded by many as a rather stuffy and aloof organisation stuck in its Victorian past.

Under new management in the late 1980s a major estate modernisation programme was launched, and management policies overhauled. However, these initiatives made little impact on Peabody's public image, and indeed the latter did not really begin to change until we began to promote adventurous new building projects like London's first *foyers* and an inhabited bridge at Bankside. Peabody began to construct mixed-use housing projects that everybody endorsed but few were prepared to undertake, and the Trust began to use cutting edge architects and competitions to produce exciting buildings.

Peabody introduced carefully branded site hoardings to create a sense of the scale of our work with projects literally spread across the capital. Internally and externally this message was reinforced by showing that Peabody had reconnected with its creative early years by embracing innovative funding arrangements, procurement and construction techniques, and by diversifying into key worker housing, low cost home ownership and community and economic development. This

has been more demanding for staff, and accordingly within the development department there was a clear need to review the levels of skills and experience needed.

While the building professionals with whom they deal have well-established academic training programmes, there is no similar training for clients. You cannot do a degree course in being a building client – which is probably why most clients do not realise that they are also developers. You have to cross over from some other profession or career, and those who come from other professions are too often looked on by their peers as having left the mainstream of professional life. Perhaps it is not surprising that many residential social landlords (RSLs) have traditionally recruited development staff from a generalist rather than professional background, including many from an earlier housing management career. While many have been effective, I tend to the view that professionals often seem to get the most out of other professionals, or at least the relationship is based on a greater degree of mutual understanding and trust. As a result Peabody currently looks for a professional qualification in one of the environmental or construction professions or a related academic first or second degree.

The cumulative result of these steps is that Peabody is now seen as a much more progressive organisation, and what it does is seen as relevant to others, so its influence has grown. I believe the crucial impact of the new building programme cannot be overstated. Our buildings, like our clothes, send out powerful messages to others about our values, our ambitions, our success, and our wealth or lack of it. Too few organisations seem to understand this. No wonder organisations such as the Church of England have difficulty in establishing their relevance to modern society when all their buildings proclaim medieval images. And no wonder image-conscious media companies have forsaken Fleet Street and flocked to Canary Wharf.

4.1
**Holland House,
Newington Green by
Rivington Street
Studio, an example
of an architectural
competition winner**

Appealing, appropriate design

So we have learnt that we can use our
buildings to say positive things about us as an
organisation but also, and I believe more
importantly, to say positive things about the
people who live within them. Society today
often seems to be embarrassed that, while
most people are well-off, we still have a
substantial impoverished minority – the socially-
excluded in current parlance. Perhaps the real
problem with the ambitious post-war housing
developments was that they were too large and
obvious. Today we seek to eliminate this
embarrassing visibility of the poor by advocating
that their homes should be indistinguishable
from those the volume house-builders are
putting up for owner occupation. Out of sight is
out of mind, but I for one am uneasy about this
attitude, not least because volume house-

builders are not concerned with long-term
fitness for purpose and economic cost in use.
Kerb appeal is what matters in the war to keep
shareholders happy.

Fortunately the best Housing
Associations have stuck to their principles, their
standards and to appointing their own
architects. As with Peabody's BedZED
development in Sutton, many other housing
associations have energetically explored the
green agenda, focusing on energy saving,
carbon dioxide emissions and ecological impact
in a way apparently absent from the private
sector. Not only do their schemes enhance their
settings, giving a real boost to the
neighbourhoods, but they are genuinely socially
responsible.

The comparison with the bottom end of
the volume builders' product is stark. Little boxy
detached houses facing in all directions are not

energy efficient, are wasteful in materials and inflexible in use by nature of their minimal space standards. But this is difficult territory. Consultation with those affected directly or indirectly by development proposals is important and sometimes leads to insights and opportunities which would otherwise be overlooked. But there is more – much more – to being a good client that simply consulting all and sundry and seeking some middle way, for there most likely lurks the lowest common denominator. Libby Purvis quotes Lord Reith's working rule for the BBC as 'to offer the public something better than it thinks it likes'. I like that point of view and I believe it is nowhere more important than in creating new buildings and in particular those for the poor and disenfranchised.

As a client for a new housing scheme, one needs to distinguish between the interests of immediate occupants and future generations of occupants. The same goes for those who live and work in the streets around. As a housing charity there is also our long-term interest in our asset base, on which our very substantial borrowings are secured. Extra attention to design enhances long-term attractiveness and is reflected in higher property values over time. Really well designed buildings can trigger the improvement of run-down areas. I believe we need to think more about the long-term and less about the short-term. Costs in use, and the appreciation and delight of future generations are important considerations – in contrast with the often fickle and fashion-led tastes of current society.

This is not easy, and it is not necessarily popular but I believe that clients have a responsibility to confront these issues, especially in areas which need regeneration. Regeneration implies a new beginning, looking forward, not backwards, and therefore needs adventurous, youthful, contemporary architecture and not reproduction building styles and an over-emphasis on reusing existing buildings.

4.2
BedZED, designed to be the UK's first carbon-neutral housing development by Bill Dunster Architects, and developed by the Peabody Trust in partnership with BioRegional Development Group

4.3   a and b.
Dalston Lane, by AHMM. A controversial modern mixed use, keyworker housing scheme

a.

b.

A quality process or a quality product?

Exploiting design to advance urban regeneration is an idea championed by Richard Rogers, but I sense an underlying tension between the important proposals put forward by Rogers in his Urban Task Force (1999) report and Egan in his report *Rethinking Construction* (Construction Task Force, 1998). Rogers sees urban regeneration being achieved through design-led construction projects, large and small. The emphasis is on bespoke solutions to deliver an ambitious vision with utopian overtones. Egan suggests that better buildings are those which are built faster, more safely, with fewer defects and more cheaply. Some contractors have interpreted this latter agenda as endorsing their view that the design process – and the architect – should be subservient to their overall project management. I find it hard to see how this model will deliver Rogers' vision.

The aspect of the Egan Report I most applaud is his emphasis on innovation at the expense of conventional and established ways of doing things. I also particularly like the stress on building quality and involving people. However, I am concerned that in the brave new world he has stimulated there seems to be more emphasis on the construction process than on the product. Perhaps this was inevitable as the organisations, particularly the Housing Forum, set up to deliver his vision are dominated by producers – by which I mean contractors and house-builders – rather than by designers, which includes architects and engineers. I for one find it difficult to conceptualise innovation in construction as being a design-free thing. For me design and construction innovation should be one and the same thing.

Which brings me back to my earlier points about the legacy that we are creating. Many of the buildings which Peabody owns have been steadily fulfilling their purpose for the past 140 years. Those we build today will last in

their turn for at least as long. Once the building is completed, the dramas which surround its creation soon fade away. Today we do not dwell on the relationship between Cubitts, who built our earlier estates, and Henry Derbyshire, the Trust's first architect. We know his designs have withstood the tests of time and that the buildings were very well built. These were long-term relationships that lasted for over twenty years – and incidentally we are proud today that a descendant of Cubitts the builders, Sir Hugh Cubitt, is Chairman of the Trust.

Long-term working partnerships are crucial to the success of organisations. There are contractors, mainly small firms interestingly enough, who are working for us today and have been working for us for the last twenty years. There are some architects, quantity surveyors and engineers about whom I can say the same thing. To me the terms of their appointments or the form of building contract is in essence neither here nor there; we like the work they do and will continue to feed it to them. Absolutely fundamental to these relationships is continuity of personnel, which in turn is crucial to a sense of mutual confidence and trust. In this context I feel some nervousness that current enthusiasm for partnering arrangements is too simplistic in that it ignores the need to build trust over a period of joint working.

I am also concerned that some people feel that a sense that all the parties are equal and share the risks equally is implicit in partnering. This is not the real world. While I am emphatically positive about close and collaborative working, at the end of the day the client carries the can. It is the client who is buying a service from consultants and contractors, and not the other way round. The product is more important than the process, and the over-attention being devoted to the latter means that not enough thought is going into the legacy which we will leave behind us. In this context I am concerned that architects and engineers are losing influence in the new arrangements.

Looking to the future, perhaps the real issues are less how we resolve the traditional confrontations between consultants and contractors than how our shared industry will be reshaped by the all-powerful forces of the global market and the Internet. While the brand is king and major corporations swallow each other in an unprecedented feeding frenzy in the rush to achieve global domination, the Internet is spawning a great proliferation of new business and niche players. While global corporations are downsizing as fast as they can, all the jobs growth is with small companies.

For construction companies and large consultancies, economies of scale and an international span are attractive goals. By comparison, most architecture, engineering and cost consultancies often appear like cottage industries. But the challenge remains to show how can you make greater size pay if there is no standardisation of your product. Perhaps California is leading the way in this new world. In Hollywood, the studios are no longer the dominant force they once were. In the new world small companies and individuals come together to create a movie then disband only to reform with different partners to create the next one. In some ways this doesn't sound that different from the construction industry we know. However, the real difference is in the way risk and rewards are shared. Increasingly all the parties will have to bear some part of the risk, and the rewards will be different too. In the future perhaps there will be no fixed fees for consultants, but a slice of the action instead. A percentage of the box office will be translated into a slice of the rental income, sales turnover, or even based on examination results for schools or rates of recidivism for new prisons.

From our experience of volumetric prefabrication, I feel the most vulnerable player in the new world may be the main contractor. We have learnt that building indoors in a factory on a production line does reduce on-site risks. Production lines impose their own discipline on

supply chains and reduce dependency on traditional building trades. Most subcontractors are in the factory and not on site. This could open the way for the emergence of dynamic new partnerships between architects and manufacturers – with designers acting as the interface between client/developer and the external environment, while the manufacturer provides the project management. Architects would have to develop new skills such as public relations, media communications, political lobbying, public consultation, financial modelling, costing their own designs and design research. Only once all these have been mastered, and a share of the risk accepted, would the reward of designing the building be earned, and with it the right to exert the dominant influence over the form and aesthetics of the building.

Valuing design

To conclude, I believe that building is a development process and should be design led – that design is about creating value, and that high value leads to a lasting legacy. When we identify a site which we want to buy and develop we reach for our architect or engineer to help us explore how we can maximise its potential and minimise any drawbacks it may have. We expect them to bring their knowledge of construction in so far as it is relevant at this stage, but generally we do not need to appoint a contractor to tell us how to build it before we have decided what we want to build. This may sound simplistic, but it is about the difference between real property development and building. The design process at its best extracts the full potential out of a site and adds both real and intangible values as well.

This crucial dimension to development has been admirably highlighted by the Urban Task Force. It is worth reflecting that nobody has a bigger stake in the success of the urban renaissance than the poor. They are already

4.4

**Murray Grove:
An example of
marriage between
exemplary
contemporary
design and off site
volumetric
construction
(architects:
Cartwright Pickard)**

over-represented in areas of lowest environmental quality and have the least choice in terms of moving to more attractive neighbourhoods, or even being able to afford a holiday in order to get a break from bleak surroundings. Creating new social or affordable housing is only part of the process. Just as important is creating neighbourhoods in which they would wish to live, and where they will find opportunities for employment and engagement with the good things of life. Improving our neighbourhoods is not something that can be achieved by simply placing standard products there.

Great architecture and urban design have the ability to raise the spirits and give a quality of life beyond the imagination of many and beyond the mundane consideration of mere utility: stunning views, private sun-drenched patios, interesting spaces, the interplay of sunlight and shadow, tactile materials, visual surprises, humour, a sense of security and comfort. These are combinations to send the spirits soaring. The essence of the excitement and stimulation of city living is something architecture can do for everyone.

A bespoke, development-led approach, using factory-based construction technologies to achieve a high quality product is the way ahead for affordable housing. The pre-contract period may take longer, but the result should cost no more if it exploits standardised construction processes. In the long run the recipe for success is to work on the basis that only the best will be the cheapest over time.

References

Construction Task Force (1998) *Rethinking Construction: the report of the Construction Task Force*, London: DETR.
Urban Task Force (1999) *Towards an Urban Renaissance*, London: E & FN Spon.

Chapter 5

The long-term costs of owning and using buildings

Raymond Evans, Richard Haryott, Norman Haste and Alan Jones

As the world becomes an increasingly competitive place, companies are being required to operate on a global basis. This causes increased downward pressure on margins. In order to outperform their competitors these global companies are seeking differentiation combined with an increasing emphasis on improving product performance and reliability and reducing cost through improvements in efficiency.

The cost of ownership and maintenance of buildings, combined with the cost of the staff who work in these buildings, is significant. The optimisation of productivity of people is a source of significant competitive advantage, particularly when the cost of ownership is considered over the medium term. The nature of work and the way that people interact in the workplace continue to change, driven not only by changes in technology but also by the personal expectations of the staff themselves.

Changes to the demands placed upon buildings mean that the buildings must be capable of adaptation to meet these new and changing requirements. Changes in the technology used in buildings not only impact on the way people within a building work but also have an effect on the way the building itself operates. They also affect the nature of the physical structure and configuration of the building. There have, in addition, been a number of developments in the way that buildings are procured. An example within the public sector is the introduction of Private Finance Initiatives. These are bringing a 'whole-life cost' approach to the procurement of various types of public buildings, including amongst others, hospitals.

Buildings by their nature have long design lives, whilst the requirements placed on them are changing rapidly in time horizons which are short, particularly when compared with the design life of the building. This can lead to complex and competing requirements throughout the various stages of the life of a building. Understanding the interplay between conflicting requirements and the surrounding issues is essential for both potential owners and managers of buildings, as well as for people involved in the production and commissioning of new buildings, in order that informed and balanced decisions can be made.

A key point of this chapter is that buildings designed for the accommodation of people generating wealth, or people providing a service, must create an environment where people will give their best. The cost of ownership and maintenance of a building is typically about 3 per cent of the overall cost of the people working in the building. A useful guide for the whole-life cost of operating and owning commercial office buildings is illustrated by the ratio 1:5:200, as shown in Figure 5.1.

Similar ratios might well apply in other types of building. There is a good deal of evidence that the building itself, if properly designed and managed, can lead to significant improvements in productivity. The split between the respective costs throughout the life of the building combined with changes in use, technology and other operational aspects, lead to complex problems and conflicting pressures when trying to improve the productivity of a given building. These issues must be addressed on a whole-life cost basis to ensure that there is an appropriate balance between the conflicting requirements.

Other industries take great care over the management and productivity of their assets. For example, an aircraft operator carefully monitors the health and usage of his aircraft and plans maintenance and upkeep accordingly. Such organised management of assets is not universal in the management and update of buildings. Whilst this chapter sets out a number of examples that illustrate how these issues can be managed, there is a need for greater awareness, further study and an increasing availability of integrated services to owners and operators of buildings to enable improvements in productivity to be realised.

A building costs money to run, and breakdowns and failures in the function of the building are unsatisfactory and result in unnecessary costs. The functional content of the building will generally be changed, at some considerable cost, at regular intervals during its lifetime. The objective of this chapter is to highlight the main issues that arise, so that in the medium term improved systems and methodologies can be developed to enable better and more objective decisions to be made at all stages throughout the life cycle of any building. This chapter has been produced jointly by a working party comprising the four authors, who individually draw on respective and complementary areas of expertise.

The role of buildings

Buildings serve a wide variety of commercial and industrial uses. These range from structures to house large and complex process systems where the demands of the process itself drive the primary requirements of the building, to buildings designed to house people operating a business where the physical requirements of the staff or customers are the principal need. Whatever the business, the underlying purpose of a commercial building is to act as a focal point to bring together knowledge and to function as a platform on which to generate wealth for the business. In a similar way, public buildings, such as hospitals, have to be built to meet their specific needs efficiently and effectively.

The management philosophies adopted within businesses change from time to time to reflect new thinking and new ideas. These new philosophies affect the basic way in which people within the building work and interact, for example, open plan, cell working and hot desking amongst many other approaches. This chapter does not address the relative

5.1

Ratios of capital cost, facilities cost and business operating cost

Construction cost	1
Maintenance and building operating costs	5
Business operating costs	200

advantages of these alternative approaches. The issue is that the building in which these philosophies will be put into practice should have the flexibility to adapt in order to cope effectively and efficiently with the prevalent philosophy at any one time.

There are also a variety of approaches reflected in the ownership or custodianship of a building. At the one extreme is an approach in which the building is constructed for a specific need or purpose. Under this approach the building forms a key part of the process that is to be performed within it. In this situation the capital cost of the whole built environment forms an integral part of the overall process itself. The process may have a limited life and therefore all the capital costs, including that of the built environment, are written off during the forecast or anticipated life of the process. At the other extreme is the 'investment' approach, where the objective of ownership is to earn an income whilst at the same time preserving the value of the asset.

The type or design of a building may also play an important role in making a statement about the owner or occupier. There are numerous examples of such buildings and for many architectural practices this element is one of the most important in the design process. Whatever the business objective, the role that a building is to play has an impact on the whole approach to the building life cycle.

The life cycle can be divided into three phases which must all be considered. These are:

1   Design and construction;
2   Operational period;
3   Demolition/recycling.

There is evidence that the approach towards building ownership is affected by cultural preferences. There are a number of differences between the approaches favoured and adopted in the UK from those preferred in the USA. For example, it is very common for major corporations in the USA to own their own buildings, with as many as 90 per cent of major corporations doing so. There is evidence that this tendency to own limits the demand for buildings that make a statement or convey an image. Whatever the overall business objective, a building must be efficient and facilitate the functions which will take place within it. In this sense providing a building is no different from any other service which must be of a suitable and appropriate quality that will enable the business to function effectively. As has been mentioned in the introduction to this chapter, the operating costs of the process carried out within the building normally far outweigh the costs of both its construction and maintainence. A key issue is to establish and use appropriate mechanisms for judging the value of a particular building against the operational productivity forecasts of the business situated within it.

In a factory or production facility it is often relatively simple to measure productivity, but it can be much harder to achieve this in a commercial or service-based business. In this situation, perhaps the best indicators of productivity are those recommended by the American Society of Heating, Refrigerating and Air-conditioning Engineers (ASHRAE) workshop on *Indoor Air Quality* held in Baltimore in 1992 (BOSTI and Brill, 1994):

- Absence from work, or work station
- Health costs (including sick leave, accidents and injuries)
- Interruptions to work
- Controlled independent judgements of work quality
- Self-assessments of productivity
- Speed and accuracy of work
- Output from pre-existing work groups
- Cost for the product or service
- Exchanging output in response to graded reward
- Volunteer overtime
- Cycle time from initiation to completion of process

- Multiple measures at all organisational levels
- Visual measures of performance, health and well-being at work
- Development of measures and patterns of change over time.

Operational productivity may be influenced by up to 17 per cent by addressing factors which include noise, temperature fluctuation, lighting and glare, comfort, relocation frequency, layout and the users' perception and level of control. One of these factors is air quality, and a recent study by Dorgan and Dorgan (1997, 1999) examined the link between the productivity of employees working within commercial buildings and the quality of the air within the buildings. Based on a number of existing research and other reports, the authors determined the capital and running costs of bringing the indoor air quality (IAQ) within all commercial buildings in the USA up to ASHRAE Standard 62–1989 and other accepted indoor air quality practices. This study concluded that the increased productivity that results directly from improved air quality provides a rapid payback period. Clearly, the actual payback periods for individual buildings vary, depending on the specific circumstances.

Overall, this study concluded that the productivity of the US economy could be improved by $55 billion per annum by a one-time investment of $120bn in works to improve poor air quality in all buildings. This benefit is achieved simply because the productivity of the people working within the building is improved as a direct result of improved air quality. This research also shows that, in addition to the productivity improvements, other cost savings are achieved in salary and related profit benefits. These benefits further reduce the payback period which, in some cases, is reduced to a matter of months.

Even if the Dorgan figures are open to discussion, there is sufficient evidence that investment by the owner/occupier in the efficient operation of the building will pay dividends in the business operating costs. A previous study by Wyon (1994) suggests that an extra 50 per cent increase in energy costs as a result of improved ventilation would be paid for by a gain of between 0.25–0.5 per cent improvement in productivity. The responsible owner and designer will want to achieve these productivity gains while still reducing energy costs, aware that these may become more onerous in the future.

Design and construction

Whilst the construction cost may represent a small fraction of the cost of ownership throughout the whole-life of the building, it is nevertheless a significant capital sum. It therefore remains important that the cost of construction should be minimised and there are a number of ways in which this can be achieved. Some owners of buildings wish their buildings to project, or be a statement about, the company itself – clearly this increases the initial costs compared to a spec-built building. The buildability of a building may be considerably improved by adopting a 'loose-fit' approach. This would include increasing the areas allowed for services so that both design and construction can be carried out more rapidly.

The cost of the extra space may be more than compensated for by a reduction in building costs achieved through simpler working with less interface and coordination problems. This approach may also speed up the construction period and therefore reduce the rolled-up interest costs accumulated during this period. Rolled-up interest costs during construction can represent a major element in the cost of the build. On a large project this interest cost, whether real or opportunity, may typically represent around 25 to 30 per cent of the overall cost during the construction phase. As an example, the introduction of additional plant space by inserting an interstitial mezzanine floor in research buildings can substantially reduce the time required for construction. As an additional benefit, this extra floor also reduces the costs of operation and the costs of changes in the future. These savings are achieved by what would initially appear to be an increase in the construction cost. This loose-fit approach will reduce the operating costs through simplified maintenance and will give greater flexibility in the use and adaptation of the building in the future.

Both design and construction can be speeded up by the adoption of modularisation and standardisation. The adoption of standard specifications for steel used in fabrication is a good example. The fabricators and the steel suppliers are continually working to introduce fewer standard sections and fewer grades of steel. This pressure will reduce the costs of buildings, but it must be handled in such a way that it does not reduce the ability to optimise buildings for owners. The construction period can be reduced by improvements in labour productivity achieved through good design, training and scheduling as well as by the effective management of the workforce. A reduction in programme time, reworking and better communication can also be achieved by the early involvement of constructors, suppliers and installers.

Sophisticated computer-based modelling tools are now available for almost all elements and issues relating to the design of buildings. The use of these techniques can have a major impact in reducing uncertainty in the construction period and therefore limit the risks of cost over-runs. They may also delay the time by which final decisions must be made during the design and construction period. These models allow some very spectacular and complex buildings to be designed and built which would otherwise not be possible. The use of modelling techniques may increase the capital cost of construction but reduce the overall cost over the life of the building. The objective of modelling techniques is to inject the maximum knowledge into the design process, helping to reduce waste and to improve the efficiency of both design and construction as well as operation.

Determining and accurately evaluating the relative advantages and disadvantages of alternative options is clearly a difficult task that would be impossible without the use of computer-based modelling techniques. The design and construction period may be reduced by the use of systems that can be integrated between the different parties during this period. These systems allow for the rapid sharing of data between all the various parties, improving coordination which results in quicker and therefore cheaper construction with a greater all-round team approach. There are numerous sophisticated modelling techniques available, but these are not currently being fully utilised. The key challenge is to develop the skills and techniques to use these tools effectively in the future, in order to derive maximum benefit and so that modelling becomes more of a science than an art, as it is now often considered. The owner or user can be informed by the effective use of these techniques during design and operation phases.

Operational period

The issues that need to be considered during the operational phase are highly dependent on the process for which the building is designed. The scope of this chapter is limited to buildings designed for occupation by human-based processes. An integral part of this phase is being able to define the need of the business and to have a clear understanding of the best means of delivery. As discussed in the Introduction, staff-related and other operating costs of the business that occupy the building are generally considerably higher than the cost of operating and managing the building itself. It is therefore important that during this phase effective mechanisms for measuring the productivity achieved are established.

There has been an increasing emphasis on environmental issues during the last few years. These relate both to the internal environment of the building and to the environmental impact of the building itself, including the disposal after use and demolition. Surveys have shown that the environmental impact of a building has now become the second most important issue for building occupiers. The rate at which this concern has grown is highlighted by the fact that as little as five years ago environmental issues did not figure in the list of main concerns of building occupiers. This environmental concern, along with other non-financial issues, must be considered.

There are a number of techniques available to reduce both the energy consumption and the environmental impact of a building. The cost, however, of constructing a low energy use building may be 10 per cent, or more, higher than the cost of constructing a standard air-conditioned building. Energy costs themselves represent only a small part of the overall operational costs of the business. Various studies conducted within the USA and UK show that staff costs are 100 to 200 times the annual cost of energy (Oseland and Williams, 1997). It must, however, be remembered that future increases in energy costs and environmental taxation could convert these issues into financial costs. Energy taxes have already been introduced in some countries, including Singapore, where tax is imposed on the thermal conductivity of the building. This tax can represent a significant proportion of the occupancy costs.

As previously discussed, the productivity of the process carried out within the building can be significantly affected by human behaviour and related motivational aspects. Achieving a 10 per cent improvement in the productivity of staff occupying the building is likely to more than repay the additional building-related costs associated with achieving that improvement. There are a wide variety of ways in which these improvements can be achieved, such as departmental adjacencies and functionality, in addition to the environmental quality issues already discussed.

BA, in its new Waterside headquarters near Heathrow, gave a lot of consideration to the environment and working atmosphere from a social perspective. The building is, in fact, a series of buildings (not ideal for modularisation) and inside the building, functions as it has been designed – to create a good atmosphere for the people who work in it.

There has been some debate about the impact of technology on the office with the possibility of teleworking and the emergence of the virtual office. Evidence so far is that this has had a more limited impact than previously forecast. Some impact has been seen with the introduction of new working methods in the workplace, such as hot-desking. This will have an increasing impact, as will integrated technology-driven systems that will allow buildings to be operated more effectively in the future, whilst allowing the occupier and user sufficient degrees of control over their immediate environment.

As discussed, the adoption of a loose fit approach can speed up the construction process and therefore reduce the costs. This loose-fit approach can play a role in reducing operating costs by improving access to services and the maintainability of the building. This approach also improves the building's ability to adapt to future needs. This is best highlighted by the problems of 1960s' and early 1970s' buildings, which now have insufficient floor to ceiling heights to accommodate current IT requirements.

Today, many offices have an annual churn rate of 50 per cent or more as departments and operating structures are constantly adjusted. Buildings and their systems must be flexible enough to accommodate this level of constant change, remaining maintainable, whilst minimising the associated disruption. Some of the key facilities that contribute towards improving a building's flexibility include additional conduits, excess capacity of services including mechanical, electrical and voice and data cabling. This flexibility may increase the original capital cost by up to 5 per cent but there is evidence (from the USA) that this investment has paid off in the longer-term.

The key issue is, of course, incorporating flexibility into the building in the right way so that it can be used in the future. This, in some ways, requires an ability to predict future changes in practices and technology that will need to be accommodated within the building. As an example, a research-based company invested in flexible benching systems for a research environment at a considerable premium. Having invested in this flexibility it turns out that the benches have never been moved and therefore the inbuilt flexibility has not been utilised – yet.

Changes in technology are happening rapidly, with IT systems lasting from 18 months to three years. This makes determining the future a difficult task. The use of higher quality, and usually more expensive, material can increase the period between refurbishment and renewal. However, this may reduce the overall life cycle cost of a building, and as a result will cause less interference with the business being carried out in the building with all the associated advantages of efficiency. This additional expenditure is wasted if the building requires significant change or adaptation for other reasons before the full life expectancy has been realised. As an example, in airports there are options of using partitions of steel construction that can be relocated, or of using dry-lining partitions that cannot be relocated. With the configuration of an airport normally lasting no more seven years, determining which is the most effective option is not simple.

There is evidence that the cost of a major refit may be no cheaper than the cost of demolishing and rebuilding. An alternative option is to design buildings with a relatively short design life that can be demolished easily with the space and waste recycled quickly and simply. This approach is adopted more commonly in the USA than in the UK. The facilities manager (responsible for achieving the effective functioning of the building) plays a critical role in maintaining productivity levels. Information, guidance, training and communication have become key issues in operating the building to achieve these aspirations. Feedback, operation, maintenance and replacement data also play a key role in informing the owner, designer, constructor and supplier with regard to future projects, and the facilities manager needs to be part of the process of measuring success.

Conclusion

Optimising the productivity of people working in buildings is influenced by a range of complex and competing issues. The solution adopted must consider a wide range of issues including the whole-life cycle cost and, most importantly, the actual cost and efficiency of the business to be conducted within the building. There is no single approach that should be adopted. The different circumstances of each situation need to be considered. Investing in a building to improve productivity would appear to offer a sound investment in many circumstances and may have a key role to play in achieving competitive advantage for the occupier of the building. However, the ability to carry out a detailed assessment requires both the costs as well as the benefits of the improvement to be quantified. This is relatively easily achieved with regard to the costs; however, assessing the productivity benefits is not so easy.

In order that objective decisions can be made, there needs to be good quality information and data that will allow informed decisions. Whilst there are a range of techniques and strategies available to achieve this, the key challenge is to use these more effectively and more widely, in order to derive their full benefit and where necessary to develop new tools. These measures may need to be tailored to the specific requirements of each situation. The cost of property is often judged in terms of the rental cost per square metre. It might perhaps be more appropriate to examine the cost of occupation in terms of the people that are able to occupy the space or in terms of the output or productivity that can be achieved from that area.

References

BOSTI and Brill, M. (1994) *Using Office Design* to *Increase Productivity, Workplace Design and Productivity,* quoted in C. Lomonace, 'Comfort and control in the workplace', *ASHRAE Journal,* pp. 50–56, September 1997.

Dorgan, C. and Dorgan, C. (1997) *Productivity Link Assessment* to *Indoor Air Quality, Creating the Productive Workplace,* October 29,1997.

Dorgan, C., Dorgan, C., Kanarek, M. and Wilman, A. (1999) 'Health and productivity benefits of improved indoor air quality', ASHRAE's Poster Presentation Award 1999.

Oseland, N. and Williams, A. (1997) *How Best Practice Can Improve Productivity: the relationship between energy efficiency and staff productivity,* Watford Building Research Establishment Ltd, EE2898, BRE/109/9/4.

Wyon, D. (1994) 'Economic benefits of a healthy indoor environment', *Proceedings of Healthy Air,* Budapest 1994, pp. 405–416.

Part 2

Case studies of added value

This section presents examples and case studies from the sectors where most research has been undertaken into the issues of achieving quality and value – offices (Chapters 6 and 7), schools (Chapter 8), and healthcare buildings (Chapters 9 and 10). Chapter 11 deals with design quality at the urban scale.

In Chapter 6, Jon Rouse describes the conduct and findings of a substantial study of high profile organisations that commissioned new buildings during the late 1990s. He set out to enquire how a number of corporate clients, whose expenditure on their new buildings exceeded the market value, measured architectural value in order to justify the extra over-expenditure. He argues that if this question can be understood – if the benefits of architectural quality and value can be demonstrated – then additional investment into the built environment can be released. His chapter contains ten case studies of bespoke buildings, and reports on the motivations of the case study organisations. All these organisations recognised the corporate benefits

from architectural investment, representing both tangible benefits of the sort that can be counted by traditional cost:benefit but also intangible benefits that are more difficult to measure. Employee satisfaction was the most highly rated motivation; human capital is the major resource of the organisations and they seek to enhance the ability of their employees to contribute to turnover and profitability. Corporate policy in architectural investment was also very important; design champions at senior levels within the organisation and corporate precedents for high quality architecture were both found to be important. For seven of the ten organisations, procuring a building was part of a much wider corporate development process – with the goals typically of transforming how the company does business; encouraging creativity, enhancing communication, promoting team work, operating less formally, encouraging flexible working and reducing hierarchy.

As for how the benefits had been quantified as part of the design process, three of the companies attempted to cost out the benefits from intangibles – corporate identity, company branding, staff recruitment and retention – using known methods. However in four more, formal valuation processes more appropriate to financial reporting than to design had been used. These had incorporated the costs of the project but failed to take account of the corresponding benefits, particularly the intangibles. This was because of the constraints and restrictions of these methods, which have their roots in company law, accountants' standards and surveying practices. Rouse's concluding argument is that we should stop using formal valuation methods for processes and purposes for which they were never intended and which distort. Instead, new tools are needed to account for value and we need to look to other disciplines – such as the behavioural sciences, engineering, psychology and economics – where potential alternatives are already being investigated.

In Chapter 7, Terry Wyatt reports on functionality and performance in the case of three major office projects, each of which demonstrates one of the key drivers identified in the Egan report – customer focus. In the case of the MOD offices at Abbey Wood, he reports on the interior lighting and ventilation systems. For the lighting, intelligent luminaires were selected that respond to daylight conditions. The additional costs of these proved to be less than expected, while savings in operating costs were larger than anticipated. Both factors resulted in a payback period of only one year; they also have the benefit of simplifying future reconfigurations. An incremental design approach was taken with the ventilation system design. A robust basic design with opening windows was selected for lightly occupied shallow offices on the northern façade. Normally occupied offices on all other orientations have displacement ventilation. Offices that are more intensively occupied and have larger heat gains have summertime cooling and dehumidification. Finally, offices

where equipment loads and the need for closer control of the environment demand it, have chilled beams and suspended chilled panels. As the project was carried out within a capped budget, the incremental approach – based on calculations comparing the costs of the ventilation systems with the loss arising from reduced staff productivity – help to direct where limited funds should best be invested.

Wyatt's second case study is the Bristol and West headquarters. The client's former accommodation was variable in quality, with much of it poorly suited to the equipment in use, particularly where high thermal gains resulted in overheating. Energy and maintenance costs were also high. Performance improvements from constructing a new headquarters were forecast to be worth £6.5m, and informed the decision to build a new building. In his third case study, he shows how the new office complex for BP at Sunbury is forecast to improve staff productivity while also reducing carbon dioxide emissions arising from the building itself and from staff transport. Wyatt's conclusion is that the sorts of calculations he describes show how staff comfort, productivity and well-being have been successfully factored into decision-making about whether nor not to build, where to build, what to build, and what level of services are appropriate.

In Chapter 8, Richard Feilden writes about design quality in new schools. For almost all of us, schools are the first buildings we experience without the security of parental support. They are the places where children spend a considerable part of their waking hours, and they leave indelible impressions. At best, well-designed schools should enhance our experiences of learning, contribute to scholastic achievement, stimulate interest in the built environment, and discourage truancy and vandalism. These expectations, when added to local user requirements and national design guidance (of which there is no shortage) together with strict budgetary constraints, create substantial demands for designers to achieve.

In his brief history of schools as a building type, Feilden notes that we have a substantial legacy of schools, many from the Victorian age, which have proved remarkably robust. The legacy from the third quarter of the twentieth century, on the other hand, when there was a great wave of school building, contains relatively few bright spots and many of these schools have suffered from constructional and environmental problems. In the last quarter of the century fewer schools were built. Among these, the work of Hampshire County Council stands out, and Feilden illustrates some key examples of Hampshire schools. He also illustrates several secondary schools, providing examples of the three main typologies: *street plan*, *campus plan* and *linked pavilions*. Drawing from all these examples, he presents ten key principles for good school design. The extent to which these will be delivered in practice depends on a number of factors, not least the method of procurement. The Private Finance Initiative is the route being increasingly used for schools. Its proponents claim that the integration of design, construction and operational responsibility will raise quality. However, it is the legal and financial challenges that have received most attention so far, and early indications are that early PFI schools have fallen below best practice (Audit Commission, 2003).

The equivalent of improved educational outcomes in the schools is improved recovery rates in healthcare buildings. Bryan Lawson discusses this in Chapter 9, *Assessing benefits in the health sector*. He reports on a carefully controlled experiment using two hospitals, one in general medicine and the other in mental health. In both hospitals new facilities were provided (at one hospital a ward refurbishment, at the other a new purpose-built replacement unit) and the study reports a comparison between patients' responses in the older buildings and the new/refurbished ones. At each

hospital, the same medical team was in place together with the same patterns of patient referral. Thus the only differences were the environments in which the patients were housed. The question focused on in the research was whether architecture contributes to the well-being and recovery of patients. In both hospitals, patients in the newer buildings expressed more satisfaction with the appearance, layout and overall design of the ward. In the newer environments, patients reported they had received better treatment – despite the treatment regimes being to all intents and purposes identical. The attributes of the new wards that patients identified in particular were the opportunities for privacy (though not necessarily for a single bed ward); views of everyday life in the outside world, apparent cleanliness of bathroom facilities; a cared-for interior appearance and a degree of control of their environment in terms of noise, lighting, windows and blinds. Measures of health outcomes also show improvements in the new accommodation compared with the old, a need for less medication and, in the mental health ward, less aggressive behaviour and better progress. Lawson concludes that there was an improvement not only for the quality of life of patients in the new buildings, but also for staff, and potentially cost saving for the NHS.

Chapter 10 *Making special places for health care* is also about healthcare buildings. Susan Francis writes about how society has accommodated those with mental and physical illness in the past, and at the principles that underlay the buildings provided for them. More than 250 years ago, observations of recovery from disease in different sorts of accommodation led to belief in the therapeutic benefits of sunlight and fresh air, strongly influencing the layouts of wards and the planning of hospitals.

She reviews five historical models for healthcare buildings: the asylum-like custodial model; the medical model exemplified by the sanatorium; the caring model typified by the hospice; the holistic model offering sanctuary and the health-promoting model in which medical care is supplemented by sports and recreational facilities. She offers examples of each model and then moves to emergent themes and discusses current trends toward patient-focused care, where clinical environments are designed to be less austere, and therapeutic environments where interior decor, lighting, views and ambience are all used to enhance patients' experiences and lift their spirits. As she explains, healthcare design is undergoing a significant shift in emphasis, with an increasing focus towards how buildings are experienced by patients, how they allow patients control of their environment, how they foster dignity and quiet, and how they encourage continuing links between patients and their community.

Finally in this section is Matthew Carmona's chapter, *Adding value through better urban design*. He presents the results of a research project whose objectives were to identify whether better urban design adds value and if so how, who benefits, and how greater value can be released. Three pairs of projects were studied in the east Midlands, the west Midlands, and the north west. The conclusions of the study were that better urban design does add value: it increases the economic value of development, delivers social benefits, and encourages development that is more environmentally supportive. His chapter gives details in support of each of these findings.

Overall he reports considerable economic, social and environmental benefits from better designed urban environments. His findings suggest a win:win situation where all stakeholders are beneficiaries. Investors see better returns, as do developers – with the added bonus of enhanced company image. Designers benefit from repeat work. Commercial occupiers benefit from improved staff loyalty and health, and everyday users benefit from an improved urban environment and an enhanced range of amenities and facilities. Local authorities also stand to gain from revitalised and viable environments, potentially with ripple effects to adjoining areas. Nevertheless, few schemes studied benefited from all the aspects of value, nor were the benefits automatic. Better designed schemes also have costs associated with them, for example for higher materials specifications. Carmona ends by identifying a variety of principles for urban design that should lead to the release of greater value in the built environment. These include the need for critical mass to support urban regeneration rather than small isolated pockets of development; strategic coordination and planning of the infrastructure; careful location and distribution of public amenities and mixed use development; and finally attention to social diversity and social inclusion so as to minimise the displacement of those in whose name urban regeneration is usually justified.

Reference

Audit Commission (2003) *PFI in Schools: the quality and cost of buildings and services provided by early Private Finance Initative schemes*, London: Audit Commission.

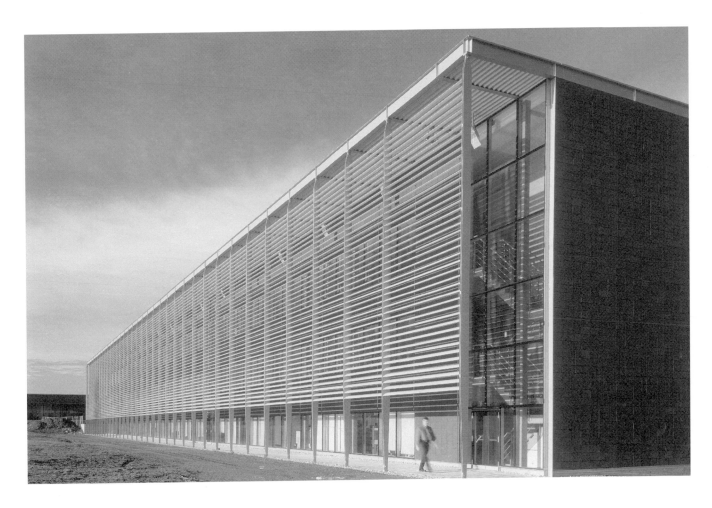

6.4
**Boots D90E
Extension,
Nottingham, 1998
(architect: DEGW)**

as a means of consolidating many of the departments back onto a single site, while at the same time stimulating a new corporate culture based on greater creativity, less hierarchy, and more teamwork. A new IT system was introduced at the same time in an attempt to increase productivity.

The building comprises three floors divided into twenty neighbourhoods, which themselves contain a mix of work layouts according to divisional requirements. Each neighbourhood also has a hub for coordinating departmental day-to-day requirements, and the whole building is served by a one stop shop. Running through the length of the building is an internal street with different amenities and informal spaces facing onto it. There are also four atria arranged in the shape of a comb. The old and new buildings are connected by a central building which also acts as a main

reception area, to the rear of which are landscaped gardens.

Lloyds Register of Shipping Headquarters, City of London

The Lloyds Register building is a 38,000 square metre office comprising 12- and 14-storey towers linked by an atrium. It is located on a relatively small foot-plate off Fenchurch Street in the City of London. At the insistence of the City, the front of the building is hidden by the listed façade of the original Lloyds building, which is again linked to the new building by an atrium. This façade has been described as an 'undistinguished Edwardian building' and has constrained both the building design and the site works. The new building features external serve cores and lifts, the first attempt at sloping concrete bracing in the UK and various energy-saving measures.

There are a number of striking elements about how the Lloyds project was managed. First, once the decision was made to proceed with the Richard Rogers Partnership, the architects were given considerable freedom. However, as a client protection device, the project managers chose the key subcontractors for the project and then novated them to the main contractor, Sir Robert McAlpine. As with a number of other case studies, the building project was used to drive a corporate change programme to modernise working methods.

Jubilee Campus, University of Nottingham

The origins of the University of Nottingham Jubilee Campus project were largely speculative, based on the opportunity to acquire 20 hectares of factory land about half a mile from the main University Park campus. It has provided an opportunity to take some of the pressure off the original campus by moving and expanding the key schools of computing, education and business. The campus is mixed-use, comprising teaching buildings, offices, halls of residence and social facilities along the edge of a small man-made lake. The design is organised as a series of bands: tree line, lake, people, buildings, parked cars and then the external boundaries. In total the campus comprises 23,000 square metres of teaching space and 750 residential spaces. An international design competition was run to select the architects, which cost the university £250,000, invested at risk, and was won by Michael Hopkins. There is a strong design emphasis on environmental sustainability, assisted by a Thermie grant from the European Commission. This is reflected in attention to life cycle costing throughout the procurement and development process.

Pearson Education Headquarters, Harlow

This headquarters building was commissioned by Addison Wesley Longman, part of the Pearson Group, in 1989/90. After a long delay, caused by shifts in corporate structure and policy and partly by a planning delay, the offices were finally completed in 1996. The company was trying to balance a need to satisfy requirements of the property investment market with a desire to create a space that would foster greater communication and creativity in staff, facilitate the increasing use of IT, be easy to maintain and cheap to run, and be a pleasure to work in.

The building is constructed as a mix of five and six storeys, set around one large

6.5
Lloyds Register of Shipping Headquarters, City of London, 2000 (architect: Richard Rogers Partnership)

1
**Beddington Zero
Energy Development,
Surrey (architect: Bill
Dunster Architects)**

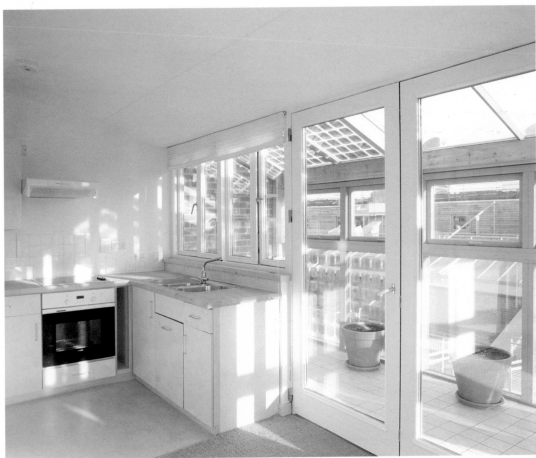

2
Interior – kitchen

3
RARE headquarters, Twycross,
Leicestershire, 1999 (architect:
Feilden Clegg)

4
Walkway detail with
water channel

5
RARE headquarters,
Twycross,
Leicestershire, 1999.
Reception

6
Capital One European
headquarters,
Nottingham, 2001.
View up the steps
to the entrance
(architect: ORMS)

7
Capital One European
headquarters,
Nottingham, 2001.
Overall view of seating
from the second floor

9
Atrium from stair tower

8 (left)
**Lloyds Register
of Shipping
headquarters,
City of London,
2000. Main entrance
(architect: Richard
Rogers Partnership)**

11
Interior

12
MOD Bristol (Abbey Wood)
1996. Interior (architect:
Percy Thomas Partnership)

13
**Greenwich Millennium School
(architect: Edward Cullinan
Architects)**

14
Greenwich Millennium School

6.6
**Jubilee Campus,
University of
Nottingham, 1999
(architect: Michael
Hopkins and
Partners)**

central atrium and two smaller atria. The west and east blocks are separately lettable, and one of these blocks was let for a time to a major supermarket chain. It is regarded as a very green building with natural ventilation, external solar shades and maximum use of natural light. Assessed under the BREEAM energy scheme, the building achieved 20 out of a possible 21 credits – unequalled at the time of assessment.

BA Waterside, Heathrow

The BA Waterside building is situated to the west of Heathrow airport. It has provided the opportunity for BA to bring many of its managers and back office staff out of separate outdated offices and into a single purpose-built headquarter business centre. BA has used the development opportunity to drive a corporate change programme based around increased creativity, greater informality, less hierarchy, more flexible working and less paper. The complex is built around an internal street sheltered by a continuous glazed roof. A stream flows down the length of the street, before emerging outside and flowing into a large lake overseen by the restaurant facilities. The lake is surrounded by 280 acres of restored parkland accessible by the local community. Six office buildings, constructed on three floors, each face onto the street. They each also overlook their own courtyard. In principle, each could be separately let or sold. The street itself provides many amenities and informal spaces include various cafés, a supermarket and a florist.

The individual office buildings reflect the objectives of the corporate change programme. Most areas have no permanent desks and little filing space. Instead there are touchdown points and hot desks to allow people to plug in computers and telephones for limited periods. There are also quiet areas for more reflective individual work requirements. The Waterside centre cost £200m, and the company estimates that it generates an average £15m per year in savings through increased productivity and lower running costs.

Selfridges Department Store, Birmingham

The design is an eye-catching futuristic shape that forms part of the regeneration of the Bull Ring in Birmingham city centre, and is part of a much larger mall development. As a company, Selfridges is in an expansionary phase. Having separated from its parent, the Sears Group, several years ago, it has already opened a new store as part of the Trafford Centre in Manchester and is looking at other UK locations for new stores.

6.7
**Pearson Education
Headquarters,
Harlow, Essex, 1996
(architect: CD
Partnership)**

Within the Bull Ring mall development, there were two department store options. Debenhams took one of these, based on the developer's original design. Selfridges took the other, but with a bespoke design of the shell structure. After complex financial negotiations, Selfridges managed the project and carried an element of risk, taking out a 35-year lease. The shell structure is carried on the developer's books. Future Systems were appointed as architects, working as part of a project team that includes external project managers and specialist consultants.

Hilton Hotel, Heathrow

The original intention was to include the Hilton Heathrow as an individual case study. However, it turned out to have been developed by a third party developer, BAA, then leased to Hilton International as hotel operator. Instead I looked at Hilton policies towards hotel design, development and operation across its recent portfolio additions.

All Hilton hotel investment options are appraised on a strict rate of return basis, comparing cost with customer income. Hilton's

6.8
BA Waterside, Heathrow, 1998 (architect: Neils Torp)

design focus is on a very standardised form of interior that maximises income-generating space while providing the customer with visual access to as many money-generating opportunities as possible. The company is not unduly concerned about external appearance except for signage. The investment priority is always the interior, particularly the reception areas on the basis that first impressions help secure repeat visits. The decision to take on the Hilton Heathrow was about securing a presence in a key location and a judgement that the architect had created a good internal environment that would enable Hilton to deliver its first priority – customer service quality. The quality of the external appearance was a secondary consideration.

In terms of hotels which the Hilton develops itself, only three UK architects are used, based on their experience in hotel design and particular knowledge of the Hilton's requirements. The architects are given strict parameters within their brief, including area

schedules, floor-plate shape and size, number of meeting rooms, size of health club, size of restaurant, and so on. There is limited room for manoeuvre.

Accounting for value

Before we talk about architectural value, it is important to go right back to first principles and get a grip of what we mean by value itself. There are two main meanings of value: one relates to use, the other to exchange. This is a crucial distinction when you talk about companies procuring buildings for their own use. We are talking about use or purpose value more than exchange value – but that may not be how the formal valuation processes actually make the judgement.

In terms of accountancy practice, what we mean by value is of critical importance. This is because companies have got to keep an eye on what the value of their asset could be at the end of the building process. The main method of valuation is what accountants term modified historic cost. It involves a number of constraint choices. On the left-hand side of the equation is the idea of use value: net current replacement cost, how much it would cost to replace what you build. What accountants do here, and this is where things start to get really blurred and fuzzy, is to use cost as a substitute for value. Cost for worth. For me, these are two totally different concepts, but in accounting there is a blurring of the distinction between them. On the other side of the equation, you have what might be called a recoverable amount, which takes you into exchange value again – market value – how much could you get for this building in its existing use, or taking into account alternative uses? Given the proximity and the closeness between the accounting and the surveying professions, these definitions of cost and value are writ large across how companies go about valuing buildings. What we really need is a much richer definition of value.

If you want to account for the value of architecture to companies, what you actually talk about is value to business. That phrase, value to business, is actually how accountants describe their method of valuation, but it is little of the sort, because the replacement cost and market value substantially undervalue the contribution of the asset to the business. Replacement cost and market value fail to account for the impact on corporate identity, the health, well-being and productivity of staff, staff retention and recruitment potential, even customer loyalty. There are all sorts of issues which a building raises in terms of its design value that are not taken into account by either accountancy definition.

In their joint study of architectural value in South-east Asia, completed in 1992, DEGW and Technobank (1992) identified that there was a composite value – a combination of exchange value, use value and image value. These overlap, and are inseparable; and to try to separate them will detract from the true value

of a building to a company. So we have a distinction between the way the accountants view a valuation problem and how economists, psychologists, and social scientists view value.

Where does the accountants' system fall down? It falls down because it has a very strict concept of prudence, which creates three problems for us in terms of design value:

- First of all, design value is intangible to a certain extent. Certain elements may be tangible – for example, if you can prove a definitive cost saving through a particular energy-saving device; obviously that could be taken into account. But the areas I am talking about – corporate identity, branding, goodwill, staff welfare, increased productivity – are intangible; they cannot directly be attributed to the design in itself.
- The second problem is one of inseparability. The accountants' system will only take account of, and allow calculation of, assets that are separately identified and traded. But of course, design value cannot be separated out from the building as a fixed asset.
- And the third problem the accountancy system has is commensurability, which basically means that there are very few comparators. If you are constructing a building which is *per se*, bespoke, then it is very difficult to find comparators that can be used for strict market evaluation that take into account the benefit of that design to a particular company.

Are new methods needed to account for value?

The next question is: does this really matter? Is this what we should be getting excited about? Are financial accounting methods going to make any difference to how much decent architecture is really procured by companies? The answer is a resounding yes, and there are three main reasons why it does matter.

The first is that there is a huge and complex debate which has been raging for the best part of ten years now between the investment representatives, like the US Securities and Exchange Commission, and the accountancy bodies that control accounting standards both nationally and internationally. Briefly, the argument is that a substantial fraction of the value of a firm, perhaps as much as 90 per cent in the case of an organisation like Microsoft, is actually not in normal financial capital, it is not in the bricks and mortar, it is actually in the intellectual capital of the organisation. Intellectual capital can be further subdivided into human capital and structural capital, as shown in Figure 6.9.

Why does that affect architecture? Because it has been explicitly recognised by companies like Skandia, and by organisations like the US Securities and Exchange Commission, that architecture spans both of these headings. Certainly a building is a fixed asset in terms of the facilities it provides, but there is also considerable intangible value – called structural capital – that supports the

competence and the attitudes of the staff in terms of what they provide, as well as the organisation's identity and its ability to undergo cultural change. Yet none of the structural capital is included in the company balance sheet. So architecture finds itself part of the debate, although the debate itself is a lot bigger than concern about the delivery of architectural value.

The second reason why the limitations of poor evaluation methods matter is that not only does bespoke design create intangible benefits which might get missed out of the equation in the accounting process, but also it creates additional transaction costs which might also get missed out, that flow from bespoke assets, but are also usually present in specific assets. Asset specificity actually reduces the tangibility of the asset. What do I mean by that? It means it is going to be more thinly traded because an organisation with a bespoke corporate identity is less likely to be taken on. There will be fewer purchasers, and so there will be a depression in its value. The problem is that traditional investment appraisal techniques, like internal return or net present value, do not properly account for all that.

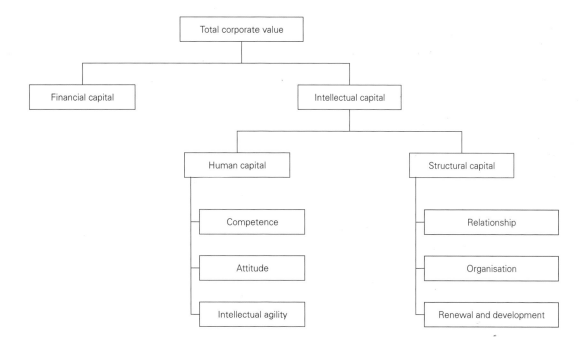

6.9
Value distribution tree (after Roos and Roos, 1997)

The third reason why it matters is more generic. It is really about the changing decision-making context. There is corporate recognition about environmental responsibility, the benefits of corporate identity, and the retention of staff, which companies are eager to try and put some sort of measurable value on. Obviously the design of buildings contributes to those issues. We have seen the emergence of corporate design champions. This is particularly relevant to one of my case studies. Vittorio Radice arrived at Selfridges and sought to direct the whole company towards an ethos of corporate identity, in which you create a retailers' theatre, an entertainment space where building, concession space, colours, layout and so on, all contribute to the customer's experience.

A final point is that investors are no longer seen as the only stakeholder that has to be satisfied; others range from local community through to critical special interests, and there is an interest in satisfying the broader range of stakeholders.

Alternatives to traditional valuation methods

If traditional valuation methods are limiting us in terms of design values, are there alternatives? The answer is, yes, there are. There are many, and they originate in a variety of other disciplines. The *analytical hierarchy process* and *multicriteria analysis* come from the behavioural sciences and engineering; *human capital measurement* comes from the human resources psychology perspective; *contingent valuation* comes from the measurement of environmental amenities and *hedonic pricing* is a similar welfare economics measurement device; *cost-benefit analysis* comes from economics; then there is *fuzzy logic* from IT. So there are many techniques in other disciplines, all of which are potentially applicable. Buckley (1988) and Voogd (1988) provide an introductory overview.

The research community, particularly in America, has started to play with some of these devices in relation to value in design, particularly with intangible benefits of design. Of those that seem to offer particular promise, the analytical hierarchy process is a multicriteria evaluation method. It breaks decision attributes down into a hierarchy of factors and uses paired comparisons to estimate relative magnitudes (Vargas and Saaty, 1981). The US Real Estate Association has looked at the application of fuzzy logic (Bagnoli and Smith, 1998). Contingent valuation is used in cost-benefit analysis (Layard and Glaister, 1994)

Let me admit that these three methods are totally untested in terms of their cost, timing, and general practicability, let alone their acceptability in this context. We are at the start of a long process in terms of adoption, although a method like fuzzy logic is now the norm in terms of intelligent machinery. If you have a programmable washing machine, it has some sort of fuzzy logic system built into it. If it's applicable there, why not in terms of intelligent buildings? This does not seem to be a huge step. But the valuation profession, in this country at least, is not in a state to take on those sorts of alternative measuring methods in their professional development training.

What really drove the case study organisations?

The most important finding from the case studies concerns what actually motivates corporate design investment. According to accounting conventions, exchange value and replacement cost are the key drivers, so cost-efficiency and disposable value would be the things that companies would give most priority to. Yet in practice, disposability – the ability to obtain exchange value – turned out to be the least important criterion for these ten organisations.

Buckley, M. (1988) 'Multi-criterion evaluation: measures, manipulation and meaning', *Environment and Planning B: Planning and Design*, vol. 15, no. 1, pp. 55–64.

DEGW and Technobank (1992) *Intelligent Buildings in Europe*, London: DEGW.

Doron, J., Shilling, J. and Sirmans, C. (1992) 'Do market rents reflect the value of special building features?', *Journal of Real Estate Research*, vol. 7, no. 2, pp. 147–55.

Hough, D. and Kratz, C. (1983) 'Can "good" architecture meet the market test?' *Journal of Urban Economics*, vol. 14, pp. 40–54.

Layard, R. and Glaister, S. (1994) *Cost Benefit Analysis*, Cambridge: Cambridge University Press.

Loe, E. (1999) *The Value of Architecture: context and current thinking*, London: RIBA.

Property Council of Australia (1999) *The Design Dividend*, Canberra: PCA.

Roos, G. and Roos, J. (1997) 'Measuring your company's intellectual performance', *Long Range Planning*, vol. 30, no. 3, pp. 413–26.

Rouse, J. M. (2000) 'How do profit generating organisations measure and manage the costs and benefits of architecture and design when investing in properties for their own business use?' Unpublished MBA thesis, University of Nottingham.

Vandell, K. and Lane, J. (1989) 'The economics of architecture and design: some preliminary findings', *Journal of the American Real Estate and Urban Economics Association*, vol. 17, no. 2, pp. 235–60.

Vargas, L. and Saaty, T. (1981) 'Financial and intangible factors in fleet lease or buy decisions', *Industrial Marketing Management*, vol. 10, pp. 1–10.

Voogd, H. (1988) 'Multi criterion evaluation: measures, manipulation and meaning, a reply', *Environment and Planning B: Planning and Design*, vol. 15, no. 1, pp. 65–72.

Chapter 7

Measuring and improving functionality and performance

Terry Wyatt

In the late 1990s, as the millennium ended, the construction industry signed up to 'Latham and Egan'. It was a defining moment and represented a commitment by the industry to make significant performance improvements. Their reports urged the construction industry to learn from other industries where radical changes and improvements had been made. The advice was to copy from the motor and aircraft industries, including the adoption of new methods such as using a 'single 3D model' for buildings and 'object-oriented design'.

In its report *Rethinking Construction*, the Construction Task Force (1998) led by Sir John Egan stated: 'construction too often fails to meet the needs of modern businesses that must be competitive in international markets, and rarely provides best value for clients and taxpayers'.

Some improvements have been made during the past three or four years. There are now integrated 'Project Databases' with better procurement through management of the supply chain. Key Performance Indicators (KPIs) have been prepared to assess and monitor improvements continuously. However, progress to date has been focused on the construction process, and little has been done to address the underlying issue of Latham and Egan, namely *customer focus*. As a result, there are as yet no measures for the performance and functionality of buildings compared with what the customer really requires, which is a better, affordable product.

Recent announcements in the press suggest that some constructors have achieved better financial performance through 'better quality' buildings, although what these better qualities are is rarely stated. Is it design, materials, construction methods, performance (such as comfort, energy use, maintenance needs), adaptability, value or just 'more bells and whistles'? In housing, it often turns out to be a case of moving upmarket, by producing fewer, more expensive homes. This hardly represents progress on construction industry performance improvement.

Better quality is undeniably required of the buildings delivered by the construction industry and, in housing at least, DTLR and

CABE have jointly launched *Better Places to Live*, a guide promoting higher standards in the design of housing developments. Several housing associations are starting to put the recommendations into practice. Yet it is an indictment of the industry that the new Part 'L' of the Building Regulations, amending the energy efficiency provisions, is at all necessary. It is also a comment on the work of designers that the document has had to be so prescriptive.

So what constitutes *better quality*? Performance and functionality of buildings are best studied by reference to actual rather than theoretical buildings. Exemplars can demonstrate how to go about assessing aspects of building performance. Three case study buildings illustrate the delivery of particular aspects of performance in terms of their *value* to the users:

1   The MOD Abbey Wood development – showing care over indoor climate design for user performance and consideration of 'travel to work' emissions as this relates to quality of life.
2   Bristol and West plc HQ – showing care over managing a business with performance indicators used in investment studies aimed at improving overall business performance and cutting costs.
3   BP Sunbury redevelopment – showing a business emissions basis of building performance, driven by the need to address the climate change agenda, and assessments that think beyond the 'perilous square metre of net floor area measurement'.

While these case studies do not illustrate the only, or necessarily the most important design issues, they serve to trigger ideas about how we should begin to focus on the customer. In each case, the customer is given information about what the building being designed for them will deliver – something we take for granted with car, aircraft or computer manufacturers.

MOD Abbey Wood

Numerous studies of the relative importance to users of various aspects of building performance have repeatedly shown lighting, ventilation and thermal control heading the lists. In this case study, lighting performance is considered in terms of use of daylight, luminaire design, disposition for flexible use of space, and lighting control.

The objective was to provide high quality lighting of workplaces at the lowest operating cost within a capped budget. The proposed 'intelligent' lighting control system 'sees' when and how much lighting is needed to supplement daylight. The system allows 'trade free' reconfiguring of workplace furniture and partitioning throughout the buildings based on a 1500 mm grid.

During the design phase, the *value* of the proposed system was assessed as follows:

• The extra capital cost of a lighting management system using 'intelligent' luminaires was estimated at £35 per fitting. Since no switches or wiring are required with intelligent luminaires this extra cost could be reduced by £10, bringing the net extra cost to £25 per fitting. The total amount for the 15,000 fittings required was £375,000.
• Operational costs for the system were estimated at the time to show a 15 per cent reduction in energy usage, representing a saving of £45,000 per year on energy costs. This was before the introduction of the Climate Change Levy, which would have added a further 15 per cent saving.
• The flexibility and adaptability of the system due to 'trade free' reconfiguring produced an additional saving on churn, that is, the movement and relocation of workplaces. This was estimated at £24,000 per year.

On this basis, the simple 'payback value' for the system was reported as being between five

7.1
**MOD Abbey Wood
Offices (architect:
Percy Thomas
Partnership)**

and seven years. In practice, the outcome has been considerably better.

- First, the actual extra cost of a luminaire was £25 which meant the net extra cost over a conventional fitting is actually £15 or £225,000 for the total installation.
- Second, operational costs measured over the first two years of full use of the building have shown that, instead of an anticipated installed lighting load of 16 Watts/m^2, the average running load is now under 8 W/m^2.

Thus the actual saving of energy costs is £156,000 per year (with Climate Change Levy this is now £170,000 per year) and, with the churn saving, the simple payback valuation is about one year.

Ventilation and thermal control performance in this case study were considered in terms of:

- enabling natural use of outdoor air whenever it is beneficial to do so
- design of system plant and air distribution
- disposition of outlets and extracts for flexible use of space
- system control.

The design approach for MOD Abbey Wood was given the acronym AIDA – An Incremental Design Approach – since it offered the best means of achieving the design objective. This was to provide the highest quality of indoor air and thermal control for optimal user performance. As with the lighting system, it had to be achieved at the lowest operating cost, within a capped budget whilst meeting targets for emissions performance. The AIDA approach ensures items are only added to the design when they represent value in what they produce in terms of performance and use. This avoids the situation where items might be included in the design regardless of need or with insufficient care to the needs of the user.

The first stage of AIDA begins with natural ventilation and perimeter heating which is then incrementally supplemented, to meet the needs of the user. The increments are:

- displacement ventilation facilities operable in 'mixed mode' and with 'heat recovery'
- cooling and dehumidification of system supply air when needed in high summer
- active static cooling by chilled panels where necessary to offset heat from user equipment

Installations are equipped with system controls that adjust to meet prevailing requirements. As with the lighting system, the air supply and thermal control facilities are disposed and installed to allow trade free reconfiguring of workplace furniture and partitioning throughout the buildings on a 1500 mm grid.

The initial 'basic stage' (Figure 7.2) has opening windows and perimeter heating for ventilation and thermal control. The windows have glare control, and the heating is adjusted centrally by reference to outdoor air temperature and locally by thermostatic valves. The structural mass is exposed at soffit for heat exchange by radiation with occupants. The façade has high levels of thermal insulation.

In the case of MOD Abbey Wood, these basic stage facilities are appropriate for lightly

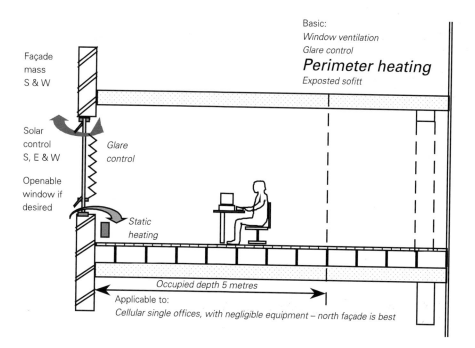

7.2
'Basic Stage' Facilities; perimeter heating

occupied offices to a maximum depth of 5 m with negligible heat gains from equipment and having a northerly aspect.

The 'first increment' (Figure 7.3) of increased facilities has the basic stage facilities augmented with a simple displacement ventilation system by mechanical plant incorporating heat recovery. The windows have solar shading control by inter-pane blinds. Façades having southerly aspects are of high mass masonry construction, and are also of high thermal insulation.

These first increment stage facilities are appropriate for normally occupied offices

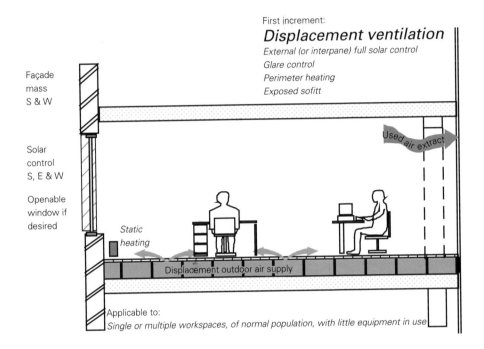

First increment:
Displacement ventilation
External (or interpane) full solar control
Glare control
Perimeter heating
Exposed sofitt

Façade
mass
S & W

Solar
control
S, E & W

Openable
window if
desired

Static heating

Used air extract

Displacement outdoor air supply

Applicable to:
Single or multiple workspaces, of normal population, with little equipment in use

7.3
'First Increment Stage' facilities: displacement ventilation

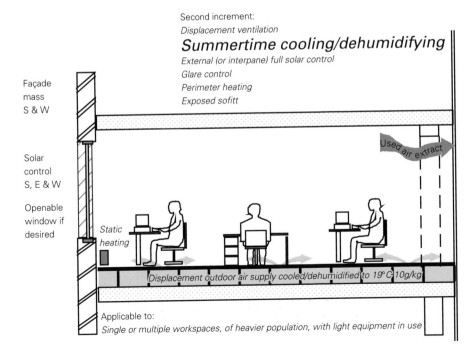

Second increment:
Displacement ventilation
Summertime cooling/dehumidifying
External (or interpane) full solar control
Glare control
Perimeter heating
Exposed sofitt

Façade
mass
S & W

Solar
control
S, E & W

Openable
window if
desired

Static heating

Used air extract

Displacement outdoor air supply cooled/dehumidified to 19° C 10g/kg

Applicable to:
Single or multiple workspaces, of heavier population, with light equipment in use

7.4
'Second Increment Stage' facilities: summertime cooling/ dehumidification

with some equipment heat gains on all elevation aspects. The 'second increment' of increased facilities has the basic stage facilities augmented with the simple displacement ventilation system by mechanical plant incorporating heat recovery of the first increment (Figure 7.4). The ventilation system is additionally equipped with mechanical cooling to maintain the system supply air temperature to 19°C and dehumidified to 10 g/kg in peak summer when the outdoor air exceeds those conditions. Windows, solar control and façades are as the first increment stage. These second increment stage facilities are appropriate for heavier population and higher equipment loads on all elevation aspects.

The 'final increment' of increased facilities has the basic stage facilities, augmented with the simple displacement ventilation system equipped with mechanical cooling and dehumidification (Figure 7.5). Windows, solar control and façades are as the first increment stage. In addition there is active static cooling consisting of chilled beams at sun-side perimeters and suspended chilled

panels applied to the lighting/acoustic units of previous stages.

These final increment stage facilities are appropriate for those areas of the building having a commensurate need arising from equipment loads and a demand for closer control of thermal conditions.

Why are the various increments so important in terms of performance of people? A dynamic thermal analysis of a model of the building was prepared in order to determine the amounts of time during working hours that indoor temperatures exceeding a series of degrees would occur (Figure 7.6). The original building model, comprising the basic stage facilities, was shown to result in indoor temperatures that would exceed 24–26°C for most of the time between April and November. For some 50 per cent of the period May to October, the indoor temperature would exceed 27.5°C. When indoor temperatures exceed 26°C, everyone complains and performance drops markedly.

The building model was then given additional facilities incrementally until the indoor temperatures were reduced to less than 10 per cent above 27.5°C to occur from July to

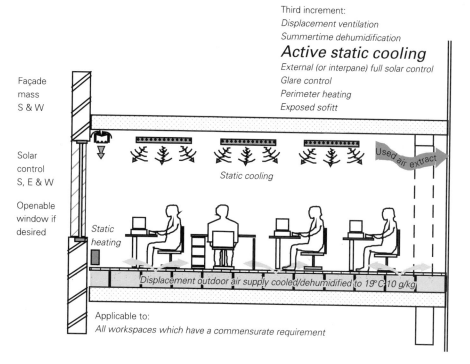

7.5
'Final Increment Stage' Facilities: active static cooling

September, and less than 25 per cent above 24–26°C during the April to October period.

This '2.5 per cent climate', a description used by DEGW in their original design briefing report for the project, means that indoor temperatures should only be beyond generally acceptable conditions for no more than 2.5 per cent of the working year. (Roughly 2.5 per cent of 2000 equals 50 hours a year.)

Research shows that worker performance is affected by the temperature at the workplace. Figure 7.7 is a graph of the relationship between workplace temperature and worker performance, based on original findings by Wyon (1996).

A computed cost of production lost – calculated by giving worker performance a monetary value based upon a production rate of

£50 per working hour at an ideal working temperature – was compared to the capital cost of each incremental facility. Using the dynamic thermal analysis of the building model, the negative impact of indoor temperatures upon this production rate could be calculated. The value was computed by reference to the length of time that the various temperatures would prevail and then amortised across the population of 5,000 workers in the buildings. By this means, installation of just the basic stage facilities was estimated to cost £1.6m with an associated cost of lost production calculated at £4.5m per year.

The capital cost of the first increment stage – providing simple displacement ventilation – was estimated at £2.6m. The cost of lost production was now calculated to be £2.8m per year. Thus the value of installing this

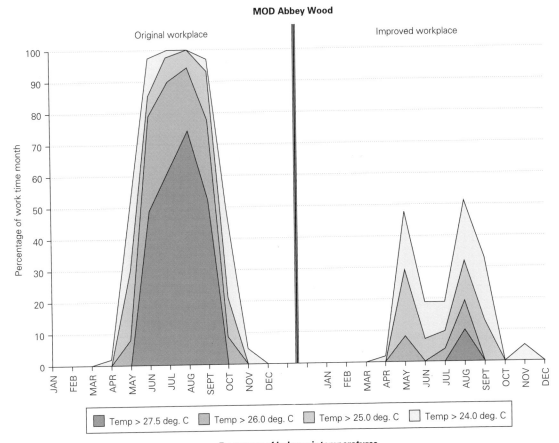

7.6
Predicted indoor temperatures

Frequency of indoor air temperatures

also appropriate to compare this management decision – to go ahead with a new building in order to save the equivalent of 40 per cent of the payroll costs – with today's all too common decision simply to dismiss staff.

In addition, further quality management decisions were made including locating the new building in the centre of Bristol, close to the railway station. This results in reduced travel to work emissions, improved quality of life and an enhanced corporate image. Workplace buildings are a vital tool of commerce and industry and their performance is crucial to business success.

BP Sunbury

The BP Sunbury buildings demonstrate how a building's performance can be assessed on the basis of 'business emissions'. Of concern to everyone today and thereby of great importance to building owners – and so a significant message to designers and the construction industry – is the Eco-Factor performance of a building. A primary element of that factor is the climate change emissions implications of the building in operation. These can be quantified in terms of the building's progress towards achieving a 'climate or carbon neutral' status which requires at least a 60 per cent cut from today's emissions.

In the case of BP Sunbury, the new buildings can be compared with those they are replacing in terms of their climate or carbon neutral performance. The existing buildings produce 150kg CO_2/m^2 pa. However, according to BREEAM, the new buildings produce 65kg CO_2/m^2 pa. Hoare Lea's own assessment

7.9
**BP Sunbury
(architect: Broadway
Malyan)**

from computer modelling suggest this figure will probably be closer to 75kg CO_2/m^2 pa. The CO_2 emissions reduction is 75kg CO_2/m^2 pa or 50 per cent.

But can a comparison based on square metres ever be a true measure of business emissions? It is surely more appropriate to consider the people producing for the business and the amount of emissions each individual generates in making that amount of production? Looking again at BP Sunbury, the buildings being replaced housed 2,200 people in 60,000 m^2, so the emission per person was some 4 tonnes carbon dioxide per year. The new buildings will house 4,000 people in 60,000 m^2, which means the emission per person will be 1 tonne of carbon dioxide per year. Thus, moving to the new buildings will cut CO_2 emissions by 3 tonnes per person per year. This is equal to a 75 per cent cut – rather than the 50 per cent cut based solely on square metres.

Further progress towards carbon neutral status at BP Sunbury is shown by other features. A BP-sponsored bus route with a service from the local rail station has led to a 5 per cent cut in travel to work emissions. The introduction of a nine-day fortnight has led to a 10 per cent cut, and the introduction of BP Hives (Highly Interactive Visual Environment Suites) video conferencing units are saving 125 air miles per person per year. In total, the carbon dioxide emissions cut for site-based business equals 3.3 tonnes per person per year which, when multiplied by the 4,000 head count, equates to 13,200 tonnes per year.

But is head count an appropriate measure of business performance? Surely productivity is a more important factor? The new Sunbury buildings give greater than 16 l/s of outdoor air per person and up to 70W/m^2 of incidental cooling. It provides a top quality indoor climate. This will certainly bring a better than 5 per cent productivity increase which would equate to cutting CO_2 emissions by some 14,000 tonnes per year for the site – an 80 per cent cut from previous emissions.

BP are committed to cut emissions by 40 per cent for every business unit, worldwide, by 2010. The businesses based at Sunbury are cutting 14 kT CO_2 per year (or 80 per cent of their existing emissions). Since BP operates an internal emissions trading system which is currently costed at $20/tonne CO_2, each business unit at Sunbury, after delivering their required 40 per cent emissions cut, has residual savings of 7kT CO_2 per year to trade. On the internal Carbon Offset Trading Market, this is worth $140,000 per year plus the value of the energy saving which amounts to $2,600,000 (@ $185 per tonne). The business unit is therefore saving $2,740,000 per year or around £1,850,000.

BP Sunbury is an ongoing development, which enables progressive, and incremental, improvements to be implemented with each new building. Operational trials are also carried out on preceding buildings to ensure they perform as was expected and to test further possible improvements. BP Sunbury is undoubtedly a growing success story in terms of business emissions and building performance: productivity is up by more than 5 per cent; carbon dioxide emissions have been cut by 80 per cent; and energy costs are down by more than $2.74m per year.

Conclusion

The important question raised by these three case studies is, why are there no Key Performance Indicators related to building performance? Being in a position to give customers information about how the building designed for them will perform is long overdue.

If procedures such as those described in this chapter were employed as standard practice, surely it would go some way to enabling the construction industry to deliver the performance improvements that are called for and so evidently needed?

References

CABE and DTLR (2001) *By Design – better places to live,* London: Thomas Telford,

Construction Task Force (1998) *Rethinking Construction: the report of the Construction Task Force,* London: DETR.

Wyon, D. (1996) 'Indoor environmental effects on productivity', *Proceedings of IAQ '96,* Baltimore, MD.

Chapter 8

Design quality in new schools

Richard Feilden

Entering a well-designed and well-run primary school is one of life's more pleasurable experiences. The buildings and their design form a backdrop inhabited by pupils and staff to provide a child-centred environment which ensures a sense of security whatever uncertainties may exist in lives beyond. If the primary school is a child's first step into a wider society, the move to secondary school will be no less significant in his or her life. Inevitably there will be a different scale and a very different environment, going from the security of the class-based junior school into a larger world where corridors and toilets can become threatening places. In both environments the architecture of the school can be shown to be highly significant, but a variety of factors have conspired so that many of our schools fall short of the standards that we might reasonably expect.

In Britain there are currently about 24,000 schools in the state sector and approximately 2,000 more in the private sector. These are buildings of huge significance in the lives of about 20 per cent of the population, they are workplaces for over 500,000 people and they are visited regularly by many more. The school is the place where children spend most of their waking hours apart from home, and it is the most significant contact that they will have in their lives with provisions made by the state. Relatively few, however, have any real architectural merit.

Designing schools is not easy. Budgets are almost invariably constrained and an apparently simple set of user requirements can pose difficult issues for designers, particularly as educational requirements become more sophisticated. Discussion about the design of schools is currently much needed in Britain, because the country is now in the early stages of a great schools building campaign that will see the reconstruction of a significant proportion of our school stock. Recently the discussion about this reconstruction has tended to focus on the means of procurement for new projects, which is frequently the controversial Private Finance Initiative (PFI). In the very complex process issues that PFI raises it is easy for the value of design quality to be sidelined by commercial and legal considerations, and there is a growing determination that this should not be allowed to happen. Debate about the importance of design is gathering momentum. *Schools for the Future*, published by the Department for Education and Skills as Building Bulletin 95 (DfES, 2002) is essential reading.

This chapter is a further attempt to redress the balance by exploring why well-designed schools matter and how they may be achieved. It explores the history of design ambitions for schools, and current views on ways in which the school estate can be improved as it is progressively rebuilt.

The value of well-designed schools

Before embarking on the main discussion, it is worth commenting on the significance of school design as an area for serious architecture. From the sheer numbers of people who are affected by school buildings, their importance will be clear. Establishing a quantifiable comparison between a well designed and a poorly designed school is, however, difficult – buildings have been described as a 'scientific nightmare' and many different factors can distort the picture and need to be adjusted to obtain meaningful correlations.

Gradually, research studies are being undertaken, mostly in the USA, but increasingly in Britain, with their findings being collated by the Commission for Architecture and the Built Environment (CABE, 2002). Positive correlations are claimed between the attributes of the building and pupils' examination results, and between quality of daylighting and progress in reading and maths; improvements of between 20 and 26 per cent going from the worst daylit school to the best are reported (Heschong Mahone Group, 1999). In Britain a team led by

Professor Brian Edwards is investigating the performance of 'green' schools compared with similar schools that do not have these features. Early results imply positive correlation between green features and pupil performance, particularly at the primary level, although caution is essential in interpreting the data since it is difficult to ensure comparability among the schools being investigated for factors such as pupil intake and staff capability. Both this research and that undertaken by Price Waterhouse Coopers (2001) on behalf of the DfES show improved staff morale and retention in better facilities.

The research is ammunition for those arguing for expenditure on improving facilities. But it does not in itself provide evidence that well-designed new buildings provide better academic results than poorly designed new buildings. The best school designs should offer genuine value for money, whether this be through improved functionality, improved performance of pupils or other issues such as improved recruitment and retention of staff. As new schools come on stream it should be possible to test their performance and explore the value for money issue further, but this will take some time. Considerable investment is currently being made in the development of a system of Design Quality Indicators, described in Chapters 15–17, which are intended to ensure design quality remains a focus throughout the design process. In the meantime we should not ignore common sense or a very simple measure proposed by the former Director of Estates from Sunderland University when he said: 'a well-designed building exceeds expectations, a poorly designed one falls short of them'.

It is also possible to argue that the quality of accommodation that we provide for different activities indicates how much we value those activities. Looking at many British schools now one might confidently argue that we value our shopping and leisure activities more highly than our children's education. While many universities achieve standards of quality that match or exceed their surrounding areas, this is often not the case with schools or colleges of further education. One objective of the school building programme that is now under way should be to reverse this position. The role of careful and skilful design in ensuring not only fitness for purpose, but also civic quality and lifting of the spirits, will continue to be debated. But even if there may be some additional short-term cost associated with good design, this will pale into complete insignificance over the lifetime of a school and thus the value of quality will be clear.

A brief history of school design and its legacy

Progressive architecture and progressive thinking in educational terms are frequently found hand in hand. John Newsom, Chief Education Officer of Hertfordshire in the 1950s,

believed that 'education was inseparable from the environment' and it is no surprise to find that his authority was one of the great commissioners during his period of tenure.

From an earlier period we still have a legacy of Victorian school buildings arising from the realisation that widely distributed education was a requirement for a modern and technological society. These buildings were based very largely around the classroom designed for 'chalk and talk' and teaching areas accounted for a high proportion of floor space. The fact that some of these buildings are still in use after more than a hundred years suggests both that the class-based model is still at the heart of our schools, and that they were durably built. They are also of interest environmentally since they were constructed at a time when natural light was virtually essential for operation, as was natural ventilation. Primary schools were typically lofty single-storied structures with tall windows so that light reached deep into the space.

8.1
Bathampton School

In urban areas it is still possible to find a significant number of 'triple decker' secondary schools where a different arrangement was required. These buildings had classrooms with a typical ceiling height approaching four metres and central corridors were lit by borrowed light from the classroom, usually with opening lights to permit cross-ventilation.

The quality of specification of finishes has meant that they are quite often more robust than modern alternatives. However, their basic configuration and the lack of flexibility that goes with load bearing construction and ageing services are beginning to render them redundant. In particular modern teaching requires more space in the classroom. This point is illustrated by current moves to revise *Building Bulletin 82*, which is the benchmark of space standards.

The legacy of school building from about 1910 to 1950 is fragmented. Many school designs still followed the principles established by the Victorians, albeit with increasing diversity of materials and the quality of construction falling short of earlier standards. Approaches to environmental issues also changed, with more reliance on artificial light and lower floor to

ceiling heights. In the 1930s Henry Morris, Chief Education Officer of Cambridge County Council, commissioned the pioneering Village Colleges which were an early manifestation of the recurring idea of community schools intended to 'touch every side of the life of the inhabitants'. The last of these colleges (1938–1940) was designed by Maxwell Fry, the early British modernist. Complete with flat roof and generous glazing offering quite new architectural messages, this was education as a progressive and inclusive activity, a fundamental element of life in the community.

Between 1950 and 1970 a new school was opened every day – a truly extraordinary achievement in logistical terms although it is not one that we have always blessed, since the output left much to be desired in architectural and performance terms. This was the era of system building, of CLASP, MACE and SCOLA, economical solutions that were backed by an architectural philosophy that revelled in the freedom offered by flat roofs and prefabrication from a 'kit of parts'. In practice these buildings were widely disliked from quite early on and with age they have become even less appreciated, as their constructional and

8.2 (below left)
Haverstock School

8.3 (below right)
Haverstock School interior

environmental failures have become apparent. This period has left a legacy with relatively few bright spots. Peter and Alison Smithsons' 'brutalist' Hunstanton School was a one-off design with individual character, but the majority of schools were the results of a production line of dubious quality.

The great wave of building up to 1975 was followed by a very different period when limited school building was undertaken. The bulge in population passed through the system and, with ever-tightening constraints on public spending, Britain hit an unsustainable low in its approach to the educational estate. There was, however, one bright spot which deserves a special mention, and this was Hampshire County Council.

The Hampshire schools

No history of school design would be complete without a description of the work undertaken by Hampshire County Council under their County Architect Colin Stansfield Smith. This programme has stimulated the whole debate about public buildings, and it is valuable to describe some of the trends that emerged and remain the starting point for any designer approaching the design of new primary schools in particular. They are fully reported in Richard Weston's splendid book *Schools of Thought* (1991) which celebrates Stansfield Smith's RIBA Gold Medal.

These schools, designed from 1974, can be seen as a reaction to the system building that provided 'universal' school building solutions that might be structurally and economically logical but did not provide individual responses to sites or users. Underlying the approach to the later Hampshire schools was the belief that carefully designed, lovingly developed individual solutions elevate the activities housed – bringing delight and enhancing the activities that are accommodated. It is a hypothesis that has fired

8.4
**Burnham Copse
Infants School**

generations of architects to greater endeavours, and the struggle between this view and a more utilitarian view has characterised much of the debate about school design.

In the Hampshire primary schools two main trends developed and both were developed exquisitely. There is a third trend which is also worthy of mention. The first trend has been characterised by Richard Weston as *the big roof*, and although there are many variants it perhaps reaches its climax at Burnham Copse infants school where the building form is akin to a giant wigwam with classrooms spiralling to the south of a top-lit central hall. The building plays with levels, the classrooms being half a level above the hall and

given their own outside space immediately adjacent and with their own outside doors. Up half a level the class bases are found – an arrangement that would be unacceptable with contemporary standards of design for the disabled. The form of this school is rather deterministic and will create inevitable restrictions on the ways that the space can be used, but the richness of the architecture is expected to compensate for these restrictions.

A second trend reached its finest realisation at Queens Inclosure First School. This much celebrated design is a long and low elegant 'shed' that is sited parallel to a wooded edge which is the last remnant of the Forest of Bere. Where the big roof buildings are often

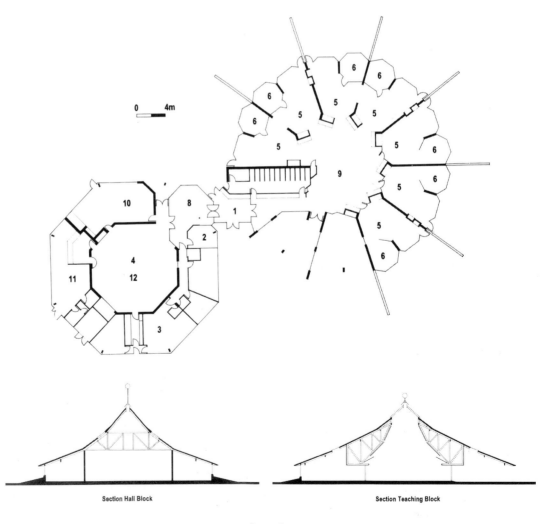

8.5
**Burnham Copse
Infants – plan**

0   4m

8.6
**Burnham Copse
Infants – section**

Section Hall Block

Section Teaching Block

0   4m

designed to give identity to nondescript sites, Queens Inclosure is designed to provide a modern but subservient counterpoint to its forest backdrop. There is also a different approach to internal planning where an extraordinarily open feeling is developed with class spaces flowing out into circulation; and 'pods' that contain specialist activities also opening into the central circulation spine that separates teaching areas from other activities. This school caused some trepidation for teachers and parents before it was constructed, but in practice it is reported to have worked extraordinarily well — allowing great flexibility of teaching which fitted well with teaching patterns, at least of the time when it was built. The head has been quoted as saying 'this is the best primary school in Britain. When I walk in every morning my heart lifts because of the way it works for children.'

The third trend to emerge in the thinking at Hampshire was of a more articulate architecture, almost Scandinavian in feel and responding to wooded sites at both Whitehill and Woodlea. In these buildings architectural formality gives way to a more organic feel, with individual classrooms expressed in a complex form relating to the slopes in the landscape and linked by stairs and ramps. Here the classroom becomes the focus again, but connects to both enclosed class bases and shared resource bases that flow out into the landscape. These are perhaps the most popular of all the Hampshire primaries, a very acceptable face of modern architecture and an environment in which anyone would be happy to work and study.

It is interesting to note that the Hampshire schools were largely developed with only limited input from the end-users and that this is an approach that is much less likely now. Perhaps because of this they were not universally popular with end-users, although they have had a very good architectural press. It is nonetheless a pity that the County did not have the opportunity to develop the typology of secondary schools in a similar way, since the current wave of school building would have benefited from a similar exploration.

8.7
**Queens Inclosure
First School**

Some more recent primary schools

The tradition of lovingly designed child-orientated primary schools has been developed in a number of recent projects, and it is interesting to note that virtually all the trail-blazing projects had rather higher levels of funding than one would expect under normal regimes which have led to rather more pedestrian results. Three schools are worth a brief mention.

The new single form entry primary school at Great Notley in Essex was the result of an architectural competition which was won by Allford Hall Monaghan Morris. A primary objective of the competition was to explore the issue of sustainability and the response is an unusually shaped building that is essentially triangular in plan. The low perimeter was a part of the strategy to reduce both energy losses and construction costs, and good natural light is achieved through a series of rooflights achieved by folding the green roof. The school has been well received, but is now due for a doubling of size that was always anticipated but proves problematic with a form that appears complete in itself.

The new primary school at Perthcelyn in the Rhondda Valley in South Wales is a beautifully crafted project that lies within the organic tradition developed by Hampshire Architects. It was also designed by the local authority architects, in this case Rhonda Taff Cynon. All the classrooms are expressed externally and face east over a spectacular view with entrances shared between two classrooms so that children can be delivered to their own room. Light is admitted to the backs of the classrooms by a combination of roof and borrowed lights, and a sense of transparency pervades the building. A two-storey shared space runs the length of the building and connects the area of classrooms to the unusually generous community facilities that are on an upper level.

8.8
**Great Notley
Primary School
(architect AHMM)**

8.9
**Perthcelyn Primary
School (architect:
Rhonda Taff Cynon)**

8.10
**Perthcelyn – interior
of the double height
void**

quality can be expected to come to the fore as one of the key selection criteria.

Proponents of the PFI claim that the integration of design and construction with the responsibility to maintain buildings for a twenty-five-year period will lead to significantly better results than the previous procurement routes. Whether this is true or not will depend on a variety of factors. First, there is the question of whether the PFI will come to be seen as a 'design friendly' process which encourages service providers to employ the best architectural practices and, in turn, is attractive to those practices. A second, and perhaps equally important, issue will be whether sufficient funds are made available to build to a quality which offers genuine value for money. This means something more than compliance with minimum area standards. It requires the creation of schools of which users and communities can genuinely be proud. Only then will the school occupy its rightful place at the heart of the community, and as a key staging post on our children's route into a civilised society.

References

CABE (2002) *The Value of Good Design: how buildings and spaces create economic and social value*, London: CABE.

CABE and OGC (2002) *Improving Standards of Design in the Procurement of Public Buildings*, London: CABE and OGC.

DfEE (1994) (Department for Education and Employment) *Passive Solar Schools – a design guide*, Building Bulletin 79, London: DfEE.

DfEE (1997) (Department for Education and Employment) *Guidelines for Environmental Design in Schools (Revision of Design Note 17)*, Building Bulletin 87, London: DfEE.

DfES (2002) (Department for Education and Skills BDH Schools Building and Design Unit). *Schools for the Future – Designs for Learning Communities*, Building Bulletin 95, London: DfES.

Heschong Mahone Group (1999) *Daylighting in Schools: an investigation into the relationship between daylighting and human performance*, report on behalf of the California Board for Energy Efficiency, Fair Oaks, CA: Pacific Gas and Electric Company.

Organisation for Co-operation and Economic Development (1996) *Schools for Today and Tomorrow*, Paris: OECD.

Price Waterhouse Coopers (2001) *Building Performance: an empirical assessment of the relationship between schools, capital investment and pupil performance*, Research Report 242, London: Department for Education and Employment.

Weston, Richard (1991) *Schools of Thought – Hampshire Architecture 1974–1991*, Winchester: Hampshire County Council.

Chapter 9

Assessing benefits in the health sector

Bryan Lawson

The vast majority of architects would probably feel in no doubt that good design and a well-cared for environment add value. Unfortunately demonstrating this unequivocally and empirically is not so easy. There are two major and many minor problems with conducting such research. First we need some measures of the success of the way the environment works. We need to know how effectively the environment supports the functions and activities housed in it. Second, such investigations inevitably have to be conducted in the field and the extent to which we can control all the other variables is therefore extremely limited.

Whilst we cannot solve all these methodological problems, and no research of this kind is ever likely to be entirely satisfactory, we believe we have carried out work reported here that comes as close as it is likely to get. To solve the first problem we have been concentrating on evaluating building types or housing activities that have a measurable output and are already monitored for other reasons. Obvious examples of such buildings would

include major public sector services such as hospitals and schools. The work reported here has been done on hospitals with the support of NHS Estates and with the collaboration of two NHS trusts (Lawson and Phiri, 2000).

We were able to identify two pairs of hospital wards where construction was planned. The first pair is in general physical medicine at Poole General Hospital and the second in mental health at South Downs in Brighton. The first pair involved the refurbishment of existing 1960s' general wards. In the original ward there were six four-bed bays and six one-bed bays. There were lavatories at each end of the ward. In the refurbished unit there are sixteen single bedrooms and three four-bed bays. The new bedrooms have a clean simple interior using natural timber and have ensuite bathrooms.

The second pair involved the replacement of two 15-bed wards in the Freshfield Mental Health Unit of Brighton General Hospital, which were housed in Victorian brick buildings with typically high ceilings, with a new purpose-built mental health unit. The new Mill View Hospital that replaced these wards is a thirty-two bed unit with single rooms with ensuite facilities.

In both cases the same medical teams and patterns of patient referral that were in operation in the old buildings were going to be used in the new buildings. Inevitably this cannot have been perfectly identical, but we are as sure as we can be that the types and conditions of the patients, and the circumstances facing them in the new buildings, were as similar to those in the old buildings as could reasonably be hoped for in real practice. Thus the only major differences were the environments in which the patients were housed. Such a research opportunity is not easy to come by. We had our work approved by the ethics committees of the two hospitals and enlisted the cooperation of the medical and clinical staff as well as the management in each trust.

We were able to study a substantial sample of patients passing through the older wards in each case, followed by a second sample of patients in the new or refurbished wards. Sample sizes were approximately 140 in Poole General Hospital where patients typically stayed for nine or ten days, and about 75 in the Brighton Mental Health units where patients typically stayed rather longer for about 35–40 days.

It is important to be clear here about what we are measuring. There are three major sets of aspects that can be evaluated in a retrospective examination of an architectural project. It is useful to think of these as the 'three Ps': Process, Product and Performance. Process includes all those aspects of a project that are to do with how it came about. It includes the procurement method, commissioning and briefing of consultants, the design team and their management of the process and so on. The Product group of issues covers all aspects of the building as a physical and aesthetic entity. The materials, systems and components of the building, how well they operate, their capital and life cycle costs and so on are included here. This project, however, concentrated almost exclusively on the Performance aspects of the projects. Here we consider how well the building facilitates the main purposes and functions to which the client wishes to put it. What is really under consideration here is what the building adds to the client's main business. Here in the case of a hospital we have considered mainly the patients, although we have done some work on the staff too. The real question the research team tried to answer was: 'Can architecture contribute to the well-being of the patients, make their enforced stay in hospital less unpleasant and even help them to recover and leave more quickly?'

Collecting evidence

We first held focus groups with a series of people involved in the commissioning, management, design and daily use of these kinds of buildings. We wanted to know what the client's expectations were, what the design team's intentions were, and what experienced users of such buildings thought important.

From these focus groups we were able to establish questionnaires that would be administered to patients at the end of their stay in hospital. These questionnaires asked them a series of questions about their stay and the building in particular. We asked them for their reactions to the building and to the treatment they had received and staff who had been looking after them. We decided in conjunction with our clinical colleagues that in the case of the mentally ill patients we would administer the questionnaires through their carers. The patients on the general wards completed their own questionnaires.

Patients were in general very happy to take part in this study, and remarkably articulate about their environment. This should not surprise us, of course, as most people are generally concerned about their surroundings. However, one architect experienced in the design of healthcare buildings had warned that this would not be so. Patients are far too focused on their illness, he claimed, to be worried about the environment. Whilst of course some may be very seriously ill and some may be very worried, in reality most patients have time on their hands. Patients are, after all, simply members of society in a particular condition at a particular time. While in hospital they spend a great deal of time with perhaps rather less purpose than in their normal lives. This may well make them even more susceptible to the environment and more sensitive to it. Over a century ago Florence Nightingale had noted the importance of their surroundings to her patients (Nightingale, 1860) and work here certainly confirms this. In fact a patient in hospital may get the personal attention of a doctor for probably only a very few minutes in a day and slightly longer periods of personal care from nurses and therapists. However, they lie in bed, or if they are lucky, sit, get pushed or walk around in their environment for many hours.

In general then we found that patients were able to assess their environment using our questionnaire. The patients in the newer building expressed more satisfaction with the appearance, layout and overall design of their wards. At Poole hospital 72 per cent of the patients in the new unit gave the highest rating they could for overall appearance, compared with only 37 per cent of the patients in the old unit. At South Downs these figures were both lower, with 41 per cent giving the highest rating in the new unit compared with only 20 per cent in the old. It may seem odd that the South Downs figures are so low compared with the Poole figures, but in reality this is not really so. We do largely expect mental health patients to report lower levels of satisfaction due to the unhappiness of their condition. What matters in this study is not the difference between

physical and mental health patients but in each case the differences between the old and new buildings. A series of other questions on the overall design and the extent to which the facilities met the patients' needs revealed similar responses. In all cases there was a highly statistically significant difference in favour of the newer building.

We had a series of questions about particular spaces rather than the overall design and again the newer buildings were more highly praised. The most significant differences were in the patients' assessment of their own private area, whether in a multiple-bed bay or a single room. We will return to this point later.

We asked patients much more detailed questions about the physical environmental conditions such as lighting, temperature, air quality and noise. Again in both sets of samples the new building tended to fare better than the old. These differences were less marked than those for the overall design and spatial organisation of the wards. Next we asked what levels of control patients had over their environment, and here we found remarkably disappointing results. Patients generally reported low levels of control over their environment, whether in the old or new buildings.

Next we asked our patients quite explicitly if they thought the environment had helped them to feel better. Both hospitals showed a significant increase in the patients' assessments of this. We had also asked patients to assess the quality of their overall treatment and to rate the staff who had cared for them during their stay. In all cases we found an improvement in these ratings in the newer buildings, although these differences were not always statistically significant. There are so many of these figures that even though there is a lack of strict statistical significance they seem to paint a remarkably consistent picture. In the newer environments patients thought they had received better treatment and that their doctors, nurses and therapists were more helpful and attentive. This is spite of the fact that treatment regimes were the same and in many cases staff were identical!

Valued features of the healthcare environment

So what were the features of these new hospital wards that have attracted these comparatively improved ratings from patients? We asked our respondents to tell us in their own words what features of their environment were either particularly good or bad. It is worth remembering here that there are two groups of factors that we commonly see on work which might be classified as 'architectural psychology'. The first and most obvious concerns the direct relationship between people and their environment. Such factors would include the colours of surfaces or the temperature of rooms. However, the second group of factors concerns the way the environment mediates the relationships between people (Lawson, 2001). Such factors would include matters of privacy or how spaces enable people to establish community or maintain 'personal space'.

It is often falsely assumed that the value of good design lies largely in the first category. Whilst this may be true for designers with heightened senses of aesthetics, in fact it is more often the second which matters more to ordinary people. This is no exception! The most commonly raised issue amongst all four of our patient samples was that of privacy. That is not to say that all our respondents were asking to be entirely private; they were most definitely not, as we shall see. However, the way the environment enabled them to be either private or not as they wished seems to be of the greatest importance.

Following on from privacy came the matter of view. The most common complaint made to us about any hospital situation by patients was the lack of view. Nurses and others working in hospitals also mentioned this

problem, not just for themselves but also on behalf of the patients. Again, however, this factor should not be interpreted as a purely aesthetic matter. There was no evidence that in general patients wanted classically beautiful views. If anything, it is views of everyday life that seem in demand here. Views in which something happens seem desirable, and views that enable conversation between patients of the events unfolding; perhaps children leaving school.

The next most frequent aspect of the environment to be mentioned was that of the bathroom/shower/toilet areas available in hospital. Yet again the same message was repeated. Patients commonly raised this in connection with the two specific factors of privacy and cleanliness. Of course patients were concerned about hygiene, or more commonly the perceived lack of it when such places were dirty. Also important seemed to be the symbolic value of a lack of cleanliness. What this seemed to be signalling to patients was the lack of care, pride and concern that the authorities showed for the environment. In turn of course this sends worrying signals to patients who find themselves forced to stay in such a place!

Next come the two obvious issues of appearance and noise. Appearance is inevitably a highly personal matter, but again whatever people's taste, they do appreciate an environment that at least appears cared for. Again not all patients want an entirely silent ward. What matters most here seems to be to have some degree of control. Our respondents mentioned this about such things as heating, the lighting, windows and blinds as well as noise. In fact the newer designed wards continued generally to offer relatively low levels of patient control of these matters. There is a long way to go it seems in convincing both clients and designers of their relative importance!

With privacy being such an important issue and our newer wards showing higher levels of provision in single bed accommodation, we decided to investigate this matter in much more detail. We had already found that the levels of satisfaction with treatment were higher for those patients in single bed accommodation. At first sight this might suggest that this is therefore generally more desirable. However, it turns out this fact was masking something more subtle and important. We conducted a pilot study at Poole hospital to see if single bed accommodation was more popular. Our data was sufficiently interesting for a full-scale study involving a sample of 473 patients.

In fact some 54 per cent actually expressed a preference for multiple bed space accommodation; 43 per cent voted for single beds and the rest expressed no preference. This majority in favour of multiple accommodation may be slightly misleading. We found that a majority of patients expressed a wish to be in the same kind of accommodation as they were occupying at the time. This may be partly due to patients getting their wish from the hospital and partly due to them not being able to imagine the alternative. Two common reasons were given for preferring multiple bed spaces – the wish for company and others to chat to, and a feeling that they were more likely to be given attention by nurses and might be forgotten about if isolated in their own room.

Some 22 per cent of patients were moved during their stay in hospital; often this was against their wish and to satisfy the needs of another patient. Such a move was often made during the night in response to some emergency.

Our data show very clearly that patients who are in the sort of accommodation they prefer and are left there, express significantly higher levels of satisfaction than others. They regard their treatment as better, rate the staff more highly and consider the overall design of the hospital to be superior. They are also more satisfied with their level of control over the environment, although this is most particularly true for patients in single bed rooms. Such patients, however, did not express any higher levels of appreciation of the appearance of the hospital.

The data confirm two interesting conclusions. First, being able to decide what levels of privacy and community you want is extremely important to people. Second, being able to control the environment is also very high on the agenda. Finally, not only does meeting these needs of people in the design lead to higher levels of satisfaction, it also transfers significantly to their general feeling about their treatment. Whilst it would clearly be foolish to advocate neglecting the appearance of the environment, these data unequivocally demonstrate that matters of privacy versus community and personal control over the environment are much more fundamental and of far greater significance.

All these results show a clear tendency for the environmental improvements to be recognised in themselves but also and importantly to contribute to an overall improvement in the sense of well-being of the patients, as indicated by their assessments of treatment and staff. It does indeed appear to indicate some real value attached to good design.

Our study also looked at the actual health outcomes of the patients. These data were recorded in the normal way by the clinical staff and extracted for us and associated with the patient questionnaires. We looked at a number of measures that might indicate improvements in health outcomes. The most obvious of these is length of stay. Do patients in better environments actually get released from hospital earlier? There was some very sketchy evidence from a couple of earlier studies that this could indeed be the case. In a frequently cited study Ulrich has shown that patients with a view from a window were discharged earlier than those without (Ulrich, 1984).

In fact both our general hospital and mental hospital patients were released significantly quicker from the new wards than the old ones. In the general medical wards at Poole, patients who did not undergo operations were released on average one-and-a-half days earlier from the new wards. This represents a reduction of about 21 per cent in the average stay of just over a week. Patients who underwent operations showed no reductions in the length of their stay post-operatively, although there were differences in the pre-operative stage. The reasons for this seemed unrelated to our study and are not reported here. In mental health wards, stays in hospital are normally longer with an average stay of over a month, so the reduction in length of stay of six days seems even more dramatic but actually represents a reduction of about 14 per cent.

The evidence is not simple to assess, and there are many other measures that can be investigated here. For example on our general medical wards at Poole there was a dramatic reduction in the amount of analgesic medication taken by the patients on the newer wards. Class A controlled pain killing drugs such as morphine, oramorph and codeine phosphate are generally administered on demand. On the newer wards the average number of days on which such drugs were administered was reduced by 22 per cent and the number of doses applied on these days reduced by 47 per cent. However, there was a slight increase in the amount of Class B drugs taken on the newer wards.

At Brighton in the new Mill View mental health unit, patients were judged by staff as significantly less aggressive, making fewer verbal outbursts and showing fewer instances of threatening behaviour. The number of instances of patients injuring themselves was reduced by two-thirds. Most dramatically the amount of time patients needed to spend in intensive supervisory care was reduced by 70 per cent from 13.1 days to 3.9 days. Finally, staff assessed some 79 per cent of patients as making good progress with their condition compared with only 60 per cent in the old buildings. Taken together this paints a picture of a far calmer and less hostile environment, with patients making better progress and being released earlier.

Conclusion

In sum, the evidence suggests not only an improvement in the quality of life for the patients, but also of course for the staff of the hospital. However, there is also potentially a significant saving for the NHS. We have not costed this yet, which is in any case a complex task. In addition to the obvious savings on drugs and bed occupancy it is likely that there are other results. Reductions in patient treatment times may in due course contribute to a reduction in waiting lists which otherwise seems to have become an endemic factor in the NHS. Certainly on the mental health side the improvement in the atmosphere on the wards is likely to rub off on the staff, who may well take less sick leave and show a reduction in turnover and be easier to recruit. Such data as we have been able to gather so far on these side effects are inconclusive at this stage. Until a larger study with access to such data can be completed it is difficult to put precise figures on the value of design in the healthcare environment. However, it is worth noting that such environments are extraordinarily costly to run, and it seems highly likely that the savings over the life cycle of the buildings may be quite considerable. We know from our data that the patients appreciated the better designed environments and that their stay in hospital was as a result more pleasant. In the healthcare environment good architecture seems to have the double value of making life more pleasant and treatment cheaper.

Finally, it is worth returning to the question of what aspects of the environment were most correlated with satisfaction and improved health outcomes. It is interesting in this regard to note that these aspects turn out to be universal rather than specific; that is to say, they could be seen to apply to all environments rather than being specific to the hospital. They may need different interpretations and realisations in buildings as varied as schools or law courts, but the lessons do seem to imply widely applicable principles. They concern such general matters as privacy and community, view, environmental comfort and control of the environment. Whilst they also inevitably involve the appearance of buildings, these factors seem very much more a matter of personal preference. However, where the appearance communicates other more fundamental issues, these factors again seemed important and generic. Untidiness and a lack of cleanliness, when they occurred, seemed important to all our patient samples. It seemed from our focus group findings that these are taken by people to indicate a lack of care, of attention or even of love of the place by those responsible for it. The communication of such values, or lack of them, is clearly disturbing and upsetting to patients who find themselves unwillingly although usually temporarily resident in them. Perhaps patients are asking themselves 'If the place is not loved and cared for, what about the inhabitants?'

The above discussion could have omitted the word 'patient' and the reader would have no idea the topic of discussion was a hospital. The factors that most seem to influence our patients' sense of well-being and their health outcomes thus have little or nothing to do with the technicalities of hospital design. In other words these issues are about good place-making. Considering that such results are arrived at in such a technically demanding building as a hospital, this suggests some wider lessons could be learned here. It is ironic that so much guidance exists for the design of healthcare buildings. NHS Estates publishes a great deal of material and many researchers have published other notes on the design of hospitals and associated building types.

Anecdotal experience also suggests that architects tackling such buildings pay great attention to the specific issues concerned with the typology. A simple experiential survey of most purpose-built healthcare environments suggests that such matters as the provision of view and enabling patients to control their environment are frequently neglected. Regrettably in UK NHS hospitals there is at present a frequent concern about lack of cleanliness. Untidiness seems endemic in such places with furniture and fittings procured without reference to the visual style of the buildings, with notices pinned haphazardly on walls, and often with later extensions and alterations leading to visual chaos.

Even the new buildings we have examined in this study are far from perfect in the eyes of patients in terms of these matters. The results nevertheless show significant improvements in the levels of satisfaction and health outcomes from better design. Is it therefore possible, with care, to create even better value through good design in hospitals? Is it also possible that many of the lessons learned in this study could apply to many other types of public buildings and places of work? Clearly our study is limited in its size and scope and much more evidence needs to be gathered on the true value of design. At the very least this study suggests that it might be possible to design places that enhance the quality of the lives of their inhabitants whilst simultaneously enabling them to be more productive. Design may well be able to offer added value rather than, as it is so often regarded, being an added financial burden.

References

Lawson, B. (2001) *The Language of Space*, Oxford: Architectural Press.
Lawson, B. and Phiri, M. (2000) 'Room for improvement', *Health Service Journal*, vol. 110, no. 5688, pp. 24–7.
Nightingale, F. (1860) *Notes on Nursing*, London: Harrison and Sons.
Ulrich, R. S. (1984). 'View through a window may influence recovery from surgery', *Science*, vol. 224, pp. 420–1.

Both projects have inspired recent developments in primary care buildings in the UK where the promotion of health and fitness and overlaps between health and social care are addressed. Many are designed with a sensitivity conscious of scale and are welcoming and generous to any visitor not necessarily ill, but wishing to take responsibility for keeping healthy. The integration of health with other community services such as social care, education and leisure is likely to lead to yet further experiments such as 'healthy living centres'.

Historical precedents and modern practice

The aim of citing these models is to illustrate a range of ideas and intentions about healthcare and medicine in relation to architectural settings. They describe an intellectual landscape from which to trace key ideas and map current concerns. The models are not intended to describe a strict chronology and indeed several may coexist at any time. But they do present architectural interpretations of particular models of care and show that by understanding the intentions behind the spatial configurations it is possible to reinterpret the plan.

The largely discarded custodial model presented a formal solution to maximise observation which, by inverting the concept, can suggest how to achieve legibility and orientation for visitors, a crucial planning concept in health buildings. This may be achieved through an atrium plan that provides a unified circulation space from which the rest of the building is visible.

The medical model embodies essential respect for process and programme. This model also highlights the hospital or complex health environment as one that consists of several discrete parts that have distinct functions. There is no doubt that health buildings need to be fit for purpose, enabling busy staff to carry out their work efficiently and effectively. Detailed studies of specific services have been documented in guidance as a way of sharing best practice designs, advisory and mandatory regulations. A great deal has also been understood about the development process from project conception, briefing, scheme development and design development through construction to completion. Whatever the particular procurement method, the route map or step by step guide to the development process remains principally the same. Guidance that sets out functional requirements and a preferred development process both assist the making of buildings 'fit for purpose'.

The caring model introduces the importance of sensual stimulation for a sympathetic environment and a dignified setting for nursing. It suggests that greater attention can be paid to how the space feels through stimulating the senses using colour, light, smell, and touch. Attention to such aspects of design can help to make spaces feel special, distinctive and particular to their location.

The description of states of healing in the holistic model translates into architectural spaces for privacy, sociability and urbanity. This can suggest a sophisticated and dynamic interpretation of the hierarchies of public and private spaces. Rather than buildings being seen as a collection of different rooms or services, they may be coded by the degree to which they offer space for public or private activities. Entrances may, for instance, be used for formal celebrations such as exhibitions and concerts. Social spaces that are more informal may create places to pause and reflect for staff and patients in waiting rooms, cafés and even corridors. Private places are essential for the many consultations and treatments between patients and clinical staff. The need for counselling rooms to talk to bereaved relatives, anxious patients and distressed staff is increasingly being acknowledged in many health buildings.

Finally the health-promoting model not only offers a proactive concept for health care environments but by acknowledging a continuum from illness to wellness privileges integration over segregation. Many community buildings are now being developed to embrace social as well as health care, legal and financial advice, educational and leisure facilities. In a way, they are developing as a new kind of community centre – one that includes health and social care with a broad range of professionals offering advice, consultation and therapy with spaces for a range of community activities.

A contemporary model for care and design

Alongside these historical precedents there are some significant emergent themes that inform the contemporary design of healthcare buildings. These include the notion of patient-focused care, the impact of new technologies, the idea of the therapeutic environment and sustainable development.

Patient-focused care

The notion of the patient-focused environment emerged in the last decade of the twentieth century. Patient-focused design has become explicit in the review of management systems to re-engineer the organisation of care to better suit the needs of the patient. For some projects, this has been interpreted as a way of achieving management improvements such as greater process efficiencies in, say, the reduction of steps required to make an X-ray. For others it has had far-reaching concerns that question the conventional hierarchies and status of patients in relation to health professionals. In some hospital projects, the idea of bringing equipment and services to the patient rather than subjecting them to long and uncomfortable journeys resulted in devolving diagnostic and treatment services to wards.

This process is now being applied beyond single buildings across the whole health economy. Mapping the process that a patient may encounter through the health system is helping to inform the reconfiguration of services to make more user-friendly and less wasteful arrangements. So, patient pathways that cross boundaries between general practice and hospitals and clinical networks that are designed across services in primary, secondary and tertiary care, ensure continuity of care as patients move back and forth between home, surgery and hospital. Whilst there are national standards and targets for health care services, it is acknowledged that variations will occur from one place to another depending on the needs of the local population and the availability of resources.

More social models of patient-centred care, such as the Planetree philosophy, propose that patients and their families play a much greater part in care. The idea emanated from America and now has a small following in Europe. The philosophy gives greater consideration to empowering patients and their carers to participate in the decisions about their treatment. In design terms this has led to the incorporation of key additions to the environment such as information centres, space for relatives in ward kitchens and special sitting rooms away from clinical areas.

A small number of studies[7] have sought to 'ask the patient' directly what is important to them about health care environments. These qualitative studies carried out the USA and the UK have relied on small samples in specific services and this kind of research has yet to be verified by more extensive and systematic studies. However, these initial pilots all suggest that the top 10 key issues for patients are:

* Privacy
* Confidentiality
* Convenience

- Good access
- Ambience
- Sense of control
- Comfort
- Being connected to staff
- Being connected to the outside world.

The interpretation of patient-centred design in recent buildings has generally resulted in hotel-like accommodation with more comfortable decor, upholstered furniture, pastel colour schemes and mood lighting. Although these designs tend to make less austere and clinical environments by focusing on comfort and control, they do not radically question the principles of a functionalist approach.

New technologies

Predicting future trends is not an easy task, and no more so in a sector which is undergoing rapid and significant changes. Technological advances affect not only medical procedures and equipment, handling of data for tests, records and administration, but also engineering and construction techniques.

The information revolution is prompting a paradigm shift in which the notion of the self-sufficient community is becoming outmoded by telecommunication networks of connected but not necessarily physically adjacent functions: the ambitious notion of the paperless and filmless hospital. The centralisation of highly serviced functions such as laboratories with networked distribution of results may enable more efficient use of highly specialised staff and expensive equipment. Linked workstations may speed information exchange between diagnostic imaging and theatres, wards and accident departments.

Another key issue for modernising the healthcare estate relates to the integration of design with construction. This means thinking about how to develop off-site fabrication to deliver improvements in quality whilst taking advantage of technology and new materials. Developing more sophisticated spatial types that distinguish between those that may be unique to each site, those that are repeatable and those that lend themselves to modular construction is the key to future integration of production quality with customisation and design aspirations. This is not about the production of standard boxes, but rather the customisation of selected parts of large-scale buildings. It makes sense in a sector that is looking to make efficiencies through scale and equity across the country but has the capacity to develop national standards with local diversity, and a combination of the best of unique craft with the elegance of repeatable production. It is expected to deliver improvements in the quality of finishes as well as greater predictability in construction time and costs.

Experimentation with new technical innovations was hampered by the largely conservative and compulsory government-standardised hospital design during the 1970s and 1980s, but may reap new ideas in this less prescriptive design era. The use of technology to provide 'smart and intelligent' buildings will be a key to future developments.

Therapeutic environments

Current theories about what constitutes a therapeutic environment all place importance on the feelings and experience of the individual. They may be broadly classified into three groups: the scientific studies test whether design can directly affect clinical outcomes; those carried out mainly by psychologists show that building features have observable psychological effects on users; and designers and architects explore the notion that design can improve healing with an implicit blurring of boundaries between therapeutic issues and aesthetics.

The scientific studies explore variables such as view, light, sound, aroma, temperature and noise, suggesting environmental improvements that would, for example, speed recovery and reduce dependence on medication. The psychological studies give important clues about privacy, control and the potential to reduce stress largely through the arrangement of the interior decor and furniture. The designers are concerned with making spaces that uplift the mind and spirits and focus on, for example, light, views and ambience.

The studies are important for the way in which they highlight issues to be addressed in healthcare design. But none provides a really adequate design theory for the future: each of the three types of study, physiological, psychological and design theory, is unable to deal with variables outside their own discipline and therefore does not describe satisfactorily the complexity of the issue of what constitutes a healing environment. We may appreciate that a room with a view is more therapeutic than one without, but how will we assess whether the room's aesthetic qualities also contribute to its therapeutic efficacy? Or the arrangement of seats may offer a place for social interaction, but so might the shape of the room.

Sustainability

As sustainability becomes a key policy factor, so health buildings will be required to demonstrate sustainable design in social, economic and environmental terms. Already key generic performance indicators are being developed and a rating system for healthcare buildings called NEAT has been devised. Evidence of the impact on the local community, whole-life costing and the fulfilling of an environmentally green agenda will be sought. This will require a fundamental shift in thinking in which design will have to make explicit such considerations as the revenue consequences of capital considerations, the

recycling of materials over sixty years, and the rate of emissions, particularly carbon dioxide, into the atmosphere.

Conclusion

The UK has just embarked on one of the most significant hospital building programmes yet. A broad-based development plan including specialist hospitals, community hospitals and health/social centres will be needed to fully realise the vision of a modernised health care service set out in the NHS Plan.[8]

The development of Design Quality Indicators (DQIs) has involved a rigorous reappraisal of the key factors of what constitutes a quality environment. Their purpose is to clarify the factors by which a scheme can be assessed for quality of design. The alignment of frameworks by Medical Architecture Research Unit (MARU),[9] NHS Estates[10] and the Construction Industry Council's DQIs (see Chapters 14–16) demonstrate consensus about the need to meet criteria relating to functional, technical performance as well as impact. With toolkits and pilot projects underway, it now remains to be seen how robust these frameworks are in supporting and reinvigorating an essential dialogue between informed clients and expert design teams.

Urban design raises issues of location and master planning for all health buildings. Whilst sustainability, regeneration and inclusion will inform the selection of sites for improved transportation, employment, amenity, environmental conservation etc., there will be additional requirements for making urban designs. The debate between campus and centre city sites, of large-scale centralised hospitals rather than devolved networks, have yet to be fully articulated in terms of urban and building design for healthcare. The master planning of vast areas of city development will be a reality for some hospitals and the need for health planners and designers to respond will be on a scale as yet uncharted.

There is broad acceptance that health buildings can contribute to the civic realm, but little understanding as yet of the idea of redefining spaces within buildings in terms other than those dominated by functional concerns. Hospitals, for example, are invariably thought of as a collection of departments with corridors to link them. Planning priorities for efficient delivery of services have determined spatial adjacencies and traffic flows. The consideration of space in terms of a hierarchy of public, social and private, a common theme in other sectors, has yet to emerge for health. Recognising the functional differences and endeavouring to create contrasting but pertinent spaces, this strategy would give more emphasis to the character and ambience of the spaces over their functions. It would encourage the design of space to incorporate and focus on drawing together architecture with art and design in all its aspects – such as product, graphic and landscape.

There is no doubt that healthcare design is undergoing a significant shift in emphasis: one that is placing greater attention on how places feel as well as how they work. It is a rich mixture of ideas and intentions that is leading to a design approach for health which:

- Embraces sophisticated technology to make therapeutic environments for care: being both high tech and humane.
- Integrates health into a broader social and physical context: making civic buildings that combine health and social care. It is about creating buildings that take advantage of modern materials and production

techniques whilst retaining their unique sense of belonging to a specific locality.

- Creates buildings that stimulate, surprise and delight as well as deliver efficient and effective spaces: it is about making social places to celebrate and communicate as well as private spaces that foster dignity and quiet; buildings that make connections between inside and outside through views and landscapes; environments that innovate and integrate art, design and architecture.

It is about making places special and making special places.

Notes

1 Thompson J. D. and Goldin G. (1975) *The Hospital: a social and architectural history*, New Haven and London: Yale University Press.
2 Cited in Christine Stevenson (2000) *Medicine and Magnificence: British hospitals and asylum architecture 1660-1815*, London: Yale University Press.
3 Forty, A. (1980) The Modern Hospital in England and France: social and medical uses of architecture, in A. King (ed.) *Buildings and Society*, London: Routledge and Kegan Paul.
4 Nightingale, F. (1860) reprinted 1996. *Notes on Nursing*, London: Bailliere Tindall.
5 Nuffield Provincial Hospitals Trust (1955) *Studies in the Function and Design of Hospitals*, London: Oxford University Press.
6 Ryan, R. (1997) 'Primal Therapy', *Architectural Review*, August, vol. CC11, no. 1206.
7 These include studies undertaken by the Picker Institute for The Centre for Healthcare Design USA , unpublished study by Cancerlink for NHS Estates and a study in progress by MARU for Macmillan Cancer Relief.
8 NHS (2000) *The NHS Plan*, London: Department of Health.
9 MARU (2001) *Building a 2020 Vision: future healthcare environments*, Nuffield Trust and RIBA Future Studies. London: The Stationery Office.
10 Department of Health (2001) *Achieving Excellence Design Evaluation Toolkit*, London: Department of Health.

Chapter 11

Adding value through better urban design

Matthew Carmona

In this chapter the notion that better urban design adds value is explored. In a contemporary development climate, commercial pressures often seem to militate against long-term investment in design quality. The problem has been compounded in the past by a public sector that has not always placed design quality firmly on its agenda. The result has contributed to a marginalisation of design, and even to a widespread perception that better design generates costs whilst benefits are often intangible and can be discounted.

This seems to be particularly the case with urban design, with its tendency to fall through the gaps left between individual professional responsibilities. Nevertheless, by offering concrete evidence that better urban design delivers better value (social and environmental, but particularly economic) practice may be changed. In particular, by placing better urban design on the positive side of the balance sheet, a sea change in private as well as public sector investment decisions may be secured. Exploring this relationship was the

objective of research commissioned from the Bartlett School of Planning, UCL, by the Commission for Architecture and the Built Environment (CABE) and the Department for the Environment, Transport and the Regions (DETR).[1]

The chapter first outlines the research method and goes on to present the key research findings and recommendations. A more detailed discussion of the evidence gathered can be found in the published research report *The Value of Urban Design* (Carmona *et al.*, 2001).

The research objectives

The research sought to address four related questions:

1 Does better urban design add value?
2 How does it do this?
3 Who benefits?
4 How can greater value be released?

To answer the questions, a three-stage programme was adopted. In Stage One, a review of literature and international research was undertaken. The aim was to deliver:

- A 'working conceptualisation' of urban design
- An 'appraisal tool' as a means to objectively assess urban design quality
- The identification and listing of 'aspects of value' as they accrue for better urban design
- A review of 'stakeholder motivations' in the development process.

A key outcome of Stage One was a 'value statement'. This combined on the vertical axis a ready-made working conceptualisation of urban design – the seven 'urban design objectives' from the DETR and CABE (2000) guide *By Design* – with, on the horizontal axis, a holistic notion of value as 'sustainable value', as opposed to 'exchange value' (the classic economic view). Sustainable value explicitly recognises social and environmental, as well as economic benefits (see Figure 11.1).

In Stage Two a case study approach was chosen as the only feasible means to gather the complex qualitative and quantitative data required, particularly given the potential commercial sensitivity of some of the data sought. Selection of case studies therefore formed an important part of the research, and available resources enabled the selection of six.

To draw meaningful conclusions from a small number of case studies, the adopted approach proposed to reduce – as far as possible – extraneous influences on value by comparing like developments in key respects except for their urban design. Limiting the case studies to speculative commercial workplace developments provided the first means to reduce such influences. By pairing developments, extraneous influences could be further reduced.

Thus three pairs of case studies were undertaken, with constituent developments from each pair broadly reflecting the same geographic and market context. Pairs were also chosen to exhibit a variety of practice in urban design, thus enabling a comparison in each of the three locations of the impact of successful and less successful design approaches. The approach effectively discounted (within the pairs) factors that could otherwise unduly influence the results: development use; location (broadly defined); market context; occupier type and developer type (speculative).

In reality, the choice of case studies was not easy, as suitable pairs proved difficult to identify. Consequently, the relative quality of practice was not always clear-cut and market contexts varied more than anticipated. Nevertheless, three pairs of case studies were sought with the following characteristics:

- Predominantly office developments, but including other uses
- Development containing significant areas of public/semi-public open space
- Developments in broadly similar locations built at roughly the same time

11.1
Value statement

Sustainable values

	A. Economic viability	B. Social benefit	C. Environmental support
1 Character			
2 Continuity and enclosure			
3 Quality of the public realm			
4 Ease of movement			
5. Legibility			
6. Adaptability			
7. Diversity			

Urban design objectives

- Developments outside the unique market context found in London (to ensure any findings had wider application).

Each case study was initially visited by the research team and an on-site analysis undertaken using a simple urban design appraisal tool based on the seven urban design objectives along the horizontal axis of the 'value statement' (see Figure 11.2). Interviews were then arranged and conducted with representatives of the investor, developer and designer organisations responsible for the development; the key planning officer(s) responsible for the area and development; an economic development officer (where one existed); at least two occupier organisations in each development; and a range of everyday users of the public/semi-public spaces (a minimum of 10 interviews per case study).

Interviews, wherever possible, sought quantitative data to back up the qualitative responses of interviewees, and followed structured proformas based on an analytical framework (see Table 11.1). The framework was derived from the theoretical listing of aspects of value derived during Stage One and structured to reflect the vertical axis of the 'value statement' – economic, social and environmental value. In addition, the proformas were suitably tailored to each stakeholder group on the basis of the review of stakeholder motivations. Interviewees (with the exception of the everyday users) were also given the opportunity to complete an urban design appraisal of their own to compare with that of the research team. The study pairs chosen were from the East Midlands, the West Midlands, and from the North West.

Case study	Assessor:	Occupation:		
Objectives	**Performance criteria**	**Strengths**	**Weaknesses**	**Evaluation**
1 Character	A distinct sense of place responding to local context			0 1 2 3 4 5
2 Continuity and enclosure	Clearly defined, coherent, well enclosed public space			0 1 2 3 4 5
3 Quality of the public realm	Safe, attractive and functional public space			0 1 2 3 4 5
4 Ease of movement	An accessible, well connected, pedestrian-friendly environment			0 1 2 3 4 5
5 Legibility	A readily understandable, easily navigable environment			0 1 2 3 4 5
6 Adaptability	Flexible and adaptable public and private environments			0 1 2 3 4 5
7 Diversity	A varied environment offering a range of uses and experiences			0 1 2 3 4 5
Summary:				Total rating ?

Note: 0 = not at all successful; 5 = very successful

11.2
Urban Design Appraisal Tool

A brief outline of the case study pairs is included in Figures 11.3, 11.4 and 11.5. Stage Three of the research involved the synthesis of the data by the research team in order to reach conclusions about where, how and to whom value is added. Based on the evidence gathered, the research questions were tentatively answered.

Does better urban design add value?

The findings suggested that the answer to the first research question was a simple 'yes'. Better urban design does add value, and in three distinct ways: by increasing the economic viability of development, by delivering enhanced social benefits, and by encouraging development that is more environmentally supportive.

In coming to this conclusion, it became apparent that the notion that better design adds value is now broadly shared across all key stakeholder groups. Furthermore, this was the clear conclusion from the review of previous research, including empirical studies in the UK, the US and Australia (Department of National Heritage *et al.*, 1996; Vandell and Lane, 1989; Property Council of Australia, 1999; Eppli and Tu, 1999) and also from the empirical case study research.

How does better urban design add value?

Based on the research evidence, in economic terms, better urban design seems to add value in ten key ways:

1 In high returns on investments, including good rental returns and enhanced capital values.
2 By differentiating development products (buildings and new environments) and raising their prestige.
3 By responding to a clear occupier demand that also helps to attract investment.
4 By helping to deliver more lettable area on sites, primarily through making higher density building politically and contextually more acceptable.
5 In reducing management, maintenance, energy and security costs (the latter through better natural surveillance and better-used public spaces).
6 In more productive and contented workforces, who are more loyal and less often ill.
7 In supporting the 'life-giving' mixed use elements in developments.
8 By opening up new investment opportunities, markets and areas, and – where available – attracting grant monies.
9 In creating an economic regeneration and place-marketing dividend that poor quality urban design is unable to match.
10 By delivering viable planning gain and reducing the burden on the public purse in otherwise putting urban design mistakes right.

In social and environmental terms better urban design seems to add value in ten further ways:

1 By ensuring that the social benefits of regeneration processes spread further beyond the immediate vicinity, into neighbouring areas and populations.
2 By avoiding the exacerbation of urban malaise potentially caused by poor quality urban design, in particular the undermining of local town centres.
3 In creating well-connected, inclusive and accessible new places to be enjoyed by society as a whole and by their occupiers.
4 By delivering mixed environments with a broad range of facilities and amenities available to all.
5 By delivering development inherently sensitive to its context.

Table 11.1 Analytical framework to assess and measure the value of better urban design

Dimensions of value		Possible indicators	Quantitative assessment	Qualitative assessment	Comments
Economic viability	**Economic performance of investment in better urban design**	• Rental values • Capital values • Vacancy rates • Take-up rates • Investment availability	• Comparison of rental values, capital values, vacancy rates and take-up rates of selected developments with average for similar types of property	• Interview questions to developers, investors and occupiers, addressing their views on the economic performance of the development	• Average figures for rents and capital values from the Investment Property Databank (IPD) or local property firms • Average figures for vacancy and take-up rates possibly from local property firms
	Operational performance of better urban design	• Management costs • Security expenditure • Energy consumption • Accessibility • Productivity of occupier • Health and satisfaction of workforce • Corporate imaging	• If available, data for individual developments on energy consumption, management costs, productivity, etc., which could be compared within cases or on a broader basis if information is available	• Interview questions to occupiers addressing the running costs of the development and the influence of urban design on their corporate performance	• Quantitative information might be possible for individual developments, but there are problems in finding comparators
	Production of better urban design	• Production costs • Infrastructure costs • Duration of planning approval process • Prestige and reputation	• Comparison of production and infrastructure costs and duration of planning negotiation for the selected developments, within sample of cases and with average for similar types of property	• Interview questions to developers addressing production costs, the planning process, infrastructure costs, and the impact of the development on their standing in the marketplace • Interview questions to local authority officials on infrastructure costs and the planning process	• Average figures for production costs from construction industry publications • Average duration of planning process from local authorities

Area regeneration/ viability impact of better urban design	• Local property values • Place-marketing • Area revitalisation	• Evolution of land and property values around the selected developments compared to the average in the locality	• Interview questions to local authority officials and local economic development partnerships on impact of development on the local economy	• Average figures for property values in surrounding area from local estate agents
Social benefit	• Identity/civic pride • Place vitality • Inconclusiveness • Connectivity • Safety • Facilities and amenities	• If available, data on footfall for mixed use cases with retail, compared to average for locality (vitality)	• Interview questions to local authority officials and sample of local community sddressing issues of place-identity, vitality and inclusiveness	• Quantitative information on vitality might be possible for individual developments, but difficulties with comparators
Environmental support	• Energy consumption • Accessibility • Traffic generation • Greenery/ecology	• If available, data for individual developments on energy consumption, modes of transport, traffic generation, commuting times etc., for comparison between cases or on a broader basis	• Interview questions to occupiers, local authority officials and sample of local community addressing the environmental impacts of the development	• Average figures for energy consumption (and possibly) traffic generation, modes of transport for users/occupier) by type of development are available from specialised research institutions

Context

Nottingham is a strong regional service and business centre for the East Midlands region. Castle Wharf sits between the city core and the station. Standard Court lies to the west of the centre just north of Nottingham Castle. The case study developments sit within a city that has for some time been concerned to offer a high quality retail centre, and which in recent years has extended that concern to other areas of the city outside the retail core. An increasingly active urban design team now exists within the Planning Department, and a range of initiatives have been directed towards producing more coherent advice on design quality. A number of high profile developments have also raised the profile of design.

Castle Wharf	**Standard Court**

Background: A mixed-use scheme comprising offices, leisure and retail space adjacent to the Beeston Canal. The site incorporates land that was originally owned by the local authority, by private owners and by British Waterways.[2] In the mid-1980s a masterplan was prepared for the site as part of a plan by the local authority to unlock development potential in canalside locations. This was later followed by a design brief. Included in the negotiation for planning permission was the construction of a new bridge over the canal, improving the links between the site and the town centre and to adjacent development. The development was completed in 1999 and was quickly sold to investors, having since won a number of local awards.

Urban design: Castle Wharf received a research team rating of 29 (amongst the highest of the case studies). Based on the edge of the city centre, the scheme helps to move the centre of gravity of Nottingham towards the south, opening up a range of other sites along Nottingham's south side. The scheme builds on the industrial canal heritage of the area to create a distinct sense of place. In a highly constrained site the development starts to make connections to the surrounding areas. The key public spaces are well articulated, animated by the range of uses, and are highly legible.

Viability: Castle Wharf represents a development in which some of the major occupiers were partners in the project with the developers and are now freehold owners. Other occupiers came in later and are now renting from the same investor. The costs of design work and especially of infrastructure and building were high – more because of the local authority's conservation requirements than because of urban design demands. The location, in particular, is now very popular, resulting in rising asset values for the owner-occupying firms. For the tenant firms this popularity is reflected in rents that are among the highest in Nottingham. The initial developers, however, seem to have missed out on the enhanced financial gains from their scheme, having sold their partial interest at a price which gave them only about half the normal return they would have expected for such a project.

Background: Standard Court is a mixed-use development comprising office spaces, residential units and three retail/restaurant units. The trigger for the development was the closure of the hospital that occupied the site. Nottingham Health Authority – the original owners – did not by themselves have the resources to demolish a 1960s tower block on the site and redevelop it, and under the advice of the design team, put forward a proposal for a PFI-style[3] operation which would attract resources from the private sector. The scheme, which started on site in 1996, was by 2001 still not completed, awaiting further residential development.

Urban design: Despite facing many of the same challenges as Castle Wharf in a similar edge-of-centre location, Standard Court has been less successful in revitalising its immediate environment. The new environment it tries to create, including a significant new public space (arena), remains largely unused and desolate. The impression is of a disconnected place, that does not invite users in to the development, and which offers users little once they are there. The research team's urban design assessment of 14 reflected these problems.

Viability: As the development is not on a busy route, its retail and catering premises could only flourish if they became destinations in themselves, which has not happened. Other new developments in the area are now largely rejecting the commercial model in favour of residential development. In the tenanted part of the scheme, rents have been below the best Nottingham levels and the investors consider the project to have been satisfactory but not excellent. The PFI arrangement has nevertheless delivered the investor an assured short – and long-term – return. Unfortunately, the development has proved less than easy to manage, in part because of the break up of the original estate – post completion – but also because of the maintenance problems associated with the under-utilised arena.

11.4
**West Midlands
(Birmingham/
Dudley)**

Context
The West Midlands has experienced rapid loss of established industrial activity in recent decades. In response, Birmingham City Centre has instigated a range of major transformations designed to raise its profile and attractiveness. The Birmingham case study focused on part of the central transformation, while the Dudley study examined a business park on a former steel-works site in the west of the region, adjacent to the Merry Hill shopping mall. Birmingham has for over ten years been at the forefront in supporting better urban design and provides a positive policy and administrative structure. Dudley has not been so proactive. Furthermore, the Enterprise Zone within which the chosen case study was developed effectively undermined any local authority concern for design that might otherwise have existed.

Brindleyplace	**Waterfront**

Background: Brindleyplace is a mixed-use scheme on the edge of Birmingham city centre with an emphasis on office space but including residential, leisure and retail elements. The scheme heralds itself as one of Europe's largest inner city developments. Development started in 1993, after a number of false starts, and has proceeded in a number of phases, utilising a range of funding arrangements. The developers have funded much of the development activity themselves and retain stakes in a significant part of the development. Work is still in progress and the development has won a range of local and national design awards. Recent phases continue to attract a range of 'blue-chip' investors (and occupiers), including BT Pension Fund, Citibank and UBK.

Urban design: Brindleyplace shared the highest overall research team rating of 29 with Castle Wharf, reflecting the high quality commercial environment that has been created. It has become a new urban quarter, with a distinct character and sense of place in which a network of well-defined public spaces punctuate the area to create a series of new activity settings. In achieving this, the centre of gravity of the city has moved across the Inner Ring Road offering considerable design benefits and linkages at a larger spatial scale. Nevertheless this is also clearly a privately owned environment with a slightly exclusive, highly commercial character. It is also to some degree an obviously 'manufactured' environment, with the range of uses more clearly zoned into different parts of the site than would be the case in a traditional urban environment.

Viability: As part of Birmingham's ambitious plans to transform the city centre in the late 1980s, Brindleyplace initially fell foul of the property collapse. The developers were therefore able to buy the site from the receiver at a relatively low price. This subsequently helped them to cover high decontamination, marketing, infrastructure, and design costs. Rents for offices and restaurants are said to have at least doubled since the start of the scheme, reaching a peak in 1996 but have since fallen back in line with regional trends. Significantly, the housing element of the scheme is now changing hands at twice to three times initial prices. In terms of wider economic impact, Brindleyplace is viewed very positively as a powerful catalyst for further development in adjoining parts of the city. Construction of the later phases continues apace offering a good indicator of optimism, as does the average yield figure of 6.5%.

Background: The Waterfront Business Park incorporates a mix of business, retail and leisure uses, and integrates part of the Dudley Canal into the scheme with a hard landscaped setting and formal border planting. In 1984, the Dudley Enterprise Zone was extended to encompass the site, as it was felt that this would offer the best prospects for regeneration. It was developed in two stages, first into the Merry Hill Shopping Centre and later into the Waterfront Business Park that commenced in 1990. The scheme is not yet complete, with further development being planned. Moreover, there is now a comprehensive planning strategy for the area, which focuses primarily on improving connectivity and the public realm, the aim being to create a new town centre within the area.

Urban design: The development provides a formula business park environment built on a recycled brownfield site, dominated by roads and parking requirements. Nevertheless, a serious attempt has been made to inject a sense of place through high quality soft landscaping, a formal layout, and through relating the development to the canal. It has also created a vibrant oasis through its range of popular bars and restaurants. Unfortunately, the realisation lacks many key urban design qualities, not least a connection of the site to its immediate hinterland. Thus users need to rely heavily on private cars to reach the development. The research team's analysis gave the development a rating of 15.

Viability: The specification of the buildings and landscape were higher than the prevailing level for the region at the time, and rents were set at a level above the norm. The scheme has nevertheless let well and rents are reported to have continued to rise. The scheme has prospered despite some major drawbacks, including the acute inadequacy of the road and public transport infrastructure and the failure to relate the scheme to the nearby shopping centre, town centre or with other surrounding areas. Its financial performance reflects the popularity of the scheme with occupiers, for whom there are no comparable alternatives nearby. The project has made a strong contribution to economic growth and regeneration in the sub-region. Considerable (and expensive) remedial action is now planned on the urban design front.

Context

The economy of Manchester has undergone a rapid restructuring in the last two decades, losing much of its manufacturing and port-related activity and replacing it with a growing tertiary sector. Barbirolli Square is a transformed site on the western edge of the centre, whilst Exchange Quay was an early development within the Enterprise Zone designated in nearby Salford. In Manchester, the experience of redeveloping both the 1960s Hulme housing estate, and the city centre (following the IRA bomb) has led to a rediscovery of urban design. In Salford, the closure of the Docks encouraged the planning authority to develop a new urban design framework for the Salford Quays. Significantly, the case study project fell outside of this framework and relates poorly to it.

Barbirolli Square	Exchange Quay

Background: The development comprises a free-standing concert hall (the Bridgewater Hall), two office blocks and a café/bar, and represents one of a number of development initiatives west of Manchester City Centre. In 1990, the 'Bridgewater Initiative' was launched as a developer/architect competition to design a new concert hall and to develop the canal basin. Planning permission was obtained in 1992 and government and funding from the European Regional Development Fund was in place by 1993. The development was completed in the late 1990s and has since won awards from the Civic Trust, the RIBA and several local awards.

Urban design: Barbirolli Square is the smallest development examined, comprising two office blocks on one side of a square faced by the new Bridgewater Concert Hall on the other. The clever use of levels allows the central space to step down to a re-established canal basin onto which a new café opens up. The result is a gently animated public space with its own distinct character and sense of place, and, despite the exposed position of the site, with a good quality of enclosure. However, although good connections have been established on two sides of the new space, connectivity on the other two is compromised. Furthermore, the 'corporate style' office buildings and the introspective nature of the offices and Bridgewater Hall leave the higher levels devoid of active frontage, leading to a research team rating of 23.

Viability: The Bridgewater Hall was financed partly from the sale of the site for office development and partly from European Funds. Initial financing for the office development was challenging reflecting the very demanding attitude of investors regarding schemes in provincial cities. The economic conditions in the mid-1990s were not very bright, and the office block (just one at that time) constituted an uncomfortably large commitment. Investors finally signed up, however, when the office scheme was split into two blocks, whilst the high quality of the urban design helped to make the case that the development would command prestige occupiers at premium rents. The history of the development has so far fulfilled the ambitions of developers, letting well and commanding rents that are the highest in Manchester. Indeed, most of the space was pre-let early on, whilst the project cost of £27m is now delivering a real estate valuation of £60m. The high capital value and associated regeneration in the area suggest that further rental growth can be confidently expected.

Background: Exchange Quay is situated on the Banks of the Manchester Ship Canal/River Irwell at the southern-most point of Salford Quays. The scheme is mainly an office development, with a limited range of retail and restaurant units intended for the occupants of the constituent buildings. Exchange Quay was conceived in the late 1980s as a type of office centre totally new to Manchester; a piece of Dallas which would attract large international corporate occupiers to a pioneering luxury enclave in a degraded dockside area. It was completed in 1991 towards the end of the Enterprise Zone designation.

Urban design: Exchange Quay was rated least highly out of the case studies by the research team (a rating of 9). The development represents a classic high-density, disconnected office development, which provides an internalised and largely car-dependent work environment. One key space forms a central gathering point including a café and a number of retail units. Unfortunately, the microclimate is poor and the amenities are minimal with the development overwhelmingly dominated by office uses and associated car parking. The buildings themselves are international in style, and the development almost completely turns its back on the Manchester Ship Canal and surrounding communities who are deliberately excluded from its spaces.

Viability: Initial investment was subscribed readily by a large number of international investors. Letting in the early 1990s, however, proved a severe problem because by then demand nationally and regionally was in strong decline. Instead of large corporate occupiers, only smaller users could be found and the offices had to be modified to fit multiple lettings. Today, rents at Exchange Quay remain below or around the regional average. Nevertheless the development is almost fully let, and the investor/managers are convinced that the 'Dallas' style of urban and building design is a feature which – together with the adequate car parking – makes the scheme enduringly popular. Unfortunately, investment returns remain low at 1–3% per annum on the original investment, although investors are in the main retaining their shares hoping for better profits in the future. However, there is little evidence of broader local economic impacts. Retailers in the scheme, for example, do not serve people from surrounding areas, nor do people who work there make extensive use of adjoining services.

6 By giving or returning inaccessible or run-down areas and amenities back to public use, for example ex-industrial areas.

7 Through boosting civic pride and image and therefore the self-respect of local populations.

8 By enhancing the sense of safety and security both within and beyond developments.

9 Through the creation of more environmentally supportive (particularly more energy efficient and less polluting) development.

10 Through revitalising urban heritage – buildings and infrastructure – such as former warehouses and disused canal basins.

Collectively, the economic, social and environmental benefits add up to a considerable design dividend. Nevertheless, the research also indicated that few schemes benefit from all the aspects of value, and the benefits are by no means automatic. Thus, issues of location, the quality of office space and value for money were key to occupier decision-making, and therefore also for developers and investors; the former who were looking for the latter, the latter who were primarily concerned to find long-term above-average income streams which were dependent on attracting good quality, preferably blue-chip, companies. Better urban design therefore offered just one part of the package occupiers were seeking to find, and developers and investors were seeking to supply.

Furthermore, better designed schemes are not without their costs, particularly those relating to the higher materials specification and time delays associated with more stringent conservation requirements. Beyond these added costs, however, no evidence was found that better urban design raised either design or development costs, or the time taken to secure planning permission. Also, the purchase of low value or subsidised land was not required. Gentrification was identified as the only potential social cost of better urban design, but

also a cost that local authorities were willing to pay in order to kick-start regeneration.

Who benefits from added value?

The findings suggest that all stakeholders benefit from better urban design and that these win:win benefits relate directly to how urban design adds value. Thus, investors primarily benefit through favourable returns on their investments and through satisfying an obvious occupier demand, although the full payoff may not be immediate. Developers, if they retain a stake in their developments for long enough, also benefit from good returns on their investments. Furthermore, developers benefit from enhanced company image, with successful schemes regularly used in company marketing, and through attracting investors and pre-lets more easily.

Designers – if able to achieve good quality – benefit because better urban design is crucially dependent on their input and is more likely to receive planning permission without delay. Occupiers benefit from the better performance, loyalty, and health and satisfaction of their workforces and from the increased prestige that their better-designed developments command with guests and clients. Everyday users benefit from the economic advantages of successful regeneration, including new and retained jobs, but also through access to a better quality environment and an enhanced range of amenities and facilities. Finally, public authorities benefit by meeting their clear obligation to deliver a well designed, economically and socially viable environment and often by ripple effects to adjoining areas. As a result of these collective benefits, society as a whole benefits through the economic boost that urban areas receive and through the creation of comfortable, environmentally supportive, well used and loved urban places.

How can greater value be released?

The research revealed clear economic, social and environmental arguments for better urban design. At the same time it also confirmed a range of barriers to delivering better design, particularly those inherent in established patterns of investment and development (see Table 11.2). The barriers suggest that a simple causal relationship between demonstrating that better urban design adds value and its more frequent delivery on the ground is likely to be over-simplistic.

Nevertheless, a change in attitude was detected amongst key development stakeholders, in particular amongst investors, but perhaps most crucially amongst occupiers too. These stakeholders are increasingly valuing urban design and its perceived (particularly economic) dividends, and where they lead, developers seem likely to follow. From the evidence presented, it was possible to suggest a number of key recommendations to help encourage a greater shared valuing of, and investment in, urban design.

The first concerns the need to promote the value of urban design, not least to spread the message that design adds value and does so for both public and private stakeholders and therefore for society at large. In particular, it seems important that the message that better urban design does not necessarily cost more to deliver but nevertheless offers distinct competitive advantages to producers and consumers needs to be spread to those operating across all sectors of the market – and not just at the prestige end. This is clearly a task for CABE, the DTLR, and local authorities, who might also enlist the support of the professional institutes (particularly those representing developers and investors) and including UDAL.

In this regard, because better urban design does not seem to cost more to deliver, it should be possible to make the case that well-designed environments can be secured at competitive rates. Better urban design can then be used as an important sales pitch to differentiate products with modest, but fundamental, improvements in urban design such as better external linkages, more life-giving uses, and configuring buildings to face public spaces. Such improvements will place better-designed developments above the competition in their local markets at relatively little (or no) extra cost.

Crucial to the success of such a message is the need to convince occupier groups whose attitudes are key to the activities of developers and investors. In this regard, some degree of education is required to convey the message that better-designed environments offer distinct advantages to companies in economic terms, in addition to the social and environmental value they contribute. This is likely to be a more difficult task because of the disparate nature of occupier organisations. Nevertheless, finding means to promote the message to potential and established occupiers formed a key recommendation of the research.

The research indicated that the role of the public sector is crucial to the delivery of better value through urban design. It confirmed that this role extends far beyond regulatory planning processes, notwithstanding the important role of such processes in rejecting future introspective, exclusive and disconnected development proposals. In particular, the proactive role that public authorities can (and did in the more successfully designed case studies) play in positively setting the urban design agenda seems crucial. This role was delivered through:

- Planning powers, which need to be used positively and up front in the process by producing design briefs, frameworks and masterplans
- Influence in providing and supporting gap funding arrangements, which should be dependent on delivering better urban design
- Involvement as key landowners of brownfield sites. The research revealed that this latter role can provide the most decisive lever to ensure better quality urban design is delivered.

Table 11.2 Barriers to better urban design

Barrier	Problem
Low awareness	Variable awareness of urban design issues amongst investors and occupiers, relating to how important they see design quality to the success of their operations. Research suggests that different sub-markets have different levels of concern and sophistication as regards design (e.g. amongst occupiers, retailers tend to be more aware of the importance of design quality than office users).
Poor information	Unreliable available information about the actual preferences of prospective occupiers and investors, especially in the case of speculative developments. This adds to the risk of diverging from standards of design quality that are perceived to be 'safe'.
Unpredictable markets	The cyclical behaviour of the property markets, because the timing of a development in relation to the ups and downs of the property and investment market will to some extent dictate attitudes towards investing in urban design quality as perceived risk changes.
Piecemeal development	The small size and uncoordinated nature of most developments as larger sites are more likely to bring to the fore the issues of 'place-making' and make it easier for investors to capture more of the 'externalities' in the form or rents and capital values.
Land costs	High land costs that can reduce profit margins and leave little room for any extra investment in quality, especially since in the property markets prices adjust only slowly and imperfectly.
Land ownership	Fragmented patterns of land ownership which can increase the time and the uncertainty of the development process and lead to fragmented design solutions.
Combative relationships	Confrontational relationships between developers and the public sector which increase the time taken to develop and consequently increase uncertainty and risk.
Economic environment	The general economic environment, which if dominated by high inflation and high interest rates (frequently the case in the UK since the 1960s), will lead to shorter-term investment decisions and to less investment in design.
Lack of choice	Constraints in the supply of the right quality of property in the desired location reducing the role of better design in occupier decision-making – if the right location does not have good quality space on offer, occupiers will go for lower quality development, rather than another location.
Short-term planning	The structure of capital markets, with planning horizons of 3 to 5 years, which makes it difficult for many businesses to engage in the long-term planning necessary for the perceived investments required for better design.
Perceptions of cost	The perception amongst occupiers that although many of the benefits of good design accrue to the wider community, it is the occupiers who will pay for it in the form of higher rent, running costs and commercial rates
Decision-making patterns	Many of the many important urban design decisions are taken not by planners, developers or designers, but by people who may not think themselves involved in urban design at all.
Negative planning	Largely reactionary as opposed to 'positive' approaches to urban design across many local authorities, and a general failure to link the two concerns for urban regeneration and better urban design.
Skills deficit	The low levels of urban design skills on both sides of the development process which represent both a significant and consistent impediment to the effective delivery of better design.

In this regard, there seems to be a clear benefit in public and private interests working together to achieve agreed economic and urban design objectives, something dependent on the early focused intervention of the public sector to clearly lay out requirements. It is also dependent on local authorities being willing to see high quality urban (and architectural) design as a positive alternative (or at least complement) to conservation-led strategies. This, to some extent, is likely to be reliant on better publicising contemporary urban design success stories – nationally and particularly locally. It may also be valuable to commission research examining rates of planning approval and the relationship to design quality to confirm (as the research suggested) that better urban design quality actually speeds up, rather than slows down, the planning process.

The research also indicated that poor quality urban design is not necessarily a result of either an active decision not to invest in better urban design, nor a lack of time and effort put into producing a high quality design product. Indeed, in their own way, all the case study developments were carefully designed and crafted products, although in urban design terms some did not deliver on their potential. In this regard, there is still a need to change perceptions about what constitutes good urban design, and to ensure that this extends beyond limited corporate image-making objectives to a more fundamental design responsibility.

The related issue of poor urban design skills was identified as a key barrier to the delivery of better urban design, and extends beyond the private sector to the public sector. Initiatives have been launched by DTLR (Arup Economics and Planning, 2000; Davies and Rowley, 2000) and CABE (Urban Design Skills Working Group, 2001) to begin to address the skills deficit, but fundamentally the gap needs to be filled across all professional education concerned with delivering the built environment

(particularly in the finance/investment related professions) and in continuing professional education for professionals in practice.

The research indicated that initiatives on this front cannot come too soon. It also indicated that a general lack of understanding (across stakeholder groups), about the potentially positive role of better urban design in reducing the environmental resource impact of development, also needs to be addressed.

Delivering better urban design

As well as the process-related recommendations the research revealed a number of findings that could – if more widely practised – lead to better urban design solutions. The intention here is not to lay out a comprehensive urban design agenda, something that has already been done elsewhere (for example Llewelyn-Davies, 2000; DETR and CABE, 2000). Instead, the following principles emanate directly from the research and seem important in informing future urban design activity:

- **Critical mass –** Delivering better quality urban design seems to some extent to rely on delivering the critical mass needed to support it subsequently. In this regard, new public spaces, infrastructure improvements, mixing uses, public realm improvements and so forth, all rely on the realisation of developments large enough to cross-fund their delivery. The finding suggests an important role for the public sector in compiling or helping to compile larger sites or in helping to better integrate adjoining schemes.
- **Coordination –** This should not suggest, however, that smaller, more incremental, development cannot contribute to the delivery of better quality urban design. Nevertheless, for urban design to succeed

by such means, clear arrangements and strategies need to be put in place (by public or private parties) to help deliver a well considered and coherent whole. Positive and proactive planning through the production of clear urban design guidance (frameworks and briefs) is likely to be the key to such incremental approaches, as well as the coordination of planning gain.

- **Lifetime costs –** Management and maintenance costs should be considered up front in the development process. This is easier said than done when many of those with a longer-term interest in developments do not come on board until later in the development process. Nevertheless, through simply adopting core urban design principles – such as clearly overlooked spaces and design that reduces negative microclimatic effects – the delivery of reduced management and maintenance costs can become a positive sales pitch at little or no extra up front cost.

- **Strategic urban design –** The research indicated that urban design has an important strategic dimension, and that where this is ignored the value (particularly social) added by development is much reduced. This positive planning at a larger spatial scale – particularly the integration of development into established infrastructure frameworks – seems key to delivering better designed environments that also carry an economic dividend.

- **Mixing uses –** The delivery of mixed-use development was fundamental to the social, economic and environmental value added by the most successful case studies. Clearly, every effort needs to made by both public and private parties to achieve such integration, particularly in light of the higher user and occupier satisfaction that results.

- **Locating spaces and uses –** Related to this key point, the very careful location and

distribution of any new public spaces and 'life giving' uses across developments is fundamental. In particular, the location of any public amenities at accessible, well-connected points in developments is vital if both spaces and uses are to succeed.

- **Sustaining social diversity –** Good urban design can make areas more attractive to higher-income residents and the businesses and services which supply or employ them, indeed this is often one of the purposes of urban regeneration. It is important, however, to minimise the displacement of existing residents and businesses in whose name urban regeneration is usually justified. In this regard mixing housing as well as housing tenures and prices into new developments should be a key objective for better urban design. For the public sector, finding means to harness the increased value of better quality development to invest in established community infrastructure would also seem important. This implies the wise use of planning gain to combat – rather than exacerbate – any disadvantage.

The need for more research

Despite the clarity of the conclusions, in reality the evidence was complex and extrapolating the research findings to make the case that better urban design adds value in all locations and for all developments comes with an important health warning. This is based on the facts that:

- The research only looked at three regional markets
- The research looked at predominantly office-based environments
- The empirical conclusions are based on six case studies only

- The evidence suggested that where development is in short supply, almost all development adds value of some sort.

For all these reasons, this research should be considered merely an early step on the road to clarifying if and how urban design adds value, with further research required to strengthen the case. Nevertheless, an initial insight into the process and form of value creation through better urban design has been offered, and the conclusions seem to confirm current UK Government policy approaches that themselves value better urban design.

Further research could both confirm the findings, and test how they relate to different contexts, markets, land-use types, and development scenarios. This would add to the critical mass of knowledge, and further inform policy measures and the decision-making processes of public and private stakeholders. In the meantime, the consistency between the findings reported here and the other UK and international research on value and urban design examined during the work should give reasonable confidence that the more detailed conclusions reported above would be substantiated by any further research undertaken in the future.

Notes

1 Now the office of the Deputy Prime Minister (ODPM).
2 The state-owned body responsible for the management and maintenance of most British canals and inland waterways.
3 The Private Finance Initiative (PFI) provides a means for public sector bodies to finance development usually through sale and lease back to the private sector.

References

Arup Economics and Planning (2000) *Survey of Urban Design Skills in Local Government*, London: DETR.

Carmona, M., de Magalhães, C. and Edwards, M. (2001) *The Value of Urban Design*, London: Thomas Telford.

Davies, H. and Rowley, A. (2000) *Training for Urban Design*, London: DETR.

Department of National Heritage, English Heritage, and The Royal Institution of Chartered Surveyors (1996) *The Value of Conservation: a literature review of the economic and social value of cultural built heritage*, London: RICS.

DETR and CABE (2000) *By Design, Urban Design in the Planning System: towards better practice*, London: Thomas Telford.

Eppli, M. and Tu, C. (1999) *Valuing the New Urbanism: the impact of the new urbanism on prices of single family houses*, Washington, DC: Urban Land Institute.

Llewelyn-Davies (2000) *Urban Design Compendium*, London: English Partnerships and The Housing Corporation.

Property Council of Australia (1999) *The Design Dividend*, Canberra: PCA National Office.

Urban Design Skills Working Group (2001) *Report to the Minister for Housing and Planning, Department for Transport, Local Government and the Regions*, London: CABE.

Vandell, K. and Lane, J. (1989) 'The economics of architecture and urban design: some preliminary findings', *Journal of the American Real Estate and Urban Economics Association*, vol. 17, no. 2, pp. 235–60.

Part 3

Delivering better buildings

Design has been defined in many different ways – perhaps that is what makes it such an intriguing issue for reflection. In terms of buildings, it is taken to be that part of the process that lies between working with the client to identify requirements and aspirations on the one hand, and on the other putting together the components and systems to construct it. A definition produced by the Construction Research and Innovation Strategy Panel said:

Design is the activity that brings together and integrates all the diverse contributions of the construction industry to produce a product that meets customer needs. Among its strategic priorities, CRISP identified design as one of five broad areas crucial to industry improvement.

(CRISP, 1999)

Giles Oliver originally wrote Chapter 12, *Design quality needs conscious values*, in the form of a report by the CRISP Design Task Group, which he chaired. As a report about research needs to support design, it contained a highly detailed set of recommendations set out as '39 steps'. In the intervening period, much has happened to promote and implement some of its original recommendations. It remains, however, a carefully constructed and thought-provoking paper which deserves to be much more widely read. For this book it has been edited and updated and, at the strategic level, its recommendations have lost none of their urgency. The chapter stresses the need to place occupancy criteria centre field. It proposes quick response research suited to the needs of industry, together with longitudinal research into building performance and value over the longer-term. Educational reform is called for to raise the profile of the built environment, to encourage trans-disciplinary knowledge-sharing, and to increase awareness of the social and ethical dimension. Sectoral frameworks for studying design quality are proposed, together with cross-sectoral

communication, and supported by evidence-based research. Perhaps most crucially the chapter calls for the development of a common language for design which releases the widest value contribution from all stakeholders within the industry and the society it serves.

If Chapter 12 stresses the importance of evidence-based design, Chapter 13 is itself written from the perspective of extensive research into how people use buildings. Its authors, Adrian Leaman and Bill Bordass, have been centrally involved in post-handover or post-occupancy studies of buildings for more than a decade, including the Probe series. The chapter, entitled *Flexibility and adaptability*, draws on their experience to identify a series of lessons for coping with change – lessons not only for design, but also for handover and occupation. Building needs and uses change, and the provision of flexibility is one way to cope with it. However, in their experience, unpredictable changes may defeat flexibility strategies. For example, over-provision of building services to meet anticipated future needs can cause excessive complexity that reduces freedom and constrains changes in work patterns, while also removing the possibility of giving occupants any control over their environment and leading to dissatisfaction. Increasing uncertainty leads to demands for built-in flexibility but, the authors ask: 'How much is enough?' They recommend that briefs should be as explicit as possible about the need for on the one hand flexibility – that is, for anticipated short-term changes – and on the other hand adaptability – less frequent but more fundamental ones. The two should not be confused with each other. They suggest it is vital to get the basics right, such as adaptable envelopes that are good at moderating selectively the external climate; inherently efficient technologies for conditioning interiors; and systems that provide adaptive opportunities so that occupants feel they have some control over their environment. It is also vital to ensure a good match between the sophistication of the building services and an organisation's ability to operate them effectively.

Where chapter 13 is mostly about the relationship between designers and clients before and after construction, Chapter 14, *Managing design and construction*, is primarily concerned with the relationship between clients, designers and builders before and during the construction process. Its author, Peter Treblicock, starts with a historical sketch of the building of Blenheim Palace. This illustrates a range of difficulties faced by major projects. These include lack of clear payment arrangements; inaccurate initial cost estimates and escalating costs; loss of trust between client, designer and builders; and claims and counter-claims among the parties. Unfortunately these problems are not just historical – the construction of buildings is fraught with difficulties, and a climate of adversity and blame typifies many projects. While several government-sponsored reports about the state of the construction industry historically have identified similar problems, the latest two – 'Latham,' and 'Egan,' – backed up with a number of initiatives to support the changes they identify as necessary to improve the industry, appear to be having a real impact on the industry.

Treblicock's chapter focuses on better integration between designers and the supply chain as one of the contributions designers can make to the new ways of working called for by Latham and Egan. In his examples he illustrates how improved management practices at the design stage – specifically better integration of the design team with those responsible for delivery of a building – improve predictability, functionality and fitness for purpose of the completed project. He describes a number of approaches concerned with forward planning, improved communication, and programmed information flow, together with more formal methods such as the use of value engineering and value management. Between them, these methods contributed to improved financial

control, greater predictability, and a reduction in variations and abortive work. These approaches will not of themselves necessarily result in buildings that are recognised as having design quality. However, they do help to ensure that if specific requirements for design quality are fed into the start of the process, there is a much greater likelihood of their being achieved in practice first time round.

Reference

CRISP (1999) *Acquiring Knowledge, Developing Tools: CRISP strategic priorities 1999*, London: CRISP.

Chapter 12

Design quality needs conscious values

Giles Oliver

This chapter was originally written for the Construction Research and Innovation Strategy Panel (CRISP). Among its strategic priorities, CRISP identified design as one of five broad areas crucial to industry improvement:

> Design is the activity that brings together and integrates all the diverse contributions of the construction industry to produce a product that meets customer needs. It has received relatively little attention in recent industry initiatives. CRISP is keen to encourage research on design which is appropriate to end user needs and to optimising the construction process. Recent and current work on integrating design and construction needs to be moved speedily into practice.
>
> CRISP, 1999

The paper was intended as a call for research across the wide field of design quality. As this book witnesses, there has been a recent burst of activity – the research has indeed begun. So if

it seems dated in parts I am glad. Perhaps its value is in the attempt we made to range across the field, to indicate the beneficial connections between design subspecies. A persistent theme is the haemorrhaging of knowledge that occurs in the absence of systematic post-occupancy evaluation of completed buildings and built environments. It is instructive that the pressure to stem this, to learn systematically, is coming from the so-called 'PFI providers' where long-term investments (thirty years or so) in new buildings prevent them 'handing on' the problems. But will they, as private companies, wish to share knowledge? That is the challenging ethical subtext which remains to be addressed. The suggestion that the historical reservoir of knowledge held by schools of architecture, known as 'history', could serve as a feed tank to post-occupancy studies and research remains to be developed. It would make a wonderful research subject, guaranteed to put the cat amongst the pigeons.

Post-occupancy research remains the next explosive and potentially enriching area for all built-environment professionals. It is inherently interdisciplinary. People have to talk to each other. There are complex issues of self-interest and public-interest involved. The Probe team (see Chapters 3 and 13) cannot be expected to cover this entire landscape, like ghostbusters dealing with the whole of New York! Project insurance could unlock this area of professional hanging back. This chapter only touches on the ownership of design research and reflection. More, much more, needs to be said about this. When something fails to be explored, or fails to reach the public domain, I would argue that that itself is worth inquiring about. What interests combine to fly in the face of common sense? 'Why' as Sherlock Holmes so acutely enquired 'did the dog not bark in the night?'

Two outstanding areas of research and practical energy have lit up the field since the paper first appeared. The work of CABE in the UK in promoting design quality at the widest level, and the Construction Industry Council's hammering out the elusive Design Quality Indicators (see Chapters 15–17). Of the 39 CRISP recommendations, approximately two-thirds now have research champions at work. From where I write, the most significant unexplored area of design research remains that of the deep study of buildings in use and through time. Clients and users find it inexplicable that the construction team melt away once the project is so-called completed. Well we, and I write as a practising architect, should spell out what we need in order to participate. If it takes legal protection, extra fees or mutual coopera-tion for us to stay with the environments we have helped design, this requires advocacy. And it is the design team as a whole that needs to do this. Complex buildings can now have up to a dozen design professionals and specialists intimately involved in the creation of satisfactory and inspiring environments. Gathered project knowledge is a valued capital potentially avail-able to clients and users over the lifetime of a building. It is routinely squandered or dissipated.

The University of Cambridge Estates Department is initiating a new contract where the design team stays on for four years to help the building settle in and to learn, under the broad heading 'soft landings'. That approach deserves research and support.

I hope the chapter reads as an attempt at 'joined-up challenging'. Analysis of causes does assist when determining why obvious improvements are failing. And analysis works only when our values are set in motion.

CRISP's terms of reference for the Design Task Group

Our adopted term of reference was to

> establish a research strategy for a sensitive methodology capable of tracking values generated throughout the design process so that clients' needs can be systematically met and expectations exceeded. Such a strategy must enable the client to monitor the design process at all stages, minimise uncertainties in performance outcome and capture extra value at all stages.

During a six-month period of intensive group discussion fuelled by members' papers, a specially commissioned research review of the field and a concluding delegate workshop to test our propositions, we developed a wide ranging set of strategic proposals. The original paper (Oliver, 2000) captures these, together with our research recommendations in the form of 39 steps.

The five main strategic recommendations from the Task Group are:

1   To raise the quality of our built environment by placing *occupancy criteria* centre field.
2   To establish *sectoral frameworks for design quality* supported by evidence-based research.
3   To initiate quick response *project-linked research* suited to the needs of the industry and occasional client.

Table 12.1 **39 Steps – the CRISP Design Task Group's recommendations**

Sectoral Value Research

1 Research into sectoral initiatives to establish design value, with systematic ordering of criteria to assist comparison and respect differences.
2 Encourage dialogue between sectors to learn from each other's evaluation systems.
3 Research successes and failures at a design level of the PFI initiatives commissioned by Government to date, by sector.
4 Urban design evaluation requires urgent integration into the emerging matrix of building studies.

Project Based Research

5 Immediate research into the design values of the Demonstration Projects offered by Industry, including conception, development, construction and post-occupancy stages.
6 Inception Research: Design Experiment with Operational Testing. Establish "Quick Response" funding for sectoral project based research, allowing 'up-front' innovation support on a project by project basis.

'Backsight' Research/Feedback & Dissemination

7 How to establish connecting feedback 'loops' so that studies take effect and are seen to do so.
8 Support for communicating research efforts to all stakeholders.

Longitudinal Research

9 Longitudinal research into building performance and value over time, including historic and contemporary 'post-occupancy' analysis.
10 Flexibility of building uses, to encourage sustainable design through time, to develop a rating system accessible to owners, users and planners.
11 Integration of building economics into parameters for change on terms understood by all stakeholders.

Educational Research

12 Raise the profile of Built Environment design within National Curriculum to equal the enthusiasm accorded to the Natural Environment.
13 Public educational support through regional architecture centres as crucibles for change, debate and visualisation.
14 Education of design professionals in production management with cross-industry placements to fertilise the construction field.
15 Education of Design Professionals to include methods of thinking, ethics, social context, communication as fundamental.
16 Research into obstacles to raising profile and status of Building Services as a career.
17 Re-integrate Architectural Research into the demand-led improvement of building Quality, Usefulness and Delight. Building types, case studies, symbolic and aesthetic contribution of architecture are all valuable and sought after.
18 Educating the current players – encouraging continuing professional education for change and feedback. Trans-disciplinary events and seminars providing specific merit awards.

Cultural Values Research

19 To investigate inhibitors to team-working training during design professionals' 'whole-life' education and illustrate successful initiatives that break this mould.
20 To assess effectiveness of the historic 'learned society' model for inter-specialist tasks and interdisciplinary challenges.
21 To investigate and monitor institutional inhibitors to client-centred improvement and demonstrate positive alternatives.
22 Encourage cross-disciplinary learning from other sectors (such as medicine, manufacturing, psychology).

International Comparisons: Learning from other cultures

23 International scoping comparison of design assessment methods in practice, including cultural identifiers (Japan, Holland, Scandinavia).
24 Scoping Review how professional institutes in other countries contribute to design awareness and value definition.
25 International survey of educational institutes initiatives at developing common design language – at primary, secondary and tertiary levels.

Communicating Design Values: towards a shared language

26 Research into best practice Briefing languages and value-systems by means of successful examples/case studies.
27 Research into effectiveness of establishing a networking exchange on buildings in use embracing all stakeholders.
28 Research into effectiveness of establishing a think-tank for industry wide research into design, embracing all disciplines across asset/revenue divide.
29 Research into the effective communication of complex processes with trans-sectoral comparisons.

Assessment Criteria and Indicators: widening the measurement path

30 Research into how can understanding of Cost, Value and Worth be improved throughout the project team?
31 Examine current cost-in-use studies in practice, their limitations and areas requiring refinement.
32 Test methods for improving industry's capacity to express its needs - in particular workshops, dialogue, deepening understanding between estranged parties.
33 Scoping studies into existing methodologies for assessing value in buildings.
34 Establish appropriate and new ways of approaching post-occupancy assessment.
35 Invite proposals to research and establish Design KPI's, from all sectors.

Change agencies

36 Extend Government sponsorship of design champions in the field of the built environment linking CABE, Design Council and Regional initiatives.
37 EPSRC/ESRC and other key research sponsors to communicate more widely its current support for interdisciplinary research teams, since such teams are necessary to capture answers to interdisciplinary problems.
38 Research sponsors to develop specific policies for design research to guide and invite the issues raised in this report and elsewhere.
39 Research sponsors to call for 'outside the box' research into interdisciplinary design issues, with experimental funding outside the conventional research review time cycle. This can underpin longitudinal research. Also encourage short penetrative research commissions (such as the Task Group Study) that publish and be damned. The industry can provide a wealth of committed individuals prepared to offer valuable support in kind provided their contribution is time limited.

4   To encourage widespread *educational reform* to support greater quality in the built environment.

5   To develop a *shared language for design* which releases the widest value contribution from all stakeholders within our industry and the society we serve.

From the outset the group focused on a number of leading questions:

- Can we agree on the meaning or essential ingredients of good design?
- What is the common language we use to assess or describe good design?
- How can we provide evidence to qualify our assertion that design has value?
- How do we actually value design?
- Do we have shared values?
- Can value be measured?

We considered these questions critical to establishing the terms of reference for design to play a significant role within industry improvement and the declared objective of meeting client and end-user needs. The debate is still, in our view, in its early stages in this country and we would encourage everyone with an interest in the outcome to contribute. We hope our efforts can serve to stimulate the reflection and debate that must underlie effective change.

Beyond the rhetoric

Recognition of the contribution that is made by good design in the built environment is now widespread. During the short period of the group's deliberations, we noted its arrival in public and government debate, perhaps triggered by the Millennium projects, by the Egan impacts and by its emergence as a significant Government theme (Blair, Prescott, Raynsford, Smith). However, what this recognition *means* is still elusive, and definitions and delivery remain unclear. Certainly public emphasis was *not* triggered by research as such. Indeed the group's studies showed a tremendous need for backing up the rhetoric in

favour of good design and design quality with understandable, robust and widely accepted definitions and empirical evidence. Our view is that behind the rhetoric is significant and correct intuition which is, in a sense, searching for a shared language and validation.

Valuing design

In our language *design* is used to describe both a process and a product. This alerts us to the fact that when design is commonly talked about we are immediately involved with an activity leading to synthesis. The term *value* is similarly charged. Our challenge has been to interrogate the powerful implications of these two terms and their interaction. The invitation to do so was not academic in the conventional sense for they are on everyone's lips; politicians, construction professionals, industry leaders, government and the media.

Mapping the field

The group's declared intention was to identify what research was required to help establish a common language in valuing design within the built environment. We asked what methods are in use to extract evidence of design's contribution and what possibility is there for agreement? Is the intuition that good design contributes value supported by evidence and rigorous research? To support our work we immediately commissioned a literature review (Macmillan, 2000a). We set out our ambitions in a field diagram to set the scope of our study and ensure wider linkages were considered (Figure 12.1).

The review proceeded through four reporting stages: examining *process, value systems* and *product*. It showed that while process was being addressed with some energy (principally from a construction management perspective) there is a paucity of research in the fields of value systems and product itself.

It was quickly felt that confining attention to the measuring of time, cost and achievement against brief failed to capture the opportunities good design offered in practice, preventing wider assessment of the product's impact within the built environment. We emphasise that in many ways process measurement *is* essential to developing a more adequate assessment culture and our observations as to its limitation are in no sense dismissive. We would rather term it *foundational* work (Figure 12.2). However, quality of process does not necessarily result in quality of product. To measure this from the supply side, as it were, limits the benefit. For clients in the widest sense, the process is of relatively less interest than the quality of the outcome.[1] If the Lean Thinking analogy is employed here, the 'pull' for quality has to be felt *from* the client, the occupier and in the widest sense the public user of the buildings and environments. If demand is currently inarticulate or dispersed, this does not diminish its importance.

As soon as we leave the measurable sphere of the project, with its cost targets, agreed product form, and time frame, the map of design opens up into a territory that is both hard to measure and filled with competing voices who lay claim to be our guides. The

principal challenge is the evaluation of what are thought of as 'subjective' criteria.

The difficulty of measuring socially appreciated goals such as 'Function, Sustainability, and Delight' (Macmillan, 2000b) alerted us to the importance of the open declaration of values. Just as the open book underpins good partnering, we suggest that *the open statement of values* could similarly assist the achievement of a shared goals. The dispersed and sequential character of the stakeholders in the construction and management of buildings is widely acknowledged. The impact is a variety of goals. We all interpret these goals differently and place different priorities on them. Most commonly noticed are the 'delivery and handover' goals of the design and construction team, while the client's aims are only just beginning – to put the building to productive use. Dialogue and assistance between the constructors and the management/maintenance teams are weakened, and the lessons to be learnt are not passed on. Lifetime costing, PFI and framework agreements are breaching this culture, but occasional clients rely on the industry to guide them.

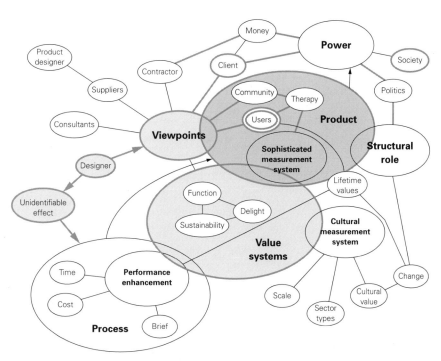

12.1
Design Realms Map

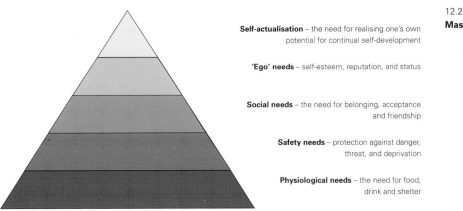

Self-actualisation – the need for realising one's own potential for continual self-development

'Ego' needs – self-esteem, reputation, and status

Social needs – the need for belonging, acceptance and friendship

Safety needs – protection against danger, threat, and deprivation

Physiological needs – the need for food, drink and shelter

12.2
Maslow's hierarchy of needs

The needs form a hierarchy, according to Maslow, because the lower-level needs have to be satisfied first. Only when these needs have been satisfied will the individual seek to satisfy the higher needs. 'Ultimately, a musician must make music, an artist must paint, a poet must write, if he is to be happy. What man can be, he must be and this is called self-actualisation'.

From the ground up: the importance of sectoral research

Just because there is no simple measure of design value it should not blind us to the important work underway in different sectors of construction; housing, higher education, offices, health and elsewhere. Some sectors proved to be much more developed and well funded than others. We attempted a brief scoping study across the sectors and immediately it became apparent that there is much to learn. But each sector has to establish its own value-programme in order to make good use of the lessons from others. Housing criteria differ from higher education criteria, for example, but both can provide some mutually useful guidance for student residences or single person hostels.

Trans-sectoral communication deserves encouragement and support. Some sectors have more sophisticated approaches to the discrimination of design value. Facing the differences and commonalities will develop each sector's powers of discrimination.

We are very cautious of the assumption that there might be a Holy Grail of universal design quality indicators because at the very least, interpretation changes with time and cultural perspective. The assumption of a universal standard measure, which research bids may claim is possible, may indeed attract funding since it appears to clean up a confusing world at a stroke. Such an approach shares with the M4I's Key Performance Indicators, an ambition to achieve a single system for all questions. Not surprisingly, the character of the post-Egan initiatives have been widely noted as evangelical.

In whose interest do we design well?

We immediately discovered that identifying values raises the challenge of acknowledging *power*. Or put more comfortably perhaps, sectional or productive interests. If Usefulness is Value's mother, then the often absent and overlooked father is Power. Large companies with sequential building programmes and relatively clear business plans have begun to establish design/constructor teams (BAA Framework, Tesco, and so on.) These are the 'professional clients'. Who is in charge is made clear from the start – the client's business goals. Hence the message of Egan from this very sector. However, the occasional nature of the construction process (when narrowly defined as new accommodation) prevents many clients, typically small and medium-sized enterprises (SMEs) from assuming such control. The occasional client is therefore invited to turn to the industry to supply the right product. Who then does the remembering? This is well-rehearsed territory and includes the bulk of construction output. What we draw attention to here is its impact on design culture and delivery of design quality.

The supply-side response is to band together to sustain the intellectual and material investment required to journey together from project to project ('virtual companies', supply chains, etc.). This is necessary and admirable, but our task is to ask the next question. How will this benefit the so-called occasional clients' design needs? Will it subordinate appropriate client-centred innovation to the more organised and powerful supply-side goals of the designer/constructor/maintainer chain? Private Finance Initiative, Design Build, Finance and Operate and, most recently, LIFT, all herald this integration process. What is missing as yet is the independent exploration of the brief, setting appropriate goals and seeing they are held to and indeed improved on. In its first phase, for example, the massive commitment to PFI hospital building demonstrated the rush to conservative design, often at a very early stage of the procurement route, with perceptible long-term social costs such as inflexibility, the loss of passive therapeutic values, repetitive solutions (Cole, 1997). This generated a reaction, and we welcome the realisation that good design adds value through functionality, whole-life costing, service enhancement and aesthetics (Treasury Taskforce, 2000). Of particular note is that a whole policy change has taken place without research to underpin it.

This example of powerful interests directing the effective design agenda away from the ostensible user goals of the project may seem obvious but it illustrates that building projects are a cocktail of competing ingredients. We recommend that research disinterestedly and courageously examines all 'inhibitors' to a better designed environment.

Research input is needed to provide evidence for productive briefing informed by innovation and thorough familiarity with past experience. The fracturing of state agencies and major enterprises into bought-in consultancy has seen a haemorrhaging of practical experience

and collective memory. There has also been a loss of research and assessment teams within major government departments, the DETR being no exception. This reduces points of access and dialogue that the whole industry can share. This shift is probably irreversible and points to a major underlying theme to this study and other CRISP Task Groups' work.

Evolving an appropriate language for design quality

We concluded that there is an urgent need to strengthen, and where possible re-establish, *sectoral wisdom*. The disinterested character of this requires an appropriate independence from Treasury-driven criteria or supply-side blandishments. The remote academic model is not an adequate alternative. All parties need to be brought to the table and informed by a robust and appropriate value system. How is it to be modelled?

Is the energy apparent in *Building down barriers* (see Chapter 14) matched by the establishment of *Driving up quality* held in briefing caucuses who view the sector's requirements in detail? Building performance hinges on a sustained grasp of detail as well as broad strategy.

Values articulated at evidence-based, pragmatic level, can transform cost or programme dominated values. Assimilation of complexity is the hallmark of civilisation. The challenge is to grasp the articulation and interdependence of the different criteria – and to do this we need a wider language which emphatically includes the rich options released by wise, informed procurement.

Wisdom is little mentioned in the excitement to praise innovation. This tendency has shaped Egan initiatives and, we suggest, reflects the covert agenda that structural change in the construction industry is the driving motive. The proper locus of wisdom and innovation is the research departments of universities. Are they fulfilling this role? Innovation is too often confused with achieving competitive advantage through product differentiation. A necessary change without doubt, involving consolidation, the driving out of waste, process alignment, restoration of reasonable profit levels and the elusive promise of capital investment by a notoriously capital-light sector. If we simply wait in a naive way for the intellectual fruits of this future tree to appear the results can be predicted. While alleviating the public purse of the burden of thinking 'for' the industry that does not fund its own thinking, the fruit will be supply-side thinking re-established at a higher (more modern) level with no guarantee that this will benefit the wider stakeholders – clients, occupiers and the general public. Poorly conceived system buildings of the 1960s remain a testament to supply-side partnering between government and construction suppliers.

It is incumbent on clients to develop measurement and satisfaction criteria. The Confederation of Construction Clients initiatives (see Chapter 2), among others, are welcomed by the Task Group; however, will this include the occupiers'/employees' interests? Can private interest fund the wider public demand for a better quality built environment? The market model can sustain its own values. Those it cannot directly engage with (in the business cycle) it leaves to government. Are socially and ethically centred professional consultants and designers capable of standing in for these orphaned values?

In this brief survey we indicate that latent and explicit values constantly drive the agenda for the built environment. People often dismiss this as politics and turn away to their preferred technical or special area of interest, competence and identity. Indeed, it is politics in the original meaning of the term – the management of civil society.

The challenge of pluralism

One of the most difficult inheritances of state-focused public construction is the expectation of monolithic value. The current situation and any future characterised by freedom is emphatically plural. Its expression is diversity. The acceptance of this and the concomitant necessity to handle, enjoy and resolve conflict cannot be delegated. Hence, the urgent need to educate design and construction professionals into their civic responsibilities, which lie beyond the single project service model.

Valuing design requires us as specialists and experienced knowledge holders to contribute our gifts appropriately. Society's investment in the often extensive training of construction professionals is significant. Research is urgently needed into the barriers to this rewarding resource reaching the public, the occupiers and the clients.

Learning from experience

We asked what cultural and practical initiative can catalyse these changes. A continuum of evaluation from inception to finished product is required. However, post-occupancy evaluation is the key, because it looks at how things are and not how they might be. It serves as a corrective to 'remotely representative' design – second guessing outcomes and ignoring lessons of buildings in use. The creative acceptance of wisdom and innovation empowers the occupiers/clients. The rigorous analysis of how buildings actually work, establishing evidence, measurability and an accessible language for this, is the necessary complement to the well-developed synthetic capacities of architects and designers. There is a real opportunity here to renew the strength and purpose of architectural culture and its academic base, and give context and direction to its research capacity. The splits in the industry and its knowledge base are dysfunctional and hinder the flow of value-generating capacity in its widest sense. Our argument and recommendations are not aimed to neaten up or codify what is, and always has been, a fantastically rich human and social activity. Rather they aim to welcome the complexity of weaving the strands into a more sustainable fabric. As any successful briefing and design process demonstrates, this is the real Holy Grail (if there must be one) in the deeper sense that the vessel is pervasive, inexhaustible and nourishing.

However, this social creativity requires a flow of enriching opportunity and innovatory encouragement from those best placed to offer their gifts – engineers, architects, landscape architects, constructors, facilities managers and creative artists, urban designers – the list can be extended and daily breaks these limits. Otherwise, the conservative and localised limitations of occupancy-based experience will confine feedback to what already does or does not work. How best to do this?

Taking time: off-line or up front?

Examples of penetrative questioning and empowering enquiry need articulating and modelling. Social science skills are required, but remodelled to elicit latent creativity. Sometimes designers respond too fast, which is why a chord is struck by the Japanese example of listening and debating at length before committing to a form or product. They are seeking understanding, not knowledge alone, and investing *time* in this process. Similar benefits can be seen in the European habit of talking at length before drawing conclusions. Nissan's UK *COGENT* initiative, aligning forty key suppliers, took several years of patient and persistent discussions. Project culture fears this time-consuming method, but suffers in the realisation stage. 'More time for design up front' is a vital slogan. 'Up front' is often the nearest a construction project gets to the celebrated 'off-line' of manufacturing and despite its limitations should be strongly encouraged and the benefits broadcast.

The listening, learning and reflective skills this process calls for are already widely acknowledged as deficient within conventional construction culture. We found too little of this in the educational frame of construction professionals, a deficiency that also directly relates to the gender imbalance. Research is

needed to identify effective means of developing this in both new and existing members of the industry. The tasks are interdisciplinary, and the impacts on our designed environment diverse and many-layered. Specialist mind frames are ill-equipped to address this reality. We argue that research models must incorporate in every stage of their development the whole spectrum of impacts. This could be called a genetic responsibility for research at this time.

International comparison

Provided that we are alert to cultural identifiers to prevent idealisation of fragmented aspects (for example, Japanese house building must be situated in its cultural context) a great deal can be learnt from regular international comparative studies. Architectural culture is open to this as is engineering, within their own disciplinary visions. The challenge, and it is primarily a European one for the UK, is to integrate a wider assessment of other built environments. Urban design is currently strongly influenced by this enriched perspective (Barcelona, Urban Task Force) and draws on growing support from popular experience of travel and emerging multiculturalism.

A framework for balancing needs

Our practical restatement of design philosophy is an argument, a proposition that deserves the strongest testing. Our intention is not to contribute a new dogma or a further burdensome set of tests, but to release creative energy dammed up by redundant frameworks, most of which are sustained internally in the minds of those best placed to reducing them. The importance of recognising the collective character of professional knowledge, practised by individuals, permits initiatives to take place at a number of levels – individual continuing professional development (CPD), institutional reform, interprofessional debate. The public dimension will alter through post-occupancy evaluation until it is no longer an exceptional enquiry but a civic habit. We should recall that the empowered client, user, occupier and passer-by are one and the same person at different times of day!

In placing such emphasis on post-occupancy evaluation, we are aware of the argument against its use as a universal mechanism of assessment, namely that the general public will not possess the same sensibilities. The needs of an unemployed youth are such that aesthetics might be very low on his priorities. Fortunately for us a lot of work has been done to understand this hierarchy of needs. Maslow's work on the hierarchy of need allows us to take into account higher aspirations while at the same time attending to basic needs. His research suggests that values are constant but interpretation may be variable and dependent upon one's situation at any point in time. The image we found exceptionally useful was a restatement of the Maslow pyramid (Figure 12.2) in which use values are foundational for the presence and construction of less measurable but nonetheless essential values.

It is natural that priorities will vary between different interest groups, sectors and timescales. This work provides us with a backdrop for researchers to interpret and balance those needs. Such a model, which implies no exclusive hierarchy, dignifies and locates the efforts of the diverse players currently active within the built environment. Potentially we can recover the intellectual and aesthetic capital that has been fragmented. It does require testing and perhaps remodelling in a dynamic manner to express the non-hierarchic and plural experiences.

In this we return to a core theme of our study, which is the call for respect for people's needs and skills. The poisoned legacy of an adversarial construction industry is a pervasive lack of respect, often class-ridden, from which design and construction professionals are not exempt. We would suggest that client-centred and occupier-centred design is marked by growing respect between all players – teams and users, and in this construction genuinely reassumes its proper place in the civic fabric we all create.

Acknowledgement

I would like to acknowledge the support and encouragement of my co-authors in the Task Group who allowed me to frame our collective concerns and insights. I also commend the CRISP Executive which originally raised the question of design research in 1999 and patiently and enthusiastically supported our work, despite the expanded agenda. CRISP continues to provide a unique (in the UK) environment for such challenging and strategic thinking from practising professionals in the industry.

Note

1   The popularity of Design and Build in the 1970s and 1980s, with its offer of cost and programme certainty, has only been tempered by the experience of significant loss of control over quality (in housing, higher education, etc.). The determination to retain certainty *and* quality characterises many current initiatives, not least the Task Group's enquiry.

References

Cole, J. (1997) 'Design Quality and the PFI', *PFI Quarterly Journal.*

CRISP (1999) *Acquiring Knowledge, Developing Tools: CRISP strategic priorities 1999*, London: CRISP.

Macmillan, S. (2000a) *A Review of Current Industry and Research Initiatives on Design*, CRISP Consultancy Commission 99/5, summary and full review available from the CRISP website www.crisp-uk.org.uk.

Macmillan, S. (2000b) *Report of the CRISP Design Task Group Workshop Proceedings*, CRISP report 99/18, available from the CRISP website www.crisp-uk.org.uk.

Oliver, G. (2000) *Capturing and Developing the Value of Good Design*, CRISP Design Task Group Report, available from CRISP website www.crisp-uk.org.uk.

Treasury Task Force (2000) *How to Achieve Design Quality in PFI Projects*, Technical Note 7, HM Treasury, available on the web at www.treasury-projects-taskforce.gov.uk

Chapter 13

Flexibility and adaptability

Adrian Leaman and Bill Bordass

This chapter is about design quality from the perspective of post-occupancy evaluation studies. We deal with the rather elusive concepts of flexibility and adaptability which should be an integral part of design quality debates, but rarely feature explicitly.

We draw upon the Probe series of post-occupancy studies.[1] We also include findings from other building studies which we have carried out, but these are not in the public domain, so the buildings are not named.

There is a growing body of literature about Probe, so it is possible to follow up some of the examples and references used here. It includes:

- the original building studies, twenty-one in all. Each of these has a short section on implications for design;
- articles based on strategic findings from Probe, another seventeen;
- third-party rejoinders, seven more.

For an up-to-date list and the opportunity to download some of these, please use www.usablebuildings.co.uk.

The Probe findings are primarily based on detailed analysis of technical and energy performance, together with occupant feedback, and backed up by contextual and observational work. Probe does not include benchmarked studies of cost, aesthetics or space efficiency/utilisation.

This chapter uses the concepts of flexibility and adaptability as a theme for exploring some of the implications for design that we have discovered in our performance studies. We do not attempt here to give detailed examples – that is a project for the future. We are looking for some of the main lessons which we draw from our observations so far. These – seven in all – are in the last section.

Everything that we are trying to say here should be relevant in some way to design decisions, however, we are not concerned only with design, but rather with the total building system that results after handover and occupation. This includes, for example, usability and manageability (which, sadly, are usually absent from mainstream discussion about design), environmental impact, and reference to the underlying social and technical changes affecting buildings, their location and procurement.

We are conscious that the terms 'design' and 'quality' are both abstract and profound (taken separately and together) with different meanings for different players. For example, unlike architects, building users are frequently concerned only incidentally with the fine points of aesthetics. They have a much more practical bent. 'Will the building allow me to carry out my tasks to the best of my ability?' 'Will it get in the way of what I have to do?' 'Will it make my life easier?' To users, a good-looking but impractical building will not win the day.

We also frequently use the word design in tandem with management. We draw on Bill Allens's aphorism, slightly adapted: 'Building research should never be more than one step away from a design or management decision.'

The myth of self-managing flexibility

One of the most common requirements for a modern building is flexibility. Clients almost always want it and designers usually say they can deliver. But it is all too easy to put a gloss on flexibility/adaptability issues and forget the downsides. We obviously need more flexible buildings, otherwise they may not meet occupier needs and quickly become obsolete, but:

* Will they be too complicated?
* Will the occupants like them?
* Will they require too much routine effort?
* Can they anticipate the unforeseeable?

Evidence from studies of buildings in use shows that flexibility/adaptability are inextricably linked with building technology and its manageability. How well a building functions, for example in terms of occupant comfort and energy efficiency, seems to be just as much, or even more, about technology-management interactions than design alone.

Figure 13.1 sums this up. From the data we have so far, the best performing buildings are either Type A or Type D: that is briefed, designed, constructed, used and managed with an upfront mandate to deal with technological complexity and manageability. The best buildings have either:

* Realistic assessments of their technological complexity combined with appropriate levels of management and maintenance skills to cope with the inevitable consequences, for example, Tanfield House (Bordass et al., 1995); One Bridewell Street (Energy Efficiency Office, 1991); or
* Minimised technological impacts, by making things simple and self-managing where reasonably possible (for example, Wood-house Medical Centre (Standeven et al., 1996); the Elizabeth Fry Building (Standeven et al. 1998a). As technological side effects are usually also environmental impacts (Tenner, 1996; Weizsacker et al., 1997) this makes environmental sense as well.

13.1
Technology-management interactions

		Technological complexity	
		Higher	Lower
Management input	Higher	Effective, but often costly *Type A*	Rare *Type B*
	Lower	Risky with performance penalties *Type C*	Effective, but small-scale and restricted uses *Type D*

3   Make habitual (formal and informal rules which help with safe, comfortable and smooth running);
4   Make acceptable (things which are not prescribed and covered by the rules, but allow scope for individuality, innovation and change).

Buildings which are properly flexible and/or adaptable will have included consideration of provision for all four somewhere in the briefing, design and operations thinking, raising issues such as usability, innovation, habit (that is, cultural norms in the organisation and user etiquette), safety, security, risk, value and uncertainty.

However, the modern tendency is to push as many things as possible into quadrant A – seek 'fit and forget' – and leave the consequences of leakage back out into the other three quadrants for someone else to worry about. Unfortunately for us all, side-effects cannot be forgotten even if they are not immediately foreseeable or includable in cost-benefit equations or risk-value payoff calculations. Examples of some of the consequences are given in Table 13.1.

Dependencies and interactions

The temptation to use technology as a get-out-of-jail-free card is often irresistible to designers and managers when faced with problems requiring quick answers. But buildings are interdependent systems with many hierarchic layers, a property which introduces dependencies and interactions, often unwanted, hidden or unforeseen. The shell-scenery-set diagram introduced in the 1970s (Duffy and Worthington, 1972) neatly summarises the hierarchic nature of buildings and their subsystems and can be helpful in separating variables and developing adaptability strategies. However, in the wrong hands such layering can actually inhibit strategic integration.

Our expanded version is in Figure 13.4, an adaptation from Brand (1994). Systems at the top of the list – site, strategy, shell – tend to set constraints for things lower down – services, for instance, are determined to some extent by the shell. Things at the top also tend to be longer lasting – centuries in the case of some sites, compared to minutes for the position of stuff on desks. The diagram has many virtues, not least of which to emphasise Russian-doll-like complexity – with systems apparently nesting inside each other – and the time frequencies of changes. The implication is that things at the bottom are more flexible, and perhaps more adaptable than those at the top, and therefore easier to change. However, this is not necessarily so: a transportable building can be moved to another site, shells and structures can be adapted or replaced. Conversely some arrangements can be impossible to change because of their interlocking nature.

Modern businesses are increasingly demanding much greater flexibility throughout the hierarchy, trying to give themselves greater degrees of freedom. Some of the symptoms are:

- Rental lease periods reduced from 25 years to sometimes 5 years or less;
- The rapid rise (and volatility) of businesses which offer high quality, very short-term, office accommodation for rent in major cities around the world, and growing investor interest in fully-serviced suites for temporary or long-term occupancy;

Adaptation?

Site
Strategy
Shell
Structure
Skin
Services
Space plan
Scenery
Sets
Stuff

13.4
Hierarchical 'layering'

- More stress on property and estate strategies;
- Renewed interest in briefing, and further consolidation of business and design targets.

Strategies based on shell-and-core or space guidelines for space planning are no longer sufficient. Space plans must not cut off options for new layouts. Potential for moving cores if necessary may even be required.

Flexibility at one level does not guarantee flexibility elsewhere – often the reverse. For example, buildings which are designed around their space plans often introduce onerous constraints. A fixed furniture system may offer occupants no options to fine-tune their seating position and furniture so that they can try to mitigate adverse effects of, say, glare or low winter sun. Any changes may have to be carried out by the facilities managers. In one instance, external consultants had to be called in every time the furniture needed to be moved! It is usually better to avoid dependency of this sort – occupants are capable of making these minor changes for themselves, they are happier and problems and costs for managers are avoided. However, the trend is towards greater dependence, not less. Occupants are increasingly having control and adjustment options taken away from them. This, in turn, places a higher burden on the technical and management systems that are supposed to provide these services – and makes them more vulnerable as well. This is why occupants say they are less comfortable in buildings that may offer relatively good internal environmental conditions, but have less perceived control options; in the jargon, fewer 'adaptive opportunities' (Brager and de Dear, 1998).

In Britain, commercial and professional pressures have tended to divide and rule so that integration between architects and engineers can be minimal sometimes, even in so-called integrated design practices. Parts of the design can easily fall in the gaps between areas of professional responsibility with no-one owning the problem. Some of these gaps turn out to be crucial for occupants' welfare, for example, the stability of the indoor environment and opportunities to change conditions quickly when required. Anecdotal evidence from Scandinavia and the Netherlands indicates that under global market pressures their previously better-integrated design cultures may be forced down this course as well.

Key considerations are:

- Develop clear strategies for flexibility and adaptability and keep them under review.
- Identify risky constraints at each level of the hierarchy and explicitly flag them up for designers or managers, making sure that they are fully 'owned'.
- Unless there are circumstances which require specialised optimisation, do not allow any one issue to dominate the others, for example, the space plan or optimising the irrelevant servicing considerations (see Bordass, 1992).
- Allow for changes at any level, including those that may be seemingly unthinkable, like the shell and structure but don't get carried away – robust simplicity is also most important; and do not forget that many parts of the building may be appropriately permanent.
- Flexibility can be hindered if options are restricted further up the hierarchy. This can be specially vexing for certain types of building services, for example, building cores obstructing the best routes for ducts, or adaptability thwarted by lack of consideration of site constraints.

Different standpoints

Flexibility and adaptability take on different meanings depending on your standpoint. Users and occupants often want short-term flexibility, answering specific local needs as fast as possible. Facility managers may be more concerned about occupant control and speedy and cost-effective changes in furniture layouts. Designers may think about possible image changes, and certainly issues like capacity, turnover, space fit, densities and layout types. Corporate managers may be more concerned with how easily they can sell or re-let the building if they no longer need it and so get locked in to property market criteria whether or not these actually benefit the users. All of them will want their needs to be met reasonably quickly, with as little fuss and cost as possible.

For any of them, it makes sense to bring the action as close to the point of demand as possible. The problem, though, is that requirements conflict and it is not obvious:

- what the needs are, especially in the future when contexts may subtly change;
- where priorities lie;
- where risks are greatest.

Specialised buildings tend to become obsolete fastest, while bespoke buildings – specialised or not – are anathema to valuers and letting agents, so stifling innovation. On the other hand there are still many spectacular examples of unlikely function changes inside seemingly specialised structures, particularly if they have become respected parts of the landscape (Brand, 1994).

Does the designer:

- Play safe with industry norms (for example British Council for Offices, 2000);
- Opt for more generic, context-free approaches, gambling on accelerating trends towards convergence of function (for example offices and laboratories becoming more similar);
- Take a longer-term view, attempting to combine this with emphasis on lower environmental impacts;
- Place greater faith in promising new technology (for example Doxford

photovoltaic building, Sunderland, UK) while gambling that accommodating new constraints (the photovoltaic wall) does not compromise other considerations (such as office layouts forms);
- Fit suitable strategies to prevailing circumstances, perhaps giving priorities to costs in use, manageability, occupants' needs, and taking a more pronounced demand side perspective.

Our view is that attention to the demand side, minimising environmental impact and carefully reviewing the extent to which generic solutions are appropriate will yield effective results in the longer-term; though it may take some time for market valuations to catch up.

Greater account must be taken of needs – and resolving conflicts between them. This implies more emphasis on:

- brief taking;
- future business and organisational scenarios;
- social, economic and technical changes in the background;

all of which give further colour to demand.

Bringing action closer to need

Bringing action as close as possible to perceived need while minimising the need for vigilance at other levels is usually an important objective. At lower levels of the building hierarchy this can be obvious. For instance, when you switch on a light (action) you want the response to give you the result you require (need). The faster the need is met by the action, the better. Any extra thought required (if the switch's operation is unclear), involvement of others (for example ringing a helpdesk) or delay in response adds unnecessary complexity, inefficiency and cost. When action does not meet need, the system is often said to be inflexible or inefficient. When it is difficult to change, it has poor adaptability.

However, things are not so straightforward as you go higher up the building hierarchy. Lags between demand and supply (the demand for space may not be in the same place as spare capacity), geographical inertia (the tendency for organisations to stay rooted to a familiar area) and longevity (only about one per cent of, for instance, the UK building stock is renewed every year and market lock-in [Bordass, 2000]) all conspire to create mismatches and inefficiencies. These inequalities drive fluctuations in property markets, giving them their peculiar character (Investment Property Databank, 1994). With individual buildings, it is unusual to find a perfect fit between preferences and the facilities provided – buildings which in the eyes of their occupants, owners, managers and designers are 'just right'. But 'good enough' is usually sufficient ('satisficing' rather than optimising). Beyond this, if the building lacks adaptability it may be replaced or abandoned.

Conclusions, with contradictions

Without being too theoretical or technical, what are the main lessons to be learned from this? Seven emerge, but sometimes they contradict each other!

1   What do you really need to change?

More uncertainty in the world leads to demands for more flexibility: but how much is really required, and where? Can simpler, more generic, but adaptable building types which get some basic things right actually prove liberating, not constricting? Is it best to adapt the building, to adapt to the building, or to change the building? Flexibility of movement within a diverse and fluid property market could make up for some of the shortcomings of individual buildings in a more static market. And how can we make better adaptive use of the buildings we already have, a significant portion of which (particularly from the 1950s to the 1970s) are now unloved not because of a lack of potential but a lack of imagination, fashionability and market value?

2   Know your timescales

We define flexibility as primarily about short-term changes and adaptability about less frequent but often more dramatic ones. Try not to confuse the two: while ideally they are complementary, in practice they can easily conflict. For example, it is not unusual for air conditioning distribution systems installed to improve flexibility to also physically obstruct adaptations one would like to make.

3   Hidden costs

Flexible concepts for buildings often provide fewer physical obstacles, particularly to any space plan which fits within the boundary conditions. However, the downside is often much higher dependency on technical and management infrastructures than anybody had anticipated. In addition, the technology has often proved to be less flexible and more prone to obsolescence than one had thought, viz: the amount of nearly-new materials and equipment which are often scrapped when an office is fitted-out or refurbished.

4   Dependency cultures

Flexibility concepts (for example, deep plans), equipment (for example interlocked serviced furniture) and technologies (for example automated internal environments) can deprive occupants of the ability to make even small adjustments, causing them to be disgruntled, make more demands upon management, or both. The costs of this – in terms of the degree to which the quality of the building needs to be improved, together with management and the expensive support services required – are often ignored, or at best badly underestimated. But if these demands are not met, occupant dissatisfaction and lost productivity will result.

5 *Hierarchical layering*

The strategic 'layering' of a building (shell, services, scenery etc.) helps to avoid unwanted rigidity by minimising interlocks between elements with different functions or with different timescales for maintenance, alteration and replacement. However, by excessive reductionism, and the splitting of activities into single issues dealt with by narrow specialists (like space planning), it can also get in the way of holistic design and strategic integration. This in turn can destroy context, reduce added value, and increase the loads a building imposes on the environment through unnecessarily wasteful consumption of fuels and materials.

6 *Generic buildings: tonic or tragedy?*

Will we benefit most from more standardised solutions or from rich and chaotic diversity? We see hope in reducing the number of unnecessary variables and seeking out more generic solutions which aim to better satisfy the needs of investors, occupants and the environment. How in practice will this differ from the North American reductionist, standardised approach which tends to destroy context and create widely-accepted, competitive, but often far from optimal, industry standards?

7 *If in doubt, leave it out*

The essence of adaptability is to invest in the outset in the things you are really going to need, and to leave to others the option of adding (or subtracting) things you are not sure about. Of course, this is not easily done in a changing world, but nevertheless it is usually possible to reach some sort of verdict.

Agendas for the future include:

- Briefs which are explicit about need, and try to make hidden assumptions crystal clear for all concerned.
- Adaptable envelopes and structures, at least in parts of the building which can benefit.
- Building shells which are better at selectively moderating the external climate.
- Intrinsically-efficient building services which adopt 'gentle engineering' principles and good controls to fine tune the environment efficiently and only to the extent needed.
- Where necessary, 'plug and play' supplementary components which can easily be obtained, installed, and relocated to alter building services' provision and capacity.
- More rounded understanding of future scenarios, especially from the perspective of businesses and their progress, and the social, technical and environmental constraints most likely to affect businesses, buildings and their locations.

So what to do?

- Consider all types of risks and constraints affecting buildings, not just the obvious or fashionable ones – acute and chronic, short-term and long-term – and work on all of them.
- Take a demand-side perspective which starts with revealed needs and preferences, especially within the immediate context of business and organisational requirements – and work towards more abstract supply-side issues, rather than the other way round as has tended to be the case.
- Think of potential downsides and their consequences, emphasising the thresholds where action meets the point of need (for example, the trigger points when people become uncomfortable and decide to do something about it; or what happens if the building becomes too big or small for you).

- Adopt a perspective which treats constraints in a positive way, so that potential bugs become features. Most great designs – especially the most usable – are like this, apparently making insuperable constraints disappear altogether. Of course, they never do; both potential and constraints have been turned to human advantage – the essence of human adaptability and the hallmark of progress.

Note

1   Probe (Post-Occupancy Review Of Buildings and their Engineering) is a research project which started in the UK in 1995 and was concluded in 2002. Twenty-one building studies have been published (20 UK, 1 Dutch) in *Building Services*: the CIBSE Journal. As well as the original Probe articles, there are many other supporting papers. An up-to-date list may be found on www.usablebuildings.co.uk by following the Probe link.

References

Bordass, W. (1993) 'Optimising the irrelevant', *Building Services Journal*, September, pp. 32–4.

Bordass, W. (2000) 'Cost and value, fact and fiction', *Building Research and Information*, vol. 28, no. 5/6, pp. 338–352.

Bordass, W., Bunn, R., Leaman, A. and Ruyssevelt, P. (1995) 'Probe 1: Tanfield House', *Building Services Journal*, Sep, pp. 38–41.

Bordass, W. and Leaman, A. (1997) 'From feedback to strategy', Buildings in Use '97 Conference: How buildings really work. London, Commonwealth Institute, February 25.

Bordass, W., Leaman, A. and Standeven, M. (1998) 'Probe 13: Charities Aid Foundation', *Building Services Journal*, February pp. 33–9.

Brager, G. and De Dear, R. (1998) 'Thermal adaptation in the built environment: a literature review', *Energy and Buildings*, vol. 27, pp. 83–96.

Brand, S. (1994) *How Buildings Learn*, New York: Viking.

British Council for Offices (2000) *Best Practice in the Specification for Offices*, London: British Council for Offices.

Chapman, J. (1991) 'Data accuracy and model reliability', *Proceedings of BEPAC 91 Conference*, Watford: Building Environmental Performance Analysis Club.

Duffy, F. and Worthington, J. (1972) 'Designing for Changing Needs', *Built Environment*, vol. 1, no. 7, pp. 458–63.

Energy Efficiency Office, (1991) *Best practice programme: Good practice Case Study 21: One Bridewell Street, Bristol*, Watford: BRECSU.

Investment Property Databank and University of Aberdeen on behalf of the Royal Institution of Chartered Surveyors (1994) *Understanding the Property Cycle: economic cycles and property cycles*, London: RICS.

Parsloe, C.J., (1995) *Overengineering in Building Services: an international comparison of design and installation methods*, BSRIA Technical Report TR21/95, Bracknell: BSRIA.

Standeven, M., Cohen, R., Bordass, W. and Leaman, A. (1998a) 'Probe 14: Elizabeth Fry Building', *Building Services Journal*, April, pp. 37–41.

Standeven, M., Cohen, R., Bordass, W. and Leaman, A. (1998b) 'Probe 16: Marston Book Services', *Building Services Journal*, August, pp. 27–32.

Standeven, M., Cohen, R. and Leaman, A. (1996) 'Probe 6: Woodhouse Medical Centre', *Building Services Journal*, August, pp. 35–8.

Tenner, E. (1996) *Why Things Bite Back: new technology and the revenge effect*, London: Fourth Estate.

van Meel, J. (1998) 'The European Office: a cultural and architectural enigma?', PhD thesis, Technical University of Delft.

Weizsacker, E, Lovins, A. and Lovins, L. (1997) *Factor Four: doubling wealth, halving resource use*, London: Earthscan

Wilson, S. and Hedge, A. (1987) *The Office Environment Survey*, London: Building Use Studies.

always more expensive either. But nor are we suggesting designers need to innovate for innovation's sake. There is a balance to be struck between innovation by application and innovation by invention.

In essence our culture demands the provision of buildings which are attractive, make a positive contribution to the environment, represent good value for money, work as they were intended, do not injure people in the process and represent a responsible use of resources. The cost in real terms must also go down.

All of these are design issues. So we first have to ask the question 'What is design?' In essence it is the intellectual task which:

- Starts with conceptualising the solution
- Develops the means by which the solution can work
- Is completed by identifying in detail how each individual component can be manufactured/assembled together to form the built solution.

In the past there was a reliance on 'craft' detailing, in a culture where designers designed, and constructors built that which the designers had designed. As a result the non-integrated set of players were unlikely to achieve the overall project objectives. However, in the current climate there is increasing recognition that the design and construction of buildings is an integrated process and the supply chain must play a role in developing quality solutions. This was the case with the master stone masons in Wren's day and is even more important with the more sophisticated building systems available today.

The relationship of designers to the supply chain

When Wren designed St Paul's Cathedral, he acted as both engineer and architect. Since his day, the design and construction process has become progressively more fragmented due to the growth in specialisation and complexity of construction methods and technologies. With this specialisation, there has been a corresponding increase in the number of organisations and people with design responsibility on a project. In Wren's day, the processes and iterative nature of design were hidden within a single mind. The task today is to understand and to manage these processes across a team of designers. There is a need for each contributor to understand and enter the province of the other.

Design is an iterative process, making the exchange of design information quite different from that of physical goods in the traditional product-based supply chain. In a product-based supply chain, physical goods move along the chain with each tier adding value through some manufacturing process until the completed product (a car for example) is available to the end-user. The product becomes increasingly complex as it passes through each stage (e.g. by combining standard components), as it is transformed from raw materials into a customised product.

In the case of a construction project, a similar supply chain can be envisaged, where value is added when construction products flow up the chain. Standardised products (such as glass, steel and cement) are combined to provide more specialised components and systems (cladding and air conditioning, for example). The suppliers in the chain will be made up of a combination of design organisations (consultants): contractors (including those with design and/or management specialists); and subcontractors, depending on the method of procurement.

As with the supply chain, where standard products are converted into bespoke facilities, solutions in the design chain become increasingly specialised and complex. Standard solutions (such as standard design details) are combined to provide more comprehensive and bespoke design solutions.

Design chains are concerned with the flow of design information between the organisations collaborating on a project (Austin et al., 2001). They differ from supply chains in not having information flowing in one direction and material in the other. In design chains information flows both ways. Designers can be found as independent architects and engineers, and within other companies that produce components, assemblies or other systems. The need for these designers to communicate effectively in both directions is an essential requisite to achieving success. The management of the overall process and the team are both vital to the project's success.

There are several facets of management in this context:

- Those involved in the management of such a process must understand the process of design.
- There has to be recognition of the breadth of design skill required – some designers will have a broad perspective on the overall building, whilst others may be task-specific specialists who will focus on their centre of activity.
- To see that project objectives are defined and communicated to all team members – they all need to understand how their individual contributions impact on the whole.
- To plan how project objectives are to be achieved.
- To view and test proposed solutions against objectives.
- To monitor progress against the plan.
- To react proactively to deviation from the plan.
- To set realistic time scales for tasks.
- To establish mechanisms by which plans, programmes and actions can be achieved, reported and monitored.
- To develop a framework to involve people for their achievements in adding value.

- To examine, test and challenge existing conventions.

Innovative approaches in practice

I will illustrate some examples where integrated teamwork has provided exemplary results. Some examples occur in circumstances which are unusual perhaps even in emergency situations. Here – as in war – the noble in us all elevates the spirit to participate as team members resolved to protect and defend the common goals and overlook selfish or partisan interests. Unfortunately in 'peace time' we often revert to circumstances where common objectives are secondary behind individual goals. Teamwork integration ought not to be evident in exceptional circumstances but be the everyday norm.

Fast track: Boots Warehouse, Beeston, Nottingham

Following a devastating fire, which destroyed a 27,000 square metre warehouse at the Beeston Site, Nottingham, AMEC was called in within five days to assist Boots in the disaster recovery programme.

An extremely accelerated fast track programme was initiated to replace the facility with a new fully automated warehouse and facilities for 400 staff. Unless the factory was rebuilt in time to stock items scheduled for Christmas sales, the consequential losses would be enormous. This sense of urgency enabled the client to adopt a more dynamic approach.

One of the key factors for the success of this fast track project was the project philosophy. Boots chose an innovative partnering agreement, which replaced a typically hierarchical project structure with a flexible team approach.

This approach featured shared objectives, good communication and prompt decision-making, which focused on achieving the very tight deadlines, rapid start-up and continuous time improvement.

The critical success factor on this project was achieving a design and construction programme of eleven months, which is significantly less than accepted industry norms. The programme was achieved without sacrificing quality or cost benchmarks by establishing the following principles:

- Co-location of an integrated project management team, made up of Boots and AMEC staff.
- Location of core design team on-site.
- Application of two-stage tendering to avoid duplication and waste.
- Encouragement of supply chain integration.
- Incorporation of work package contractors within the design team, with co-location where practicable.
- Positive avoidance of traditional contractual disincentives.

As a result the first phase was handed over in eight months with the overall building completed in ten months. The materials handling system was finished one month later.

Building Down Barriers: MOD Sports Complex, Aldershot

Two projects at Aldershot and Wattishham were identified by the Ministry of Defence to serve as research and development initiatives to inspire project delivery, as part of the Building Down Barriers initiative (Holti et al., 1999). Results from these projects have been disseminated, and key success factors fed back into the MOD procurement regimes.

AMEC were involved in a sports complex at Aldershot. The project incorporated

a 6,000 square metre, two-storey building and featured an Olympic-size swimming pool, a double-sized sports hall that could be divided into two separate fully functional gymnasia, six squash courts, a weights and fitness suite, changing and office facilities and a cafeteria.

The MOD client identified their key drivers for change. These were to:

- Improve delivered functionality
- Reduce costs through the project
- Improve value for money
- Improve predictability of performance
- Remove conflict
- Improve quality and safety.

Their objectives – summarised by their project title 'Building Down Barriers' were:

- To develop an approach to facility delivery based on supply chain integration
- To demonstrate the benefits in terms of improved value for the client and profitability for the supply chain
- To assess the tolerance of the approach to the UK construction industry.

Seven principles for Building Down Barriers
The MOD established a philosophy which manifested itself in seven principles:

1 Compete through offering superior value
2 Make 'value' explicit: design to meet functional requirement for through-life cost
3 Establish long-term relations with key specialists
4 Involve the supply chain in design and cost development – using target costing, value management and risk management
5 Manage the supply chain through specialist clusters
6 Develop continuous improvement within the supply chain
7 Collaboration through leadership, facilitation, training and incentives.

14.4
**MOD Sports
Complex, Aldershot**

14.5
**MOD Sports
Complex,
Aldershot – gymnasium**

14.6
**MOD Sports
Complex, Aldershot –
swimming pool**

AMEC utilised a series of tools to incorporate the principles into the thinking and performance of the team. These are summarised in Figure 14.7.

Selection of the supply chain
As the road to improvement is almost inevitably paved with change, the selection of supply chain members was not to be based on lowest tendered price, but on a series of criteria including common cultural understanding, ability to work in teams and the commitment to achieve the overall objectives. These criteria were considered just as important as commercial competitiveness. Table 14.1 summarises the principles underlying the supply chain selection.

Benchmarking – a means of demonstrating value
As the long-term whole-life team performance was more important to the client than achieving the lowest capital cost, the team compared critical data relating to each component which demonstrated its long-term value. Evaluation criteria included:

14.7
Key Tools

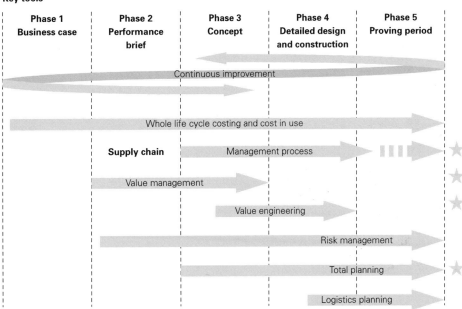

Table 14.1 Supply chain selection

What was different	What was the benefit/challenge?
• Specialist selected on 'soft' issues	• Compatibility with innovative nature of project • Need to produce a result which demonstrably meets the objectives
• Organisation offering potentially better value rather than lowest cost	• Gave rise to the need to demonstrate that value had been achieved • Need to motivate against tough targets
• Willingness to become involved in R&D – sharing results – exposure of working methods	• Capability to change • Culture not always present throughout the business

- Cost per unit/system
- Time (procurement, lead in, execution)
- Operating and maintenance costs
- Improvements in functionality – i.e. can one component to do the job of two or three?

Clustering

This is a term given to a group of specialist subcontractors who may have similar responsibilities and common characteristics i.e. the external envelope cluster may include roofing, cladding, windows and door subcontractors/suppliers.

Instead of packaging work to each individual and relying on them to resolve conflicts through technical queries with the potential for interface problems to fall in the gaps in between; the clustering concept brings all parties together to resolve interfaces, set common support elements and agree other issues face to face. Hence the parties work in collaboration with focus on a common objective. Figures 14.8 and 14.9 summarise the operation of clusters.

Some of the benefits of clustering are that it:

- Creates an opportunity for designers to interface directly with key suppliers.
- Focuses on key objectives.
- Focuses on long-term relationships and cooperation amongst key suppliers.
- Promotes supplier involvement.
- Promotes a collaborative team culture.
- Delivers enhanced performance.
- Removes interface issues and promotes common working methods.
- Can reduce preliminaries.

Value management

Another key tool used to capture priorities and subsequently evaluate proposals against them is Value Management (VM). This tool is often implemented through a series of facilitated workshops. The benefits include:

- Helps the client to crystallise requirements and priorities.

- Avoids use of alternative designs as 'Aunt Sallies'.
- Provides reference standards to test design options for best fit.
- Provides a brief which is:
  - Comprehensive
  - Understandable
  - Capable of easy communication.
- Provides a reference point for subsequent changes in clients' requirements.

In Building Down Barriers the sponsor developed the performance specification. The integrated project team established value criteria using value management methods. The

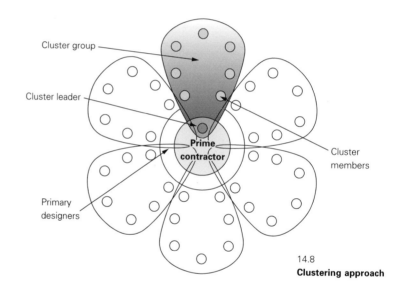

14.8
Clustering approach

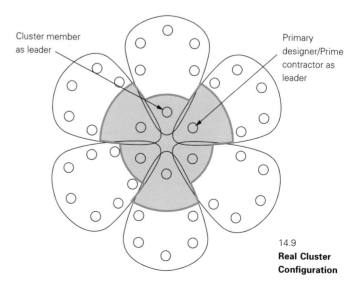

14.9
Real Cluster Configuration

project concept was developed by using value management techniques, incorporating end-users' knowledge, and applying specialist contractors' skills. Table 14.2 summarises the principles underlying the use of value management.

The main outputs from the value management and value engineering exercises were:

- Key stakeholder/end-user's requirements better understood
- Significant reduction in client variations
- Functionality and value for money achieved

- Programme saving
- Significant life cycle cost saving by using a combined heat and power (CHP) unit.

Planning and programming
Traditionally design teams manage their own design programmes, and the contractor issues his own construction timetable. At some point the contractor would usually make a request of each party – whether design or subcontractor, for the final release of information to adhere to the relevant programme milestones.

AMEC chose to undertake a totally integrated planning approach with all

Table 14.2 Value management principles and benefits

What was different	What was the benefit
• Involvement of user groups	• Ownership and buy in to the drivers and adopted solutions – few change
• Involvement of integrated project team	• A deeper understanding of clients' needs and improved functional efficiency
• Involvement of specialist supply chain members	• Major component selection and buildability resolved at the right stage

Table 14.3 Value engineering principles and benefits

What was different	What was the benefit
• Involvement of supply chain specialists	• Significant reduction in cost and improvements in manufacturing delivery and erection
• Considered component selection over 35-year life cycle	• Robust maintenance and replacement cost predictions
• Considered building performance over 35-year life cycle	• Robust prediction of utility usage

Table 14.4 Total planning process changes and benefits

What was different	What was the benefit
• Important of techniques from other industries	• Increased clarity of the process
• Total team input	• Team ownership of the result
• Fully mapped processes	• Greater certainty and predictability of outcome and opportunity to improve efficiency
• Planned to a high level of detail	• Real aid to production at the work face
• Use of last planner technique	• Caused focus on finishing activities, NOT starting

contributions integrated into the design, procurement and execution process. Each member was made aware of the criteria influencing the success of each party.

Results and lessons learned from Building Down Barriers
The key results, which can be benchmarked against other projects of the Building Down Barriers process on this project, included:

- Functionally superior design solution (Architects FaulknerBrowns)
- Only seven client variations
- Whole cost reduction of 13.7 per cent
- Significant improvements in team efficiency including reduction in waste and abortive work.

At a subsequent MOD conference the client reported the benefits as:

- Labour efficiency levels reaching 65–70 per cent (this is exceptional when compared with the Building Research Establishment (BRE) best practice level of 54 per cent and the industry norm of around 30–40 per cent).
- Up to 113 per cent improvement in productivity of blockwork.
- Up to 60 per cent reduction in cost of substructure.
- Material waste approaching 0 per cent compared to best practice benchmark of 10 per cent and industry norm of around 30 per cent.
- Reduction in construction time of 25 per cent.
- Reduction in through-life cost target of 10–14 per cent.
- Only 0.2 per cent rework (below industry norm of 10 per cent).

The whole approach also highlighted several lessons that have been developed and applied in subsequent projects:

- Importance of continuous training and facilitation of the integrated team to bring about cultural change – a major effort.
- Alignment of IT for easier communications.
- Importance of performance measurements to monitor achievement and provide information for current and future improvement.
- Recognition that not all organisations/individuals have the capability to change or add value.
- Importance of accurate and ongoing benchmarking to establish criteria for measuring value and improvement.

Partnering: BAA and the 'Pavement Team'

The logical development of a single project integrated team is to harness the benefits through utilising that same team for repeat work. BAA have demonstrated their commitment to achieving these ongoing benefits by selecting architects and other consultants and contractors to work with them on a partnering basis. Repeat business offers the opportunity for stable business, increased profits and, most of all, better managed projects with the same participants continuing to provide valuable feedback and year on year improvements for the client.

Following the award to AMEC by BAA of their first partnering agreement, AMEC has pioneered a new age in civil engineering procurement. After many years experience in producing high performance pavements for the demanding civil and military airfield environment, AMEC undertook all BAA airport pavement works at Heathrow, Gatwick, Stansted and Southampton, as part of a £150 million rolling programme of work. The 'Pavement Team', as they are aptly known, are based at Gatwick and had a £30 million annual turnover, with an aim to slash pavement costs to US levels. A five-year framework agreement has brought many benefits, including reduced overheads, a better planned workload and continuity of expertise. Central to partnering is the use of the New Engineering Contract with its clear definition of the sharing of risk.

Other tools and techniques to aid team integration

Beyond the examples cited above there are other tools and techniques designed to aid total team integration and the consequent smooth running of projects. They include:

- Common software systems
- Electronic documentation transfer
- Common CAD systems
- Web-based (paperless) document storage and retrieval
- Project intranets
- Simplified procurement methods using e-trading and framework agreements
- Adopting mechanisms to protect continuous profits whilst encouraging drive for increased value and reduced costs
- Integrated CAD/CAM software to ease the transfer of design information from consultants through to fabricators
- Site-based integrated teams
- Regular client/team feedback sessions where key learning points are captured and incorporated in working methods
- Adopting a blameless culture – relying on team and peer pressure to perform and where the team take collective

responsibility for the overall project results and problems which arise.

Conclusion

In his report on the UK Construction Industry *Constructing the Team* (1994) Sir Michael Latham highlighted the fuzzy edge between designers and the supply chain as a significant cause of poor performance in construction. This was – and still is – a key issue which the industry needs to address. It is only through the cooperation and integration of all parties in the construction process, and the widening of understanding across all team members of each other's roles and interests, that the management of design and construction will achieve the project benefits possible.

Acknowledgements

The assistance of Gerald Osborne in the preparation of this chapter is acknowledged.

References

Austin, S., Baldwin, A., Hammond, J., Murray, M., Root, D. Thomson, D., and Thorpe, A. (2001) *Design Chains: a handbook for integrated collaborative design*, London: Thomas Telford.

Construction Task Force (1998) *Rethinking Construction*, London: DETR.

Holti, R., Nicolini, D. and Smalley, M. (1999) *Building Down Barriers: prime contractor handbook of supply chain management*, London: Ministry of Defence.

Latham, M. (1994) *Constructing the Team*, London: HMSO.

Part 4

Measuring quality and value

Can design quality be measured? What are the implications if it cannot? If it can be measured, how should this be done and by whom? What are the advantages of measurement of quality, and what are the disadvantages? The four chapters in this section of the book address these difficult questions head on. In Chapter 15, *Inclusive maps*, Sunand Prasad makes a key observation – that for projects where there has to be public accountability, if something cannot be measured it is deemed not to exist. Such an attitude puts qualities like elegance, invention and wit at risk. Paul Wheeler makes a similar point in Chapter 18 in relation to the development of Housing Quality Indicators – that when value for money is being assessed, costs are easily identifiable, but value is much more difficult to measure. If there are no adequate means of differentiating between options on grounds of quality, the least cost option will always be chosen. The consequences for social housing, as Wheeler's chapter explains, were that quality was being driven down.

In his carefully written essay, Prasad discusses the issue of measurement, notes how intoxicating the numerical capture of value can become and, at worst, how over-simplistic evaluation can displace difficult questions of judgement in spheres like aesthetics and ethics. He suggests too that measurement is often seen as a threat to those things that are held as most precious in architecture – the surprising, simultaneous, civilising and place-making aspects of the built environment. However, as he also explains, to reject measurement is to ignore its value for communication and transparency – and for making explicit the relationships between subjective and objective criteria. He illustrates how widespread numerical evaluations are, even in subjective areas like judging vegetables. And he notes the growth of a measurement culture nationally, including its introduction into construction via the Construction Task Force's *Rethinking Construction*.

Rethinking Construction proposed two remedies for construction – lean thinking and performance measurement – both of which had been successfully employed in the manufacturing sector. But the Key Performance Indicators which emerged for construction were concerned almost entirely with the process – measuring completion on time, to budget and with an acceptable site safety record. As Prasad explains, the Construction Industry Council recognised that the quality of the product remained unmeasured and was at risk of being considered not to exist. In consequence, the CIC launched a research project to devise Design Quality Indicators (DQIs), which are intended to provide a framework for including both objective and subjective criteria and to ensure that so-called unmeasurable issues are not confined to the margins of debate but are retained at the centre.

Where Prasad describes some of the philosophical issues surrounding measurement, in Chapter 16, *Achieving quality in building design by intention*, Michael Dickson continues the story of the Design Quality Indicators in a pragmatic vein. The DQIs draw from a wide range of initiatives that can be traced as far back as the Vitruvian principles of firmness, commodity and delight. They also draw on the criteria used in various construction industry awards, as well as on the Housing Quality Indicators and similar initiatives. The Indicators are organised as a series of attributes, grouped under three sections of *functionality*, *build quality* and *impact*, each of which is further subdivided into subsections. Building projects can be assessed against these at various stages between project inception and handover. The Indicators benefited from pilot studies, followed by trail-blazing by up to sixty organisations.

Chapter 17, *Building indicators of design quality*, gives the research background to the development of the Design Quality Indicators. Its authors, Jennifer Whyte, David Gann and Ammon Salter, are the team formerly at the Science Policy Research Unit responsible for the development of the DQIs. They argue that

performance measurement is vital to improving performance, and that there is better understanding of design value in other sectors such as manufacturing, that benefit from better connectivity with customer preferences. In the built environment, design quality is more difficult to understand and to measure – particularly where there are more stakeholders. The team reviewed a number of indicators both within and beyond the built environment, concerned with building performance, construction process, value management, and sustainability. They considered in detail the criteria that underpin design awards. Their chapter describes the ambitions for the DQIs in terms of its ease of use, its ability to capture the diverse views of various stakeholders, and the importance of flexibility – in that it should be sensitive to the differing objectives of various types of project. The chapter describes the conceptual framework that was established, the data-gathering component, and the weighting mechanism.

As might be expected from something concerned with design quality, visualisation of the results was carefully considered. The DQIs were piloted on five different building projects and a wide range of issues emerged – for example how to capture a full range of responses to a building that was used by many different occupants, and how to combine them to provide an overall evaluation. Other questions to be faced are: if resources are limited, whose views should be sought? and if few evaluators are used, how representative can an individual's judgement be? The pilot studies also revealed previously unanticipated uses for the system of Indicators – as a means of assisting clients in procuring better buildings, as a briefing tool to encourage design team discussion, and as a means of comparing and contrasting the results for different buildings. As the Indicators become more widely used and a databank of the results builds up, it will be possible to look at the patterns in the evaluations and identify the strengths (and weaknesses) of modern buildings. This should provide feedback for the design professions and help to raise design quality.

In Chapter 18, *Housing quality indicators in practice*, Paul Wheeler discusses the background to the HQIs, together with their purpose and development. Wheeler provides a specific instance of a general point made by Prasad in Chapter 15 – that in the absence of an accepted measure of quality (other than meeting minimum standards set by regulation) cost became the dominant criterion for social housing from about 1980. A decade later, there was a realisation by government that meeting regulatory minimum standards did not ensure quality or value for money in housing provision, nor whether the dwellings were likely to meet the current and future needs of occupiers. As an antidote, the HQIs were developed in the late 1990s to evaluate both social and private-sector housing, in a way that made them both practical in use, and defensible. There are ten quality indicators, each of which is made up of about twenty to thirty different criteria.

The system of HQIs was extensively piloted in thirty-one housing schemes from twelve different developers, and including both private sector and social housing. The pilots provide considerable experience of evaluating housing, and a dataset from which a number of checks could be undertaken. These included correlation between the assessments of different assessors – such as researchers, developers and residents – of the same scheme, and also the pattern of indicators across all schemes. The pilot studies revealed the importance of assumptions built into the Indicators, for example about space standards in private versus social housing, about urban versus rural locations, and about circulation space versus living space. They also revealed that the HQI system is time-consuming in use, and a need for extensive briefing or training in HQI assessment to ensure consistency and accuracy. Most significant of all is Wheeler's closing remark – that if we are to provide design quality in housing, a deeper understanding of how homes are used is required.

Chapter 15

Inclusive maps

Sunand Prasad

The sign of a truly educated man is to be deeply moved by statistics.

Bernard Shaw

Every time a new set of statistics comes out, I can't help feeling some of the richness and mystery of life gets extinguished.

David Boyle, the *Observer*, 14 January, 2001

Microsoft assets amount to 6% of what the company is worth – 94% is in the intangible assets that the accountants cannot measure.

Charles Leadbetter[1]

There is today an understandable and widespread discomfort about the tyranny of measurement – especially in the version that has spread in modern administrative culture, for example in Britain post-1979. It appears that in this culture *what cannot be numerically measured is deemed not to exist*. Scores,

targets, performance indicators, league tables and business cases often dominate judgements of worth, and without them it is difficult to satisfy standards of public accountability and indeed to obtain funding for public projects.

But how is one to measure art, elegance, invention, wit?

A notable ancestor of this culture of hard measures, Jeremy Bentham, defined poetry as a literary form where the lines don't reach the margins. It was from such post-enlightenment antecedents that modern architecture in its turn developed a reductivist version of functionalism. For Hannes Meyer, one of the most ardent champions of pure functionalism, the subjective was inadmissible in the activity of designing buildings.[2] What could not be apparent to Meyer was that his own great skill as an architect – rather than his method – was responsible for the quality of his buildings, particularly their formal strength.

In one way or another architecture – of all disciplines the one where science and art should be creatively reconciled – has continued to have difficulty reconciling the objective and the subjective. Partly in reaction to the poverty of narrow functionalism, there is amongst architects a strong undercurrent of opposition to any attempt to systematise the evaluation of the work of architecture. There is a real fear that measuring quality will have a corrosive impact on architecture as art, and reduce it to mere infrastructure.

But if the guardians of the public purse believe that *it does not exist if you cannot measure it*, how do you even begin to argue a case for the value of design – for the real economic and social value that high quality design can add?

Rethinking construction

In 1998 the Government's Construction Task Force – one of then sixty or so task forces initiated by the recently elected and most managerial of British Governments – one that set 8000 numerical targets in its first three years – published *Rethinking Construction*, also known as the Egan report after its chairman (Construction Task Force, 1998). The report's trenchant and well-argued criticism of the construction industry and its proposed remedies were underpinned by two key theologies: *lean thinking* and *performance measurement* (leaving aside for the present a third and tacit belief that *big is beautiful*). Both of these approaches have shown spectacular results in modern manufacturing, for example in motorcar production and in electronics. For Egan, with his background in the motor industry, there were clear parallels with the state of the construction industry. He had seen car manufacture draw away from outdated methods of mass production to make goods that responded far better to customer's and indeed (because of emission and safety regulations) society's needs while becoming relatively cheaper. To do so, deeply entrenched habits and attitudes had had to be overturned.

An industry which had been in a mess had managed to achieve a real culture change and provided there was the will, construction could do the same, though in its own way.

At the conclusion of the Construction Task Force's work the Government set up the Movement for Innovation (M4I) to encourage action in the public and private sectors in response to the report. The key agents for change were to be: (a) demonstration projects that used innovative methods, and (b) an industry standard performance measurement tool – called Key Performance Indicators or KPIs. These indicators were concerned almost entirely with process. A building project would be deemed a success if it was completed on time, to budget, with an acceptable site safety record and a reasonable score for client satisfaction. There was no mention of the quality of the product in any other terms. The danger loomed that process measures would become the sole criterion of project success. It became clear to a number of people involved with M4I that putting in place parallel performance indicators was the only way to register the profound importance of a building's design for the quality and productivity of its inhabitants' lives. The Construction Industry Council raised funds to devise Design Quality Indicators (DQIs), which are described more fully in Chapters 16 and 17.

The decision to devise DQIs might be taken then to contain all the intellectual rigour of the position: *if you can't beat 'em, join 'em*. But it would be more accurate to describe it as an act of appropriation. We have to distinguish between measurement and the uses to which it is put. To fear measurement is no more or less logical than to fear technology. Those with a critical and indeed sceptical attitude to measurement are best placed to make good use of it. *Measurement is too important to be left to the measurers.*

Less prosaically, the DQI exercise has forced us to confront more precisely the possibilities as well as the limits of measurement in the realm of phenomena that contain a mixture of the objective and the subjective, which is just about everything around us. The exploration of measurement has forced a gentle enquiry into the fundamental nature of the constructed world, of language and of the relationship between art, science and morals.

On measurement

Yes, the fear of a world reduced to numbers is understandable. But look at what we routinely and enthusiastically subject to measurement systems: gymnastics, pedigree dogs, prize vegetables, flower arrangements, ballroom dancing and song contests. Numbers tell us the quality of electronic goods, cars and domestic appliances. Numbers are part of everyday language and what is more, *numbers entertain*. When the skating judges hold up their placards – putting decimal points to the quality of a triple axel with a double lutz – we are thrilled. These numbers don't appear to be impediments to admiring or enjoying the artistry. We may not agree, and indeed nor do the judges amongst themselves. Because it occurs in a well understood context the numerical judgement becomes an adjunct or an aid to critical appreciation.

At the Crufts Dog Show each breed has a breed standard – a written description of the ideal dog of the breed. The judges compare the dog to this, but additionally they look at the 'dog's condition, coat movement and temperament' – all subjective values.[3]

A piece on 'Judging Vegetables' in the US magazine *Kitchen Gardener*, describes how Charles Dell has been judging vegetable contests for forty years in the Southern States. What does he look for? For example, 'an unblemished tomato that is true to type will always trump one with a cracked skin'. . . But even perfection does not guarantee blue

ribbons . . .' he adds mysteriously, ' . . . there's more to it than that'.[4] We can be sure that whatever this mystery ingredient may be, it's not food value or taste – when judging vegetables, in an inversion of the functionalist doctrine, visual appearance clearly comes first.

These numbers and systems are not a substitute for judgement. The important statistic is not that the performance scores 5.8 but that four out of five judges considered it the best. Numbers help us put the expert in context.

In a similar way consumers are able, through numerical analyses in specialist magazines, to inform themselves about the various aspects of goods – their functionality, their quality of build and manufacture, their performance, their appearance and style. They are presented with a sophisticated and differentiated range of numbers: hard measures, such as fuel consumption data; 'soft', often subjective assessments of experts; and survey data that converts 'soft' responses from customers into the hard fact of satisfaction levels. People may avidly read *What Car?*, *Which Hi-Fi?*, *Which?* and J. D. Power but then they, better informed, make up their own minds. Otherwise we would all be driving Subarus.[5]

Indicators and their purpose

At the outset the DQI exercise quickly confirmed the obvious – the factors that go to make up design quality are far more numerous, and interact in more complex relationships with each other than any of the examples cited above. In trials it is just this complexity that has been a key reason for the DQI tool's warm reception.

The DQI's development and logic is summarised in Figures 15.1 to 15.11. The tool is a map that helps people to consider the whole landscape of design quality. The three

Designing Better Buildings

quality fields of *functionality*, *build quality* and *impact* resonate with deep truths about the nature of the way our minds have constructed the world. The logic of the subsets of attributes within the fields and the simplicity of the method of considering them allow 'hard' and 'soft' values, the objective and subjective to be given due place in an inclusive way.

Design Quality Indicators are not intended for working out in any absolute sense which is the best design or building in any given context. It is possible people will use the tool to compare buildings, but the prime purposes are:

- To provide a framework to guide the setting of a holistic vision and intent for a building
- To test the progress of the design and the finished product against this intent
- To help conduct post-occupancy evaluations of buildings in use.

Universalist, officially promoted tools such as quality and performance indicators cannot be aimed at encouraging genius. They are for *raising the average*. In a condition where there is so much mediocre and worse-than-mediocre architecture and design in both the public and the private sector, raising the average is, if anything, a greater challenge than producing isolated works of brilliance. There appears to be no evidence that, by itself, the appearance of buildings highly acclaimed by architectural cognoscenti does much for encouraging quality and clients' aspirations generally. What is needed is to reach in a direct way those commissioning buildings and provide them with the means to raise their game. We have to increase the level of critical awareness amongst commissioning clients, the professions and the industry so that we all get a steadily improving built environment.

There is a whiff of gentlemen and players in architects' resistance to measurement. Builders, still essentially craft based in most trades, are subject to precise requirements for standards of workmanship and materials. Is it easier to capture numerically the quality of craft than art? Perhaps, but a considerable amount of the architect's role is craft and science. If we accept that in the best architecture all elements of design are beautifully integrated, then we cannot downgrade the craft and science components. And if we accept their presence there is little excuse to resist measures of quality, at least in these aspects.

It is a key strength of the DQI tool is that it visibly gives place to the contributions of the many and intricately linked attributes whose excellence in realisation will make a building a success for the client and user and possibly a notable work of architecture. It maps and registers these attributes in both a cognitive and structural way. It is an inclusive map.

Any seminar can generate large numbers of valid but mixed-up quality headings for aspects of design. This can easily lead to a boring checklist or a set of design tick-boxes. So what is the logical structure for a really serviceable design quality tool? First we have to see how all these headings or attributes belong to different categories.

15.1
Possible quality headings

spheres of aesthetics and ethics. Second, not only is the objective realm easier to capture through numbers and the written word, but this ease of capture finds a ready use in the demands of representative democracy. So there appears a new need for such ready packaging of purported value. Soon, if it can't be measured, it does not exist. The imperative of accountability, itself a consequence of manifest democracy, leads to an aversion in the public sphere to risk-taking. Reliance on measurement is both a consequence and a promoter of this condition. If decision makers can distance themselves from decisions by basing them on statistical fact they reduce the risk of censure on the grounds of poor judgement.

So the art of architecture is caught in a pincer movement between popular demystification promoted through numbers and administrative accountability based on reductivist measures. But to reject measurement and numbers is to ignore their value as language and their potential to increase transparency. If such systems are the vehicle for carrying a precious idea into parts of the culture it is not reaching, then so be it: *getting in under the radar*. The only way out of the pincer is to transcend the crude polarity between the objective and the subjective.

There is some evidence that a parallel realisation is taking place in science. Richard Wasserburg (2001) in a recent *New Scientist* argues strongly for that side of science which is not directly about being useful – 'impractical' science – and coming clean about the pleasure in its pursuit. A pleasure that can be shared with a wide public. A pleasure that is remarkably akin to the pleasure that art and architecture can give.

The Enlightenment's insightful and progressive differentiation between arts, sciences and morals has now to give way to a reintegration of these realms. In architecture there seems to be ready arena for practical action to this end. If we divorce the realm of subjective value entirely from the realm of numerical value we do violence to the integrity of architecture as a practical art – as distinct from a fine art – in the sense identified by Colin St John Wilson and others.[7] This does not mean that we have to make numerical prisons for subjective value fields. What is important is to make explicit the relationship of the subjective fields to objective and ethical fields: to construct a framework for the judgement of value which is inclusive by honouring and placing in a proper relationship all aspects of the art.

But will the means of judgement become embedded in the methods of creation? If we place the subjective – the quality field of 'Impact' – too precisely in the context of the objective – functionality and build quality – will it promote a crude differentiation of the complex elements of the act of design?

It is impossible to forecast what effect a judgement system will actually have in practice. Did British architecture suddenly refract into disjointed components as soon Sir Henry Wootton translated the Vitruvian triad as 'Commodity, Firmness and Delight?'[8] Architecture then did not have to deal with the intrinsically ossifying tendencies of evidence-oriented bureaucracies, the Private Finance Initiative and European competition rules. Although there is a danger that like all systems and tools, the DQIs will be applied too mechanistically and their intent corrupted, this putative harm seems less of a threat than the real harm being done by the poverty of average standards of design of buildings today which are leading to real waste of public resources and a legacy of mediocre public buildings. The interesting aspect of the standards of design being criticised by the Commission for Architecture and the Built Environment and other bodies is how they are failing for the most mundane of reasons – lack of daylight, poor space allowance, and a downbeat environments for building users.[9] Transparency of evaluation criteria must make it more likely that quality will be addressed on a broad front, even if this is done as a checklist exercise. More profoundly the presence in the DQI tool of searching questions about the character of buildings, their appeal to the intellect, their integration with the urban and social realm demands explicit attention to such vital components of good architecture.

Nevertheless, the danger of a simplistic numerical approach to design derived from the DQI structure demands vigilance from its promoters and developers. The recognition that real design quality relies on the integration of all aspects must be embedded in such measurement systems. The rest is reliant on the level of critical awareness that will surround their use.

products, most notably cars. The manufacturer Subaru has consistently been placed first in recent years, as reported in magazines such as *What Car?*

6   Sir Henry Wootton *The Art of Building*, 1624: 'Well-building' hath three conditions: Commodity, Firmness and Delight'. Vitruvius used the words *Utilitas, Firmitas* and *Venustas*. (Marcu Vitruvius Pollio, De Architectura Libri Decem, 1st century BC).

7   A distinction made by T S Eliot as elaborated by Colin St John Wilson (1992) *Architectural Reflections*, Architectural Press, Oxford.

8   Sir Henry Wootton, *The Art of Building*, 1624.

9   CABE (the UK Government's Commission for Architecture and the Built Environment) has produced internal reports on schools built under the PFI which details these shortcomings. Similar criticism of health buildings have been widely reported. CABE has noted that such failings are not particular to PFI but to much design of public buildings. See also Audit Commission (2003) *PFI in Schools: the quality and cost of buildings provided by early Private Finance Initiative schemes*, London: Audit Commission.

Notes

1   Quoted in David Boyle (2001) *The Tyranny of Numbers*, New York: HarperCollins.

2   '. . . architecture as emotional act of the artist has no justification . . . building is nothing but organisation: social, technical, economic, psychological organisation'. Hannes Meyer, from a lecture at the Bauhaus, 1928.

3   Kennel Club website – www.crufts.co.uk

4   *Kitchen Gardner*, no. 23, Taunton Press, Connecticut, Oct/Nov 1999.

5   J. D. Power dominates the market in customer satisfaction surveys in connection with a number of

References

Construction Task Force (1998) *Rethinking Construction*, London: DETR.

Kant, I. (1929) *Critique of Pure Reason*, trans. Norman Kemp Smith. New York: St. Martin's Press.

Kant, I. (1956) *Critique of Practical Reason*, trans. Lewis White Beck. Indianapolis, IN: Bobbs-Merrill.

Kant, I. (1987) *Critique of Judgment*, trans. Werner S. Pluhar. Indianapolis, IN: Hackett.

Wasserburg, R. (2001) 'That's entertainment' *New Scientist*, 3 November.

Wilber, K. (1996) *A Brief History of Everything*, Boston: Shambhala Books.

Chapter 16

Achieving quality in building design by intention

Michael Dickson

Le Corbusier would have said that client, user, architect, engineer and constructor were all the same but different. Indeed we have to work holistically and in integrated supply chains for the successful creation of value in construction.

In the assessment of design quality, each individual responds differently to the artistic or scientific elements of a design. Le Corbusier argued that there needs to be creative tension between 'spiritual man' and 'economic man' for success. Nowadays one might add 'between different parts of the supply chain – clients, designers, specialist suppliers, and constructors'. In his model, knowledge 'of man' and of 'physical laws' are the drivers of creative imagination, beauty, freedom of choice and indeed of material, statistics, dynamics and calculation.

The actual response to a building or construction by each individual comes from the balance of their individual response to the range of stimuli – social, spatial, acoustic, visual, thermal – to the environment. In the real world this has to relate specifically to the discussions

about how the budget breaks down into its elemental parts – in the case of building development, between access and site development, landscape, entrance, built form and material usage, services and finishes, and indeed towards overall quality of specification. Without early resolution of the budgetary aspirations between client, users, designers and construction team, little real progress on quality is possible.

How is quality perceived?

The CRISP Design Task Group (see Chapter 12) whose focus was on capturing the value of good design, produced an interesting map of the pressures which range around the process of delivering the quality of product (see Figure 12.1 on page 138). The significance of this map is that it places *value systems* as the links between *product* and *process*, and acknowledges that the product is compressed by viewpoints, power, politics, and lifetime values.

This requires a sophisticated measurement system for tangible as well as intangible components. The diagram relates value systems of *delight*, *function* and *sustainability* to the therapeutic use of the product where user and community are both customers. There is, of course, also an alternative route embodying a slightly different value set via a more structured approach responding to political and financial influences. Another expresses the importance of monitoring the quality of both the *product* and *process* outcomes through the feedback loop. I find this diagram a useful starting point from which to discuss measurement of design quality in the context of delivering a product.

The Egan Report *Rethinking Construction* (Construction Task Force, 1998) placed an emphasis on a culture of measurement, monitoring and continuous improvement. This led to the development by the Movement for Innovation (M4I) of Key Performance Indicators (KPIs). Initially KPIs were all about measuring the *tangible* aspects of the process of construction; predictability of time, cost, freedom from defects and customer satisfaction. The work on Design Quality Indicators (DQIs) extends the method of assessment and monitoring to the design quality of the built product itself in order to evaluate the relative quality of a particular building.

The Construction Industry Council research programme is aimed at linking the M4I indicators in the construction process, *upstream* to the briefing and concept stages and *downstream* to the satisfaction experienced by end-users, developers, owners and society at large during occupation and use. It seeks to promote balance between the efficiency and effectiveness of the process, to delight and satisfaction with the product, which, after all, is destined to operate over many years and in different guises.

Design is recognised as having two distinct phases:

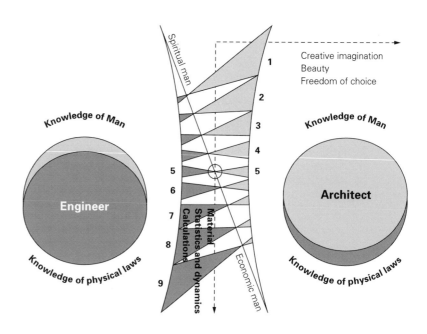

16.1
Creative imagination

- design for concept
- design for procurement.

The outcome of design can therefore be measured in two separate ways:

- satisfaction with the end product (CIC DQIs)
- realisation of the product (M4I KPIs).

Figure 16.2 shows this diagrammatically. It links the M4I 5–4-7 construction process improvement map to the activities of briefing, design, commissioning and operation.

The need for indicators for design

In 1989, The Building Centre Trust organised a seminar on 'Principles of Modern Building' at Templeton College in Oxford. Regrettably, the contracting side of the industry was poorly represented – a feature which at that recessionary time reflected the withdrawal of some of the major contracting companies from concern with design and construction to a primary focus on management and finance. The subsequent and substantial initiatives by

16.2
**Improving the
process and product**

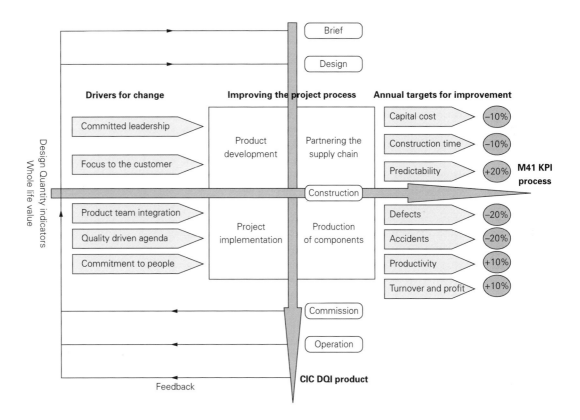

Latham *Constructing the Team* (Latham, 1994) and Egan *Rethinking Construction* (Construction Task Force, 1998) in the industry have attempted to correct this misalignment.

One of the outcomes of the Templeton workshop was *The Idea of Building* (Groak, 1992). In this slim and incisive work, Groak attempts to define *effective demand* which, for the following reasons, he finds complex:

- It is not clear who is stating the requirements: client, user or society.
- Participants have different ways of expressing their wants.
- Different people have different preoccupations – whether image, budget, purpose, or timing.

To quote:

> To build – speculatively or for a given purpose – means the creation of an economic asset, whether or not that was the prime motive. The large shift of

resources and the long lifetime of this asset and the costs of sustaining the building over a period, have meant the development of a set of large industries and complex financing methods. Their coherent management is only now beginning to be understood. Today many circumstances combine to make this process of building definition even more speculative:

- Demographic changes (for example, longer lives, urbanisation worldwide)
- Changes in location and nature of the workplace
- Changes in access to communications
- Changes in the organisational structures of industry and commerce
- A greater awareness of the environmental and energy impact of buildings and associated processes
- An increasing amount of consumer protection legislation, diminishing the significance of the traditional commercial warning 'let the buyer beware'.

In a way, he was building on earlier work from other cultures, such as that of James Marston Fitch in *American Building: the environmental forces that shape it* (Fitch, 1975), and American behavioural research (US National Bureau of Standards, 1974; Figure 16.3).

Contemporary to Groak is *Aesthetics of Built Form* (Holgate, 1992). This book was written primarily for the benefit of student engineers, to counteract their inclination to respond: 'Well it's just a building. Why should I have feelings about it?' Of course we all must – whatever our home discipline!

Towards measurable indicators

The CIC Steering Group comprised engineers, surveyors, architects and contractors, joined by representatives of the Confederation of Construction Clients, lay assessors and constructors. The research itself to devise the DQIs was contracted by the Science Policy Research Unit (SPRU) at the University of Sussex, and the principal researcher was David Gann.

At key stages the work has been discussed with the Commission for Architecture

of Built Environment (CABE), M4I, the Treasury, the Office of Government Commerce (OGC), the Urban Design Alliance (UDAL) and the Major Contractors Group. The DQIs build on various evaluation systems, particularly the evaluation criteria used in deciding awards for outstanding developments such as the British Construction Industry Awards (BCIA), RIBA and Civic Trust Awards, and so on. It also builds on the pioneering work on indicators by NHS Estates, as well as the Housing Quality Indicators, and studies by the Construction Industry Research and Information Association (CIRIA), CRISP, BRE and several other significant institutions in the field. Many were represented at the interim workshops run by the research contractor.

Among the individual influences on the development of the DQIs was a framework for evaluating design quality prepared by Susan Francis of the Medical Architecture Research Unit (MARU) presented at the CRISP Design Task Group workshop (Macmillan, 2000). She identified the overlapping features of therapy (delight), function (purpose) and sustainability (resources) in which:

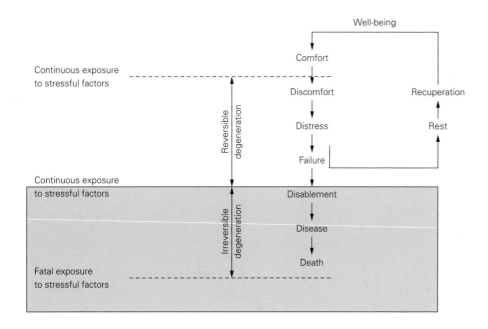

16.3
The impact of environmental factors

- Therapy relates to user perception, to psychology and to the appeal of form and space.
- Function to use for health care, of the site and satisfactory operation.
- Sustainability to social purpose, economics and environmental performance.

A similar set of design quality indicators emerged from the work conducted by the Quality Directorate of MOD in the *Breaking Down Barriers* initiative (Holti, Nicolini and Smalley, 1999). Here the terms used are:

- Architectural merit
- Internal quality
  - suitability for purpose
  - future adapability
- Accessibility
- Cost in use, ease of maintenance
- Environmental friendliness and energy efficiency
- Viability of the proposed procurement route
  - programme
  - construction method
  - use of materials
- Value for money (soundness of cost provision/risk assessment)
- Involvement of artists and crafts people.

Certainly quality in design is a difficult proposition to assess and measure. Giddings and Holness (1996) separate two components:

- Quantifiable performance attributes
- Non-quantifiable amenity attributes, such as contextual impact, aesthetics, and symbolic significance.

It is also possible to distinguish between environmental qualities that are subjective and those that are physical (Table 16.1).

Development of the Design Quality Indicator

Drawing on this wide variety of influences, the Steering Group and its research contractor developed what it believes to be a robust tool for indicating design quality. Chapter 15 has already shown some of the philosophical background and how the tool resulted from applying the design philosophy of Vitruvius to the practical, social, environment and financial constraints of procuring modern buildings, including the remarkable fact that the Vitruvian triangle of firmness, commodity and delight was found to be suitably robust as a starting point for twenty-first-century usage. Suitably updated, these became the sub-indicators of function, of build quality and of impact (see Figure 15.10 on page 181).

By considering the levels at which any particular element contributes to quality – defined as basic, added value or excellent, and by identifying within each of the three main sub-indicators the attributes that contribute to it, the overall DQI framework for assessment of relative quality was constructed (Figure 16.4).

Table 16.1 Distinguishing between subjective and physical qualities

Environmental quality (subjective)	**Environmental quantities (physical)**
• Character	• Temperature
• Atmosphere	• Illuminance
• Ambiences	• Sound levels
• Images etc.	• Ventilation rates etc.

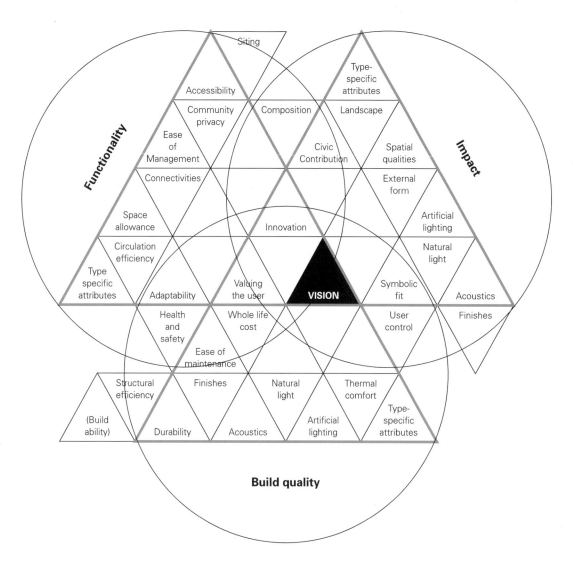

The drivers and conditioners of successful development – a necessary framework

Buildings are constructed, used and adapted within the constraints of finite resources. The end quality and value of a building have to be judged in the context of the aspirations and resources that its creators had for it and its location. Every building can therefore be said to be the product of the restraints of conditions consciously applied to its birth.

Consequently at its inception, every building project requires a clear perception of the conditions which apply to its delivery in order for it to be considered an all-round success. The approach to the value placed on the whole-life of that product and the value of the service, which its successful construction facilitates, is most significant – so-called *whole-life value*. Diagrammatically, the assessment of design quality then becomes constrained by the framework of development – finance, resources, time and whole-life value (Figure 16.5).

Such questions as:

- How long is the facility required to be in service (design life)?
- What is the likely comparison of initial capital costs of the construction itself as against the cost of occupation and maintenance of the facility (capex versus opex)?

16.5
**Constraints acting
on the framework of
development**

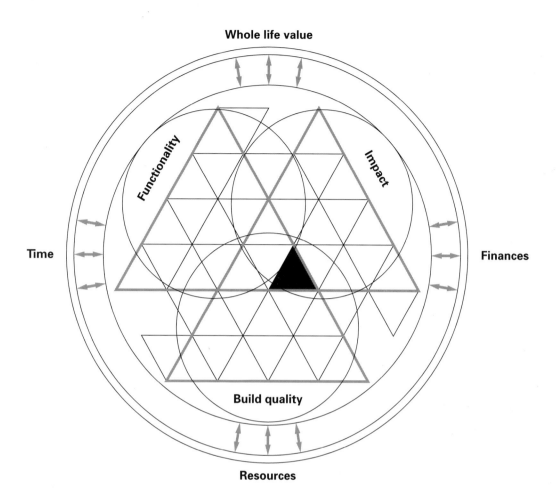

Whole life value

Functionality

Impact

Time

Finances

Build quality

Resources

- What are the opportunities for improving the productivity and comfort of operators (occupational opportunity)?

Then there are the immediate pragmatic concerns of:

- What are the financing arrangements or needs for procurement and operation?
- What are the time constraints which apply to practical completion and the income-generating requirements of the facility?
- How do the available technical, material and skills resources and legislative framework affect the development plan?

Such questions need addressing so that available budgets can be allocated and available resources apportioned to reflect the apparent risk, available time and required duties. Indeed

the successful building is often the direct outcome of creative response to these very constraints.

Process of design

Design is the activity that brings together all the contributions of the construction industry to produce a building that meets the customer's needs. It is essentially an holistic process which needs to draw together the skills and experience of a wide range of contributors working across discipline boundaries.

To make some sense of a measurement system for the value of design, consideration has to be made of the design process itself. There have been many descriptions of the design process but the clearest is a series of stages which divide into analysis, synthesis, evaluation and communication (Figure 16.6).

The overall design and procurement process can be seen as a series of decisions that lead progressively towards the built reality. The process is a stage by stage one with each stage described in the same terms, even though the content of each stage is different. To stand a hope of achieving broad-based design quality in the final product, many separate values have to be introduced into the recipe. These might be described as quality indicators which drive the development of the product model and are evaluated by a performance feedback loop in the stage (Figure 16.7).

The achievement of a good building requires a range of people with different education and interest to contribute to the process, all of them often doing different jobs and providing a variety of experience and skill. It has to be recognised that the quality of the process itself does not automatically result in a quality product.

The tool for design quality assessment has been designed to be applied at any stage of the Gershon gateway process of procurement and operation for buildings (Figure 16.8). It applies from the definition of the business case, through design, to procurement and onward to effective and productive operation in use. Primarily it allows one to track whether the initial intentions for the project have been met in the completed product.

Questionnaire

As a result of considerable development work, a simple questionnaire written in plain English for professional and layman alike, and intended to take no longer than twenty minutes to complete, has been formulated (see Figure 17.2 on page 200). The respondent is asked to score quality under the three principal sections of *functionality*, *quality of build* and *impact*, by

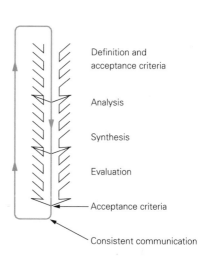

Definition and acceptance criteria

Analysis

Synthesis

Evaluation

Acceptance criteria

Consistent communication

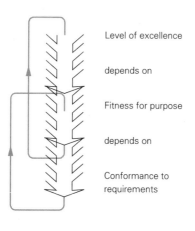

Level of excellence

depends on

Fitness for purpose

depends on

Conformance to requirements

16.6
The design process

Stages		Lead contributor	Value
Conception	DQ1	Client and architect	User productivity
Selection of form	DQ2	Architect and engineer	
Detail design	DQ3	Engineer and architect	Fitness for purpose
Detailing and fabrication and erection	DQ4	Contractor – Fabricator and engineer	
Operation and use	DQ5	User, owner	Delight

DQI

16.7
Levels of excellence

giving opinions on a range of subsections, shown in Table 16.2. Further details of the scoring and weighting mechanisms are given in Chapter 17.

Pilot studies

As part of the development programme, the DQI tool was successfully piloted on five projects, receiving positive responses from a wide range of respondents. Further details are given in Chapter 17. Each pilot enabled the team to refine language and to produce a tool that bridges the cultures and language of client (in the widest and narrowest sense), constructor, architect and other designers. The approach has been tested on a number of

representative bodies throughout the construction industry. The findings imply:

- real enthusiasm for the idea
- the conceptual structure is acceptable
- the questionnaire is about right
- the results are valuable and of genuine use.

It has also been agreed that the methodology is capable of being sectorised to a greater level of detail as required, for instance by the NHS Estates, for the assessment of performance of health buildings.

Although the value of using such a tool is now becoming widely recognised, this is very much still work in progress and it will need still further refinement. Such improvement will need additional time and further *beta* testing on a

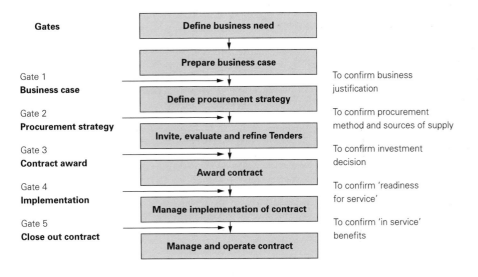

**16.8
Gershon Gateway
Process**

Table 16.2 The sections and subsections of the DQI tool

Section 1	Section 2	Section 3
Function	*Built quality*	*Impact*
• Location	• Construction	• Contribution to community and place
• Siting	• Engineering systems	• Form and materials
• Access	• Robustness	• Internal environment
• Space	• Performance	• Identity and character
• Use	• Integration	• Innovation and inspiration

range of completed buildings in order to achieve a genuinely interactive web-based version.

Conclusion

Initial feedback suggests the DQI tool is robust and readily understandable, applicable generically to all building types. It is designed to be used by professionals and lay people alike, and is intended for all who wish to see the quality of the built product improve. It complements existing indicators covering sustainability and construction process. It is aimed at addressing all parts of the industry – developers, designers, constructors, users and neighbours – by bridging cultural divides and easing communication between parties. It can be used by all parties at any stage of the design, procurement and occupation process to inform on the compromises that need to be made in the process to achieve affordable, enduring quality.

Acknowledgements

This paper is the result of an initiative started by Robin Nicholson when Chairman of the Construction Industry Council, and I would also like to acknowledge the assistance of the members of the CIC Steering Group and the research contractor, SPRU.

References

Construction Task Force (1998) *Rethinking Construction*, London: DETR.

Fitch, J. Marston (1975) *American Building: the environmental forces that shape it,* second edn, New York: Schocken Books.

Giddings, B. and Holness, A. (1996) 'Quality assessment of architectural design and design award schemes', *Environments by Design*, vol. 1, p53–68.

Groak, S. (1992) *The Idea of Building – thoughts and action in the design and production of buildings*, London: Spon Press.

Holgate, A. (1992) *The Aesthetics of Built Form*, London: Oxford University Press.

Holti, R. and Nicolini, D. (1999) *The Role of the Architect in the Integrated Supply Chain*, Tavistock Institute document CSNRO/168, December 1999.

Holti, R., Nicolini, D. and Smalley, M. (1999) *Building Down Barriers: prime contractor handbook of supply chain management,* London: Ministry of Defence.

Latham, M. (1994) *Constructing the Team*, London: HMSO.

Macmillan, S. (2000) *Report of the CRISP Design Task Group Workshop*, CRISP reference 99/18. Available on the CRISP web site at www.crisp-uk.org.uk

US National Bureau of Standards (1974) *Building for People – behavioral research, approaches and directions*, Washington, DC: US Department of Commerce, National Bureau of Standards SP474.

Chapter 17

Building indicators of design quality

Jennifer Whyte, David Gann and Ammon Salter

Performance measurement has become a vital part of the machinery to improve practices in the UK construction sector (Construction Task Force, 1998). The basis for most of the new approaches to measurement has been adapted from methods used in the manufacturing sector, with the main emphasis on process management and logistics. Lessons have been drawn from the literature on *lean production* and Japanese approaches to quality management (Monden, 1983; Schonberger, 1982; Womack and Jones, 1996). This has resulted in the introduction of a suite of benchmarking techniques and the development of key performance indicators (KPIs). The focus has primarily been on the measurement of processes, in which headline indicators have included metrics relating to time and cost of production. Measurement associated with the quality of production has also been developed and implemented, with the focus on waste and defects.

The development and use of performance measurement tools are more advanced in some areas than others, with the emphasis on performance in processes, rather than on the quality of design of products. Experience of performance measurement in some areas has also highlighted the dangers of becoming too reliant upon the issues that are easy to quantify, leading to ignorance of other factors which may be equally important, but difficult to measure. For example, it is more difficult to measure the whole-life value of a building than it is to measure its initial cost.

Design quality is an area that requires better understanding and which is difficult to measure. Following the successful development of indicators to measure the performance and sustainability of construction processes, various projects have attempted to develop indicators to measure design quality. The authors have been involved in one of these projects, which is developing and piloting generic Design Quality Indicators (DQI) for buildings.

As von Hippel (2001) argued, the users of products often have considerable information and ideas about what a product must achieve and do. Yet this information is sticky. It is often hard for users to express their preferences – they often do not speak the proper technical languages, they respond to products in immediate and direct ways with little structure. Companies use a wide range of techniques in trying to capture these reactions and integrate them into their new product development processes, but often after the fact and through a set of mediated relations, such as external consultants. In some areas of manufacturing there tends to be a better understanding of the value of design embodied in products and also better connectivity with customer preferences. For example, techniques such as Quality Function Deployment are used in the motor vehicle industry (Ward, Sobek *et al.*, 1995; Smith and Reinertsen, 1998; Clausing, 1994).

In the design of buildings, efforts at understanding customers often take place after the product has been developed and constructed. Information from users is not transferred to the design team in a shape and form that can be useful for reshaping the design. It arrives either too late or in a format that cannot be used by front-line designers and engineers. More often than not, sales and marketing or service departments receive this information and then pass it along to the production and design teams. This limits the direct flow of information and experience from customers to designers and producers.

The Design Quality Indicator (DQI) is an extension of the Egan agenda of mapping, measuring and managing the design and construction process. It places particular emphasis on the quality of design embodied in buildings – the outputs of construction. It therefore seeks to complement the existing mechanisms for examining the performance, providing feedback and capturing different perceptions of the value of design.

Measuring design and involving users

A review of the literature on design and design quality enabled us to identify gaps in the current range of tools available in the construction sector. It showed that although there have been a number of bespoke tools developed to assess quality in specific sectors, such as housing, there was no generic tool for assessing the design quality of buildings.

Quality measurement

Different indicators either in operation or in development include:

- End-user studies, such as Probe and those developed by DEGW and Hoare Lea. As Zimmerman and Martin (2001) point out, it is a common finding in social research that designers and clients/occupants evaluate buildings differently. Post-occupancy evaluations provide commissioning clients, design and build teams, and occupiers with useful snapshots of users' views.
- Value management tools, including the Institute of Civil Engineers' value management tool (Male, Kelly *et al.*, 1998).
- Housing Quality Indicators developed by the DETR (see Chapter 18).
- Design activities, integration and flexibility of the design process and a variety of different design methodologies.
- KPIs for the construction industry projects – on the Internet at KPIzone.com – although none of these deals explicitly with design quality.
- Sustainability of buildings – BREEAM and Ecopoints systems predict energy use buildings, but fail to incorporate life-cycle issues of sustainability. The SpeAR tool of sustainability indicators developed by Peter Braithwaite of Ove Arup is likely to prove useful for this.

- Legal, financing and procurement, planning and research and development mechanisms – comparing the institutional framework with European construction industries.

We drew upon lessons from the development of these tools during the creation of the DQI. There is some overlap between our tool and several of the previous attempts to explore design quality.

Design intent is developed throughout the design process, as the problem and its solution co-evolve. However, the opportunity to influence the design of a building diminishes rapidly over time. Path dependency sets in and projects become locked in to particular sets of solutions (Arthur, 1987). In spite of useful work by Brand (1994), Harbraken (1972, 1998) and Duffy and Henney (1989) not enough is known about the consequences of path-dependency and how to manage it in the context of design requirements to meet changing user needs.

The DQI project aims to measure the quality of design at different stages in the design process: inception, design, construction and use. It is designed to be used by anybody involved in the process, and to be short, simple and clear.

Performance measurement tools

The second step of the review and gap analysis was to assess the literature on development and use of performance measurements. This showed:

- Performance measurement is a process, not a product. To be successful, the indicators must fit the way people understand their work and their projects.
- Historically, there has been very little attention placed on design quality in government initiatives to improve the performance of the construction industry.

With the publication of *Better Public Buildings* (with a foreword by the Prime Minister) (DCMS, 2000) and the foundation of the Commission for Architecture and Built Environment (CABE), there has been a sea change in government attitudes. The DQI helps to support this movement towards better design.

- The instrument used to collect information needs to be simple, clear and concise:
  - ➤ It should take no more than one hour to complete.
  - ➤ It should combine subjective (attitudes toward design) and objective (specific features of the design) indicators.
  - ➤ It should include the views of as a wide a number of actors in the project as is possible.
  - ➤ It should be piloted widely and intensively.
  - ➤ Results should be fed back to all participants in the project.
  - ➤ It should be flexible – no magic number, but a set of indicators expressing the differing objectives of different projects.

Design awards

The third step in the literature review and preliminary data collection was to examine the mechanisms used in design awards for assessing design quality. The RIBA awards focus on commodity, firmness and delight: does the building work, does it feel right, does it stimulate and engage the occupants and visitors? Quality is judged in respect of:

- Its fitness for purpose
- Its relationship to its context
- The spatial experience
- Appropriateness of its structural and servicing systems
- Selection and detail of materials.

The British Construction Industry Awards, on the other hand, recognise excellence not only in the overall design, but also in the construction and the delivery of buildings and civil engineering projects. The judges take particular note of the quality of architectural and engineering design and of construction, value for money, application of quality management, performance against prediction and client satisfaction.

More detailed factors considered include:

- Concept: fitness for purpose, originality, application of research findings, benefit to the community.
- Design/planning: efficient use of materials and labour, appropriate standardisation, appearance and environmental harmony, pre-planning, selection and involvement of subcontractors, predictability of time and productivity, team-building, value engineering.
- Construction: management and teamwork, enterprise and ingenuity, workmanship, safety, economy, application of R&D findings, performance against programme.

The DQI tool

The DQI project was managed by the Construction Industry Council (CIC), supported by a Steering Group and a Reference Group, made up of over forty representatives from different parts of the design and construction community. The former Department of the Environment, Transport and Regions (DETR) funded the project. The main research contractor was the Programme on Innovation in the Built Environment at SPRU – Science and Technology Policy Research, University of Sussex. The research team moved to Imperial College London, in 2003.

The original aim of the project was to develop a tool for benchmarking design quality.

The main output of the project was to be a flexible tool that would allow participants in design and construction to measure the design quality of a building. The aim was to develop a generic tool, usable by professionals and users across a wide range of building types. The tool sought to cover all stages of a building's life, including conception, design, construction and in-use.

The DQI tool acts a mediator between the front-line customer or end-user and the producer. It structures questions about the process, providing information that is easily accessible to the designer and producer. It enables the designers to see where there are differences in the expectations across the two populations. The tool was developed with the assistance of a group of leading architects, engineers and clients, all of whom wanted a practical tool that they could use in their everyday building projects.

Design quality is multifaceted, involving a wide number of different interests and views. Any attempt to assess the design quality of product should attempt to cover diversity of activities and views associated with that product. It should reflect the divergent character of design quality. All products are multidimensional. They have to fulfil a function but also to appeal to users across many different levels. For example, an office not only provides shelter for work, it also creates an environment that has a major impact on the performance of the organisation.

The DQI tool was conceived of as consisting of three parts: a conceptual framework, a data gathering tool and a weighting mechanism. The relationship between these different parts is shown in Figure 17.1.

Conceptual framework

Design quality is considered to be multifaceted, involving a wide number of different issues, and the conceptual framework for the DQI

Results of the pilots

A vast amount of data was generated during the piloting process, and only a small portion of this information is described here. Major issues were encountered and resolved. Examples are:

1   Respondents found it difficult to know whether to answer with regard to aspirations, or perception of design. The introduction to the questionnaire has been changed to clarify this.
2   Respondents did not relate the priorities sections used for the weightings to the terms used as subcategories headings. To clarify this, questions regarding priorities at the subcategory level were moved into the sections themselves.
3   It is difficult to capture *excellence* in the questionnaire, and yet sometimes things are far better than *good* on a project. In one pilot, the phrase 'in harmony with the local ecology' was questioned as there are more trees on the site now than there were in the first place. The questionnaire was revised with regard to this type of occurrence.
4   For many of the pilots, the buildings in question were multi-user. The users may be widely different, for example, the question 'The building reduces stress for users' was difficult for the project team at the National Ice Centre to answer for this building – there are so many different types

of the overall project than the architect and engineers. This reflected the clients' concerns about the lack of specificity in the current state of the design. The results were presented to the project team. They helped to facilitate a debate among them about the state of the design. This is an example of the benefits of the tool in use that the research team did not consider during its design stage.

Within a project the views of the project manager, facilities manager and user, employer's agent and quantity surveyor, architect and engineer are represented in Figure 17.4. Their aggregate views are combined in Figure 17.5. These representations break the results down crudely at the section level only.

17.4 (below)
Contrasting evaluations by different members of a project team

17.5 (below right)
The project team's aggregated views from Figure 17.4

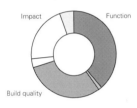

1 *Project manager*   DQI   5.447
   Good quality, flexible, cost-effective office space

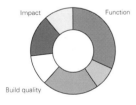

2 *Facilities manager and user*   DQI   4.074
   To provide a high quality, well maintained environment for staff. The building should enhance the image of the firm – proving us to be an employer of choice. To encourage new recruits to join

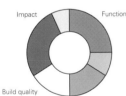

3 *Employer's agent and qs*   DQI   4.167
   A functional and aesthetically pleasing building which is completed within the client's budget. A building which is easily lettable

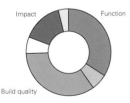

4 *Architect*   DQI   5.113
   Full tenancy, satisfied/comfort for the tenants, architectural awards for its contribution to the growth/planning in the area, no maintenance problems, longevity of materials and appropriateness for function

5 *Engineer*   DQI   3.717

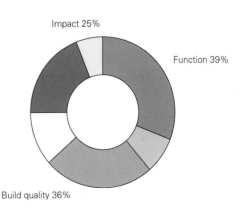

of users – rock groups, amateur and professional ice skaters, members of the public who come skating, maintenance staff, people who work in the building. This has been resolved by emphasising the role of the person filling in the questionnaire.

5 Participants were confused as to whether the questionnaire should be filled out from a personal point of view or as representative of one of the groups in the projects – 'Is this a personal thing? It's not a company thing?'

6 For many of the pilots the buildings in question were multifunction. The questions asked may not apply equally to the different parts of the building. For example, the Peabody Trust housing at Dalston Lane has both residential and commercial space. Wheelchair access is available in some parts but not in others (shops/housing). Is this a failing of the project? Respondents felt it was necessary to separate out primary and secondary functions – car park with office and some shops. The questionnaire has been changed to deal only with the primary function of the building.

7 Defining the constraints and enablers which form the resource envelope was particularly difficult. On all of the pilots it was recognised that time and money were important constraints, and that it was necessary for the tool to reflect on the constraints. However, it was difficult to shape questions to capture these constraints. For example, questions on good value for money and the profits of the organisation were inappropriate for Peabody Trust, as it has a social agenda rather than a financial one.

During the piloting of the DQIs, many previously unanticipated uses were suggested and discussed by pilot participants.

- As part of a training package to train building procurers in better design. This use of the DQIs would fit in with the work of the Office of Government Commerce (OGC).
- As a briefing tool to enable discussion within the project team, and between the project team and client and user groups. In this usage the differences between answers for the same building are most interesting and significant. One member of a project team said that the questions 'touched on things we clearly haven't thought of'. He said that there were minor items that 'we must not miss' and that the questionnaire was useful as 'a sort of checklist as we go through for things we must look at'. Another felt the DQIs should 'be client-led, and undertaken from the beginning of the project. They could set a benchmark for the project'.
- As a standardised procedure for measuring and monitoring product performance, through comparing and contrasting the aggregate answers for different buildings. Clear procedural rules about who fills in the DQI are required to enable this form of application.

Conclusion

This chapter has explained the development of a new generic tool which aims to explore the quality of design in buildings. The tool explicitly recognises that there is no single, universal result of design quality. Rather, it caters for multiple viewpoints from communities of design professionals and from user groups including lay people. The tool has a unique starting point in that it is designed to allow individual respondents to calibrate the intentions and weightings they wish to give to different design attributes. It therefore suggests an interactive, user-focused approach.

The tool is based on a method that integrates measures of 'hard' physical attributes and 'soft' perceptual viewpoints about the performance of buildings in relation to design decisions. The former are typically found in areas such as *build quality* and *function*. The latter tend to be found in the measurement of *impact* or delight.

The DQI is also capable of illustrating different levels of design value, moving from *basic* through *value added* and on to *excellent*.

While we have proven the success of the first stage of development of the DQI, there is still further work to be done in refining its use for different applications across all building types. We have embarked upon a second phase of development including an improved questionnaire with a web-based interface to allow respondents to complete it online. Moreover, we are developing new ways of visualising the results to enable rich levels of analysis. We also plan to include new approaches for eliciting information about the enablers and conditioners that underpin the parameters of design. It is hoped that this approach will lead to a more informed debate about the value of design in buildings and will complement approaches to measuring performance in design and construction processes.

References

Arthur, B. (1987) 'Path-dependent processes and the emergence of macro-structure', *European Journal of Operational Research*, vol. 30, pp. 294–303.

Brand, S. (1994) *How Buildings Learn*, New York: Viking Penguin.

Clausing, D. (1994) *Total Quality Development*, New York: ASME Press.

Construction Task Force (1998) *Rethinking Construction*, London: Department of the Environment, Transport and the Regions.

DCMS (2000) *Better Public Buildings: A proud legacy for the future*, London: Department for Culture, Media and Sport.

Duffy, F. and Henney, A. (1989) *The Changing City*, London: Bulstrode Press.

Frampton, K. (1980) *Modern Architecture: A Critical History*, London: Thames and Hudson.

Harbraken, J. (1972) *Supports – an alternative to mass housing*. Oxford: Architectural Press.

Harbraken, J. (1998) *The Structure of the Ordinary – form and control in the built environment*, Cambridge, MA: MIT Press.

Jesinghaus, J. (2000) *A European System of Environmental Pressure Indices*, Ispra: European Commission, Joint Research Centre, Institute for Systems, Informatics and Safety.

Male, S. Kelly, J. *et al.* (1998) *The Value Management Benchmark: a good practice framework for clients and practitioners*, London: Thomas Telford.

Monden, Y. (1983) *Toyota Production System*, Norcross, GA: Industrial Engineering and Management Press.

Schonberger, R. (1982) *Japanese Manufacturing Techniques*, New York: Free Press.

Smith, P. G. and Reinertsen, D. G. (1998) *Developing Products in Half the Time: New Rules, New Tools*, New York: John Wiley and Sons, Inc.

von Hippel, E. (2001) 'User toolkits for innovation', *Journal of Product Innovation Management*, vol. 18, pp. 247–57.

Ward, A., Sobek, D.K., Cristiano, J.J. and Liker, J.K. (1995) 'Toyota, concurrent engineering and set-based design'. In J. K. Liker, J. E. Ettlie and J. C. Campbell (eds) *Engineering in Japan*, Oxford: Oxford University Press.

Womack, J. P. and Jones, D. T. (1996) *Lean Thinking: banish waste and create wealth in your corporation*, New York: Simon & Schuster Inc.

Zimmerman, A. and Martin, M. (2001) 'Post-occupancy evaluation: benefits and barriers', *Building Research and Information*, vol. 29, no. 2, pp. 168–74.

Chapter 18

Housing quality indicators in practice

Paul Wheeler

The Housing Quality Indicator (HQI) system was developed by DEGW on behalf of the then Department for the Environment, Transport and the Regions (now the Department for Transport, London and the Regions) and the Housing Corporation. This chapter describes the HQI system and discusses issues relating to accuracy, usability and application which emerged from the first large-scale pilot trials of the system.

Problems of quality in housing are widely recognised. Age of housing stock is a particular problem in some regions of the United Kingdom, particularly London, where 59 per cent of the housing stock was built before 1945 (DTLR, 2000a). However, more recent housing is not necessarily of higher quality.

There is a long history of efforts to ensure quality standards in social housing. However, explicit attempts to ensure quality, such as those established by Parker Morris in the 1960s, were abandoned in the 1980s. Minimum standards in social housing were established by instruments such as the Housing Corporation Scheme Development Standards (in England) and Tai Cymru Pattern Book Plans (in Wales), while in the private sector, instruments such as the Building Regulations and Health and Safety Executive regulations provide minimum standards. However, the fact remains that large parts of Britain's housing stock are below the standards that would be expected in other north European societies. A comparative study of the control and promotion of housing quality across Europe found that the lowest standard for the minimum size of dwellings is found in Great Britain, with neither statutory requirements or conditions of subsidy relating to size of dwelling (Sheridan *et al.*, 1999).

In the absence of some explicit measure of quality, from the 1980s onwards cost has been an increasingly important factor in the funding of social housing. There is a widespread perception that in recent years reductions in housing cost have been achieved at the expense of quality. Cost was used by the Housing Corporation as one of the key criteria for Housing Association bid selection, leading to

18.3
Scheme 30: Despite thoughtful refurbishment, as a result of small room and overall unit size this development achieved the lowest score of the sample

built into the system between number of occupants and provision of living and eating space. For example, dwellings score poorly where there is insufficient space for all occupants to sit around a table and eat together.

Private sector developers noted that the assumption of 'full occupancy' described above runs contrary to the designed and actual use of their housing. In private housing, the number and size of rooms reflects ability to pay rather than need; bedrooms do not tend to be occupied permanently or to their full capacity. Within the HQI system there was no scope for designating a room as a spare bedroom, i.e. one that was only occasionally occupied. Few large dwellings, where some of the bedrooms are spare bedrooms, provide dining rooms of sufficient size for an assumed 'full occupancy'.

Reassessing schemes on the basis of developer estimates of likely occupancy resulted in dramatically improved scores for Unit size. Reassessing a large detached private house led to the score for Unit size rising by 19 per cent and the overall HQI score rising by 3 per cent.

Another issue of accuracy which was raised in the pilot trials related to the assessment of location. Participants in the trials expressed some concern that the HQI system exhibited an urban bias and discriminated against rural developments as a result of the inclusion of 'location' as a Quality Indicator. The inclusion of this category generated considerable discussion during the development of the HQI system. The locational features assessed are not qualities of the housing development, but of the surrounding area, with scores based on proximity of amenities and liabilities.

It could be argued that the inclusion of location into the system extends the scope of the Indicators beyond housing quality. However, the decision to include location as an Indicator is based on the view that context is an

which the existing system could be used in assessing private sector housing and a wider range of types of housing, such as new and recently refurbished housing. A number of issues relating to this emerged during the trials.

Social and private housing markets are clearly driven by different factors, and some of these differences have implications for the accuracy of the HQI system. One such difference is that whereas the size and layout of social housing are based on the need to house people, the size and layout of private-sector housing are driven by customer expectations and their ability to pay for these.

HQI scores for private sector developments were consistently and significantly reduced due to assumptions built into the HQI system about occupancy levels, and the form in which some questions were expressed. The HQI system assumes 'full occupancy' of a dwelling in relation to the number and size of bedrooms. Therefore a house with two double bedrooms and a single bedroom has an assumed occupancy of five people. The level of occupancy impacts significantly on a scheme's scores for Unit size and Unit layout, as a result of the relationship important contributing factor in good design: locational context contributes to the experienced quality. Assessments of quality must therefore take locational context into account.

During the pilot, use of the HQI system to assess rural developments did not seem to pose particular problems. Rural schemes' scores were lower in the Location category due to travel distances to amenities. However, overall there was no significant difference between the scores for rural and urban schemes, suggesting that lower scores on location were compensated for by higher scores on other Indicators. Indicator 3 assesses access to open space: rural schemes typically and understandably gained higher scores than urban schemes in this Indicator.

Some organisations found completion of the Location Indicator difficult and time-consuming, while others found it straightforward and uncomplicated. Ease of completion of this Indicator appeared to be influenced by the extent of the assessor's knowledge of the area and understanding of the context within which the development was located.

A third issue relating to accurate measurement of quality was highlighted by the performance of the most innovative housing scheme included in the sample. This scheme was located in a rural village and was described as:

Pair of semi-detached houses completed in 1999, built as an innovative prototype housing project. The houses incorporate numerous energy saving and environmentally friendly technologies. Isolated rural village with few amenities and poor public transport links. Village with mixed housing types – thatched cottage to RSL prefabricated houses.

This scheme outperformed all other schemes in the sample. Its score was well above average

for all Indicators except (1) Location, in line with other rural schemes, as discussed previously. It was the only scheme to score highly on Indicators (8) Accessibility within the unit, (9) Energy, green, and sustainable issues, and (10) Performance in use. The scheme performed particularly well on (9) Energy, green and sustainability issues, reflecting the energy saving technologies incorporated and the green approach to construction. The research team found it encouraging to see a highly innovative housing solution scoring so well.

However, the scheme's score for Indicator (6), Unit layout, was depressed (although still above average) as the scheme was based on an open-plan, flexible layout. Open plan layouts integrate living space and circulation space, whereas the HQI system awards higher scores for unit layouts where circulation space is separate from living areas. Whether open plan layouts genuinely reduce quality is an open question. While a large family may find the separation of circulation space from living accommodation important for their quality of life, this separation may be considered unnecessary by other types of occupants and may lead to a poor utilisation of the available space.

18.4
Scheme 28: This innovative and highly energy efficient development achieved the highest score in the trials

Usability of the HQI system

The HQI system was developed with ease of use in mind. An important element in its ease of use is the fact that assessment can be based on analysis of plans and other information, removing the need to enter individual units. However, although plans and other information are available for new developments, they may be difficult to acquire when assessing older developments.

In order to gain understanding of the usability of the system, HQI assessments have been carried out by the builder or developer responsible for the scheme. These participants were briefed on the overall aims of the pilot and on the HQI system and then left to complete the assessment themselves. Once the assessment had been completed the research team returned to debrief them on the problems and issues that had been raised in the process.

Size of scheme had some impact on usability of the HQI system. As expected, the surveys of larger schemes proved more difficult and time-consuming to complete than those of smaller schemes. The HQI system is based on assessment of each unit in a development, and the pilot trials demonstrated that this may be impractical when assessing very large developments with numerous unit types. To address this problem suggestions have been made on when sampling techniques can be used to simplify the process. In addition, it was found that schemes split over multiple sites posed significant assessment problems, and it has been recommended that in such schemes each site should be assessed separately.

Outside of sheer size and complexity, completion of Indicator (6), Unit layout, proved the most time-consuming and difficult. Recognising that housing quality is dependent not only on size but on layout and configuration, Indicator 6 assesses units on their usability.

Fifty per cent of the scores for this Indicator are awarded on the basis of the 'furniture exercise'. This exercise raises some questions about how quality should be assessed, and will therefore be examined in some detail.

The HQI system specifies for each room in a dwelling the furniture that should fit in the room. In addition the activity and circulation spaces are specified. Units that can accommodate all the specified furniture and activity zones achieve mid-range scores; higher or lower scores can be achieved by fitting in more or less furniture or activity zones than specified. This 'furniture exercise' seems a highly prescriptive approach to achieving quality. Not only is a furniture list specified for each room in a dwelling, and the number of items on this list correlated with the number of occupants, the dimensions of each item of furniture are specified.

There was considerable discussion over this Indicator – the research team involved in the pilots were initially sceptical of its utility. There was some discussion over whether the furniture exercise should be replaced with a simpler form of assessment based purely on room dimensions and proportions.

If we consider how the HQI system is designed to be used, the exercise makes much more sense. The HQI system was not primarily designed to be used as a post-construction audit; at that point opportunities for improving quality have been lost until the next project. The HQI system was developed to be an integral part of the design process, employed throughout the evolution of the design to enable designers to track the quality impact of their decisions. At this stage the designers should be thinking about how occupants will use the space being created. Some occupants may choose far more minimalist furniture layouts than those allowed for in the HQI system. However, a design that accommodates the furniture-intensive layout will also accommodate more minimalist solutions.

The 'furniture exercise' was either not completed, or only partially completed, by a number of developers during the pilot. In these cases the research team completed the exercise. In addition the research team reassessed some schemes on this Indicator to check that the exercise had been completed accurately. As a result of this the team gained direct experience of the usability of this Indicator. Our conclusions were that when assessing small, poorly-shaped rooms considerable effort was required to achieve a reasonable score. However, given a well proportioned room of reasonable dimensions assessment was swift and straightforward.

With regard to prescriptiveness, the exercise does prescribe in the sense that to achieve a high score a unit must be able to accommodate a certain quantity of furniture. The exercise does not prescribe particular room dimensions or proportions. While, as noted above, small irregularly shaped rooms achieve low scores, large irregular rooms can score highly. In keeping with the overall ethos of the HQI system, Indicator 6 does not suggest that there is only one route to achieving quality.

The research team did recognise that when performing an assessment post-completion, particularly in cases where plans are unavailable or incomplete, Indicator 6 is time-consuming and difficult to complete. To ameliorate this problem the team suggested that an alternative assessment method should be included. This recommendation has been adopted in the revised version of the HQI system as Room Matrix Approach. This alternative assessment method is based on room proportions and dimensions. However, it is noted that developments assessed using this alternative system are likely to achieve lower scores, particularly if room proportions diverge from the 'ideal', than when assessed using the 'furniture exercise'.

Finally, the piloting process revealed a need for extensive briefing of participants before they were able to carry out an assessment. While this was in part due to unfamiliarity, the research team feel that consideration should be given to the development of a more comprehensive briefing document.

Conclusion

This was the first real live pilot study of the HQI system across a diversity of housing types. The results suggest no significant problems which could not be solved through slight revisions to the HQI. These revisions have now been incorporated into the revised version. No major discrepancies between quality as perceived by housing professionals and as recorded by HQI scores were revealed in any of the housing schemes surveyed.

The HQI system will become easier to use as its application becomes more widespread. Training for HQI assessors should also ease problems relating to completion and ensure accuracy.

One further conclusion may be drawn from the experience of the pilot. We know relatively little about how homes are used. The majority of housing built today differs little in terms of the designed space use from housing built 100 years ago. Over this time the nature of the household has changed dramatically, as have many other aspects of our society. It may be that there is no need for housing design to change to adapt to our new social patterns. Perhaps traditional designs have an inherent flexibility allowing them to accommodate these changes. There seems to be little research that would enable us to tell. The development of the HQI system represents a step forward in the struggle to improve the quality of housing and the build environment in general. Ultimately, if we are to continue making progress a deeper understanding of how our homes are used is vital.

Acknowledgement

The author would like to thank his colleagues in DEGW for their contributions to this chapter and would also like to thank the individuals from public and private sector organisations who gave their time to make the pilot exercises possible.

References

DETR (1997) 'Housing Quality Indicators: feasibility study', *Housing Research Summary No. 70*, London: DETR.

DETR (1999) *Housing Quality Indicators: research report and indicators*, London: DETR.

DTLR (2000a) *Housing Statistics 2000*, London: DTLR.

DTLR (2000b) *Best Value in Housing Framework*, London: DLTR.

Sheridan, L. *et al.* (1999) 'A comparative study of the control and promotion of quality in housing in Europe', *Housing Research Summary No. 99*, London: DETR.

Index